The Sex
Life
of the Foot
& Shoe

The Sex Life of the Foot & Shoe

William A. Rossi

Wordsworth Editions

First published in Great Britain by Routledge & Kegan Paul, 1977.

This edition published 1989 by Wordsworth Editions Ltd,
8b East Street, Ware, Hertfordshire, under licence
from the proprietor.

ISBN 1-85326-939-5

Printed and bound in Great Britain by Mackays of Chatham PLC.

Contents

I
_____

The Erotic Foot
and the Sexual Shoe

The foot is an erotic organ and the shoe is its sexual covering.

This is a reality as ancient as mankind, as contemporary as the Space Age. The human foot possesses a natural sexuality whose powers have borne remarkable influence on all peoples of all cultures throughout all history. Podoerotica bears its influence on our everyday lives today.

The shoe has also played an active sensual role throughout history. The shoe is no simple, protective housing for the foot, nor a whimsical decoration. It serves chiefly as a sexual covering for the foot's natural erotic character. Footwear fashion is podoerotic art.

Today, Americans spend some $11 billion a year for the approximately one billion pairs of footwear they consume. About 80 percent of this footwear is designed, produced, fitted and sold primarily for sex attraction. This motive is sometimes naively referred to as "fashion appeal," which is simply a patronizing term for sex appeal. The shoe is the erotic foot's pimp and procurer.

The evidence of our natural podosexuality is abundant, accumulated by anthropologists, psychologists and psychiatrists, clothing historians, sociologists, medical researchers, and other qualified observers. The influence of podosexuality has been implanted in the laws of nations; in the religious books of the Hindus, Christians, Hebrews, Mohammedans, Buddhists, and others. It's found in the customs of most societies, in legend and mythology, in the traditions and mores of most cultures; in the arts, and in the writings of poets, dramatists and philosophers; in the rituals of courtship and marriage, birth and fertility; and profusely in the medical literature.

But its most dramatic evidence is seen in the everyday use to which the foot and shoe are put to express sexual feelings and communicate psychosexual attitudes.

Americans have been among the slowest of peoples to confront the realities of foot and shoe eroticism. Even the huge footwear industry, living on the front lines of this podoerotic phenomenon, has a child-like innocence about the sensual truths of its products and the sub-conscious sexual motives for which these products are bought and worn. The doctors, like the shoemen, are cloistered in the same virginal cocoon.

The *Boot and Shoe Recorder*, an industry trade publication, stated in a special "Sex and Shoes" issue of 1964, "The erotic attractions of the foot and shoe are positive and clear-cut. And though they've been with us since ancient times, it's only now that Americans are discovering what the rest of the world has known for thousands of years."

But can that "innocent" and remote foot really be an erotic organ? Does it truly play an influential role in our sexual and psychosexual lives? Yes, in very positive ways. Just for a start, let's see what some authoritative voices have to say about these podosexual realities.

Havelock Ellis, in his monumental work, *Studies in the Psychology of Sex*, says, "Of all the forms of erotic symbolism, the most frequent is that which idealizes the foot and shoe. . . . It would seem that even for the normal lover, the foot is one of the most attractive parts of the body."

Dr. G. Aigremont, the German psychologist, states in his classic study, *Foot and Shoe Symbolism and Eroticism*, "The naked foot exists as a means of sexual charming. There is a close connection between the foot and things sexual."

Renowned psychiatrist Karl A. Menninger, writing in *The Human Mind*, declares, "The mythologies and folklore of all nations are rich in material whose significance hinges on an intimate bond which links the foot and sex ideas together. In some places and at some times the natives have been more ashamed to expose their feet than their genitals. In many parts of the world it is considered disgraceful for a woman to expose her feet, even though shod, to public view. . . . Women dress their feet and legs in such a way as to attract attention to them. This emphasizes their sexual significance. The foot is a frank sexual symbol for numerous reasons—it is an appendage, it is dependent, it slips into the shoe, etc."

Dr. M. Straker, the noted Canadian psychiatrist, states that "the feet and legs have special psychological values, both conscious and unconscious. They represent highly sexualized and therefore highly valued organs." Mary Lou Rosencranz, University of Connecticut sociologist, asserts in her book, *Clothing Concepts,* "Shoes and feet have been used as symbols of sex by many peoples."

Psychologist Bernard Rudofsky, in his book, *The Unfashionable Human Body,* writes, "To uncover the feet of a person of the opposite sex is a symbol of sexual possession. Indeed, the word 'feet' is often used as a euphemism for the genitals."

Casanova, who made his reputation as a satyr, declared in his memoirs that all men who shared his interest in women are sensually attracted by the female foot. C. Willet Cunnington expresses agreement in his book, *Why Women Wear Clothes:* "Woman's foot has exercised extraordinary powers of sexual attraction."

Except for the male genitals themselves, the foot is the most common and persistent phallic symbol of the human anatomy. There's no mystery to this. The human foot has a powerful evolutionary, psychological and historical claim to its phallic association. In Eastern Europe, for example, foot phallicism is strongly implanted in tradition. In the Slovanish language the penis is called *trétja noga,* or "third foot." In the area around Naples, on the feast day of St. Cosimo, a large phallic object called "the big toe of St. Cosimo" is offered up to him. In ancient Greece, the goddesses were frequently depicted as having a second toe longer than the first. This protruding second toe supposedly gave the goddesses special male phallic powers in addition to their female attributes.

Even the footprint has made its phallic mark in sex legend. The Zuñi Indian women, while their husbands are away, keep the soil of their husbands' footprints where they sleep, believing this possession will dampen the sex urges of their men and ensure their fidelity. The ancient Romans revered the Egyptian goddess Iris. Her footprint was considered sacred, having the powers to make barren women fertile.

Dr. E. T. Renbourn, of Brookside Hospital, Surrey, England, states in his study, "The Foot and Shoe in Body and Mind," "To the primitive mind there was a sympathetic connection between a man or his feet and his footprint—in which he believed the soul resided." Examples of this can still be found in Florence, Turin, Alexandria and elsewhere in the "foot memorials" to Roman and Egyptian gods. These were tributes to the foot's phallic and fertility powers. In the folklore of middle Europe there still exists a recipe wherein the big toe is anointed with a mixture of vegetable oil and Spanish fly. This, like an aphrodisiac, is supposed to ensure rigidity of the penis by working through its phallic symbol, the big toe.

This podophallicism is enmeshed in our psychosexual structure as a subconscious "presence." Says Straker, "In my own practice, dream analysis consistently reveals the substitution of genitals by the feet. Injury to the feet in dreams often symbolizes injury to the genitals." As an example, he cites the case of a young man suffering from sexual impotence. The impotence was traced to "psychological shock" resulting from the time this man's big toe was amputated following an injury. Loss of the big toe equated with loss of the penis or castration. Psychotherapist Otto Fenichel, among others, describes cases in which the foot-genital association plays an important role in psychic and emotional disturbances.

WHY IS THE FOOT EROTIC?

Why has this long and universal tradition of podosexuality developed? Is podoeroticism biologically and psychologically implanted in the human organism itself? There's strong affirmative evidence to give the foot rightful claim to its natural erotic character. For example:

It's one of the body's most sensitive tactile organs, possessing its own "sexual nerves"—and capable of the most intimate sensations in touching and being touched.

It's rich with vibratory and electromagnetic powers linked to earth contact—which is one reason for its age-old association with human fertility and the reproductive process.

It has played a major role in the evolution and development of many of the erogenous features of the human anatomy—buttocks, bosom, legs and thighs, abdomen, hips, etc. What we refer to as "the figure" or the voluptuous architecture of the body, owes much of its sensuous character to the foot, which was responsible for the upright posture and gait that altered the entire anatomy.

The unusual structure of the human foot which made the upright posture possible, also made possible frontal human copulation, a coital position unique in all nature.

As an extraordinarily tactile appendage, the foot's phallicism is psychosexually inbred.

The foot, intimately linked to our emotional, neurological and psychosexual activities, is a reflex participant in sexual foreplay and coitus.

Of all the known sex-related fetishes, those associated with the foot, toes and shoes are by far the most common.

The sensuality of the human gait, unique in all nature and one of the most erotic features of the human anatomy, especially in women, owes its sensual character to the foot.

The foot possesses and expresses the strange power of "podolinguistics" or foot language—an innate ability to communicate feelings, attitudes, desires, especially as sexual and psychosexual symbols.

The foot has sex-attractive features of its own—its contours and sinuous movements, its arch, instep, ankle, toes, etc., which are equipped with proven erotogenic powers.

The universal human desire to dress the foot in sex-attractive ways with shoes and other ornamentation, is further evidence of the foot's natural erotogenic character.

But what proof exists of the foot's actual erotic power and influence? The evidence is overwhelming, much of which will be shown in this book. This erotic foot, for example:

Created a podosexual mania among five billion Chinese that lasted nearly one thousand years.

Has given rise to a legion of millions of foot partialists and shoe fetishists who have found their sexual outlets as "pedic lovers" for at least five thousand years, and who are found profusely in the population today.

Has been the target of censorship for centuries by popes, kings and emperors, moralists and reformers, governments, the clergy, the press, etc., on the grounds of indecent exposure of a "sexual" part.

Has inspired a ceaseless parade of prurient footwear fashions which over the centuries have been designed and worn for their sex-arousal and sex-communicative value.

Has given rise to what today has become a multi-million-dollar industry providing "podocosmetic" products designed to enhance the erotic qualities of the foot.

Has brought to light, via modern sex research, what has long been known or suspected: that the foot, with its natural phallicism and podosexuality, is commonly used in sexual foreplay and even coitus.

Why, then, has this naturally sensuous foot, in the minds of so many Americans, been assigned a lowly and utilitarian position, in sharp contrast to most other parts of the world where the foot is extolled for its beauty and its erotic and aphrodisiac powers? There's little mystery to the answer.

Only in America is there such exaggerated and distorted propaganda about sick feet, ugly feet, tired feet, odorous feet, etc. Of the countless articles on "foot health" that appear in magazines, newspapers, and other media, over 95 percent deal with foot ailments. It is one thing to make the public foot-conscious, but quite another to make them *negatively* foot-conscious.

Thus we've been made to see ourselves as a nation of foot-cripples while the real truth is concealed from us: the truth that the foot is a vital member of the erogenous family and the shoe is its sensual partner. In the subsequent chapters we'll see the real foot and the real shoe in their natural roles in our sexual lives and our psychosexual patterns of behavior.

2

Pedic Sex

The eroticism of the foot extends far beyond "symbolism." The foot has long played a *direct* role in sexual activity in foreplay and even in coitus. These practices are by no means limited to fetishists or offbeat sexual adventurers, but occur liberally among normal people the world over.

One day in London a few years ago, I was discussing the subject of foot and shoe eroticism with a friend who was editor of a British shoe publication. He smiled curiously and said, "Seeing is better than talking." That evening he took me to a sedate home which, I later learned, was known as The Palace of Pedic Pleasure. Inside we were greeted by a matronly woman, the madam. The place was furnished in good though not lavish taste. Several men and women, fully clothed, were sitting around talking and drinking.

But soon, some of the men, paired with their selected women, disappeared. My friend and I sat and chatted with the madam. Her clientele, she explained, was composed of "sexual sophisticates," which included Europeans as well as Britishers; and, she added, an occasional American who had heard of her unique establishment. What did The Palace of Pedic Pleasure offer its clientele? She explained:

"Our girls are very special. The most important thing is that their feet must be beautiful—slender, very mobile feet with smooth skin and long, flexible toes. Then we teach the girls how to become experts at pedic lovemaking."

"What do they do with their feet?" I asked. "Or what do the men do with the girls' feet?"

She smiled patiently, as though with a child. Then in blunt terms she explained, "All our clients are what you'd call 'normal' men. They're here to get laid. But they have something in common—they enjoy sexual foreplay with the feet. It can take all kinds of forms: having the penis massaged by the girl's feet; or putting the penis between the girl's feet; or sucking the toes of the girl; or using the big toe to insert into the vagina; or holding or kissing the girl's feet while they're being laid. Lots of different ways."

"Then most of them are foot fetishists," I said.

"Hardly any," she explained. "Some men like foreplay with the breasts, others with fellatio or cunnilingus, or tonguing an ear, and so on. Each to his own. Our men get their kicks out of foot-lovemaking. Many of our clients never had this experience until they were introduced to it here. Now many of them are regulars."

"One thing puzzles me," I pressed. "You run such a specialized house. Are there enough of these—well, foot-lovers, to support it?"

She smiled again. "We've been in business over ten years, and the clientele keeps growing. We're not alone, either. You can find places like ours in Paris or Berlin or Naples or Copenhagen and other cities in Europe. Maybe even in America. Those foot-lovers, as you call them, are a bigger minority than you think."

It's hardly uncommon for a person to derive sexual gratification from having his genitals fondled by his partner's feet or toes. Mirabeau, in his extensive work, *Erotika Biblion,* mentions that some women in Greece and the Middle East develop the skill of using their feet to gently manipulate the male genitals and provoke orgasm. Aigremont cites that in Alsace-Lorraine there has been a long-time practice of the male's manipulation of the partner's labia and vagina with his toes in pre-coital play. Havelock Ellis adds, "Simultaneous mutual masturbation by means of the feet is by no means unknown today."

Psychotherapist Harvey T. Leathem, who has made deep investigations into sexual partialisms, states, "Many a man has experienced a sudden surge of eroticism when a creative girl friend impulsively stopped stimulating his erection with her hands and, drawing up her legs into position, began to 'manipulate' the organ between her feet. . . . Therefore, the feel of a girl's feet gently caressing a man's genitalia is erotically exciting to nearly all men."

If the Olympic games ever included a contest for coital gymnastics, then certainly the Oriental gentleman who posed for an old painting, long admired in China, might easily take the Gold Medal. The painting shows the man in sexual intercourse with five women at once, "so that he may experience the divine joy of five orgasms simultaneously." One woman sits astride him, his penis inserted. With each hand he has a finger inserted into the vagina of two more. And with the remaining pair he has made a vaginal insertion with each of his big toes.

The theme of this painting, however, has been popular in various parts of the world for centuries. In India, for example, in Rájasthan, there is a famous painting showing Rája on his terrace having sexual intercourse with five of his wives simultaneously, two of them via podocoitus. The painting is aptly titled, "The Ancient Heroic Ideal." The coital heroics are obvious—and the ideal is a fantasy that has intrigued the imagination of sexually ambitious men since the beginnings of *Homo sapiens*.

The foot is also a direct participant in sexual arousal and intercourse in a psychosomatic or psychosexual sense. It is erotically responsive to sexual feelings experienced by the whole body. Here, for example, is a comment from Kinsey's *Sexual Behavior in the Human Female*:

"Outside of the movements of the gluteal adductor and abductor muscles (of the thighs), the muscular reactions which are next most noticeable during sexual activity involve the feet and toes. The whole foot may be extended until it falls in line with the rest of the lower leg, thereby assuming a position which is impossible in non-erotic situations for most persons who are not trained as ballet dancers. The toes of most individuals become curled or, contrariwise, spread when there is erotic arousal. Many persons divide their toes, turning their large toes up or down while the remaining toes curl in the opposite direction. Such activity is rarely recognized by the individual who is sexually aroused and actually doing these things, but the near universality of such action is attested by the graphic record of coitus in the erotic art of the world. For instance, in Japanese erotic art curled toes have, for at least eight centuries, been one of the stylized symbols of erotic response."

The reflex action of the foot and toes during sexual intercourse is but one of many such examples of the foot's instinctual participation in sexual activity—its ability to "feel" and respond to sexual arousal.

It is equally common during intense sexual foreplay or in heated petting sessions, though, as Kinsey points out, this reflex action is seldom noticed by the participants. But why this response? Because the foot itself is an erotic organ with a direct line of sensory communication to the body's sexual processes and erotogenic experiences.

Cosmopolitan magazine, whose audience is composed largely of liberation-oriented young women, recently presented a four-page feature article entitled, "The Other Erogenous Zones." The foot was cited as one of these zones. Said the article, "Girls, like kittens, *adore* being stroked, petted, pampered, fondled, fussed over—from head to toe! . . . You must make them (the other erogenous zones) utterly irresistible, kissable, caressable, in all the ways you can. . . . Feet are surprisingly sensitive. To make him want to make your toes curl with pleasure, spend some time on them."

Thus the common expressions of feeling sexual arousal "to the tips of the toes" and "making the toes curl," are no mere figures of speech but podosexual realities. All parts of the body aren't invited to the party, only those with erotogenic credentials. The foot is always among the honored guests.

FOOT-KISSING

Podosexuality abounds about us every day, expressed in both innocent and deliberate ways. One simple example of this is the instinctive toe-sucking habits of infants. This has the same psychosexual motive as thumb-sucking, and is universally regarded as the infant's first recognition or expression of its sexual identity. The kissing, nibbling, feigned biting, caressing and fondling of babies' feet and toes by mothers and family relatives is universal and instinctive.

G. Stanley Hall, writing on podosexual tendencies or symbolism in babies and children, in *The American Journal of Psychology*, states, "Some children become greatly excited when their feet are exposed. . . . Many infants play with them as if fascinated by strange, newly-discovered toys. Children often handle their feet, pat and stroke them, offer them toys and the bottle, as if they too had an independent hunger and ego of their own. . . . The interest of mothers in babies' toes, the expressions of which are ecstatic and almost incredulous, is a factor of great importance."

But foot-kissing isn't at all limited to "innocent" forms of caressing, as with infants. The adult foot, as an erogenous part of the anatomy, is kiss-prone for peoples all over the world. This takes two forms: as a traditional act of humility or homage, and as a direct expression or act of sexual pleasure.

The kissing of the feet of kings, popes, emperors, slave masters, and the statues of saints or gods has for thousands of years been practiced as a gesture of submission, humility, or petition. This custom is instinctive and compulsive, and is found in almost every culture.

Also, we kiss the foot because it is a symbol of power, of life itself. Our words "impede" and "impediment" (*ped* meaning "foot") come from that concept. To immobilize the feet is to remove their natural powers or functions—the equivalent of castration. The link between the foot and castration is as common in modern psychiatry as it was in past centuries. In the Middle Ages, it was customary for a nobleman or landlord to step on the right foot of a vassal, denoting ownership of that person. The bridegroom went through the wedding ritual with his foot on the foot of the bride, symbolizing possession of her and her inability to move without his permission. Hence the foot symbolized freedom or slavery. To "impede" a person was virtually to emasculate him and deny him the right of personal liberty. To kiss the foot was a recognition of the life-giving and emancipatory powers of the foot.

Foot-kissing with *sexual* motives, however, is quite common. In private, many persons obtain an uninhibited pleasure from foot-kissing as a part of sexual foreplay. Dr. Leathem writes, "Some non-masochistic partialists indulge in various forms of foot-kissing. Sometimes a man and woman will stretch out atop one another, but inverted in such a way that his head is pressed against her feet, and vice versa."

"In India," says Aigremont, "in the art of love there exists a toe kiss, which serves as an exceptionally strong and successful erotic arousal. The woman kisses the big toe of the man in order to arouse him to love." This not uncommon gesture is due to the phallicism associated with the big toe, and is actually a symbolic form of fellatio. Xaviera Hollander, in her recent best-seller, *The Happy Hooker*, frankly describes one of her many sex-play scenes: "Then I took him to bed and started to make real love to him, starting at the toes, sucking each one as though it were a cock."

Are such instances unusual or isolated? Hardly. For example, on Manhattan's East Side, an establishment called The Golden Tongue Salon advertises its services "for the liberated woman" and offers "ten straight men" specializing "in a wide variety of sexual tongue applications, including toe-sucking." Similar establishments can be found in many major cities of the world. For a few years, one American photography magazine was devoted exclusively to photos of toes and sexual toe-play scenes. Also, a well-known West Coast photographer was advertising a repertoire of "toe movies" for sex-selective devotees. The inevitable question must follow: How can such enterprises be profitable unless there is a substantial clientele to draw upon?

Foot-kissing, however, even as a socio-religious gesture of humble submission can often be linked with sexual motives, consciously or subconsciously. In the opera *Parsifal,* a virgin male, tempted by a seductress on Good Friday, washes and kisses her feet, signifying that he is pure and holy. "He kissed her on the foot with joy and gave himself to her." By his "holy" act he loses both his virginity and soul, but at the same time saves her soul to make her eligible for redemption and heaven. Here, then, is the joining of the holy and unholy, the pure and the prurient, symbolized by the single act of foot-kissing.

The following story is reported to be true. One evening a jealous Mark Antony stormed into Cleopatra's boudoir. She languished on a luxurious couch, clad only in a diaphanous robe. Antony, arms folded firmly across his chest, looked down at her and said sternly, "I am here to talk about Caesar." Cleopatra slowly stretched her bare, perfumed foot toward him, toes moving sinuously as though in rhythm with the undulations of the small live snake that was frequently entwined around her ankle. She reached out and touched Antony's naked thigh with the tips of her polished toes. He grasped her foot and covered it with ardent kisses. She looked up and said softly, "Now, I am not prone to argue."

We've just begun to recognize the foot for the erotic organ it genuinely is. But what about the shoe, its sexual covering? Does the shoe, like the foot, have a legitimate claim to sexual purposes? It certainly does, often in clearly prurient ways. In the next chapter we'll begin to see the shoe's role in pedic eroticism.

3

Sex Symbols at Your Feet

For ten thousand years or more the shoe has been worn as a sex symbol and an article of sex communication because it is the housing for the erotic foot. Shoes are designed and worn, consciously or subconsciously, to convey psychosexual messages.

The sexual kinship of the foot and shoe has been inevitable. While the foot has always been a phallic symbol, the shoe has always been a yoni, or vulva, symbol. This male (foot) and female (shoe) relationship is both ancient and universal.

Freud comments, "The foot is a very primitive sexual symbol. . . . The shoe or slipper is, accordingly, often a symbol of the female genitals."

Robert Riley, design consultant at the Brooklyn Museum and an authority on the history of clothing, says, "Several clear observations on the sexuality of the foot come to mind. Most obvious is the male phallic symbolism of the big toe and the female symbolism of the clefting between the toes. Equally obvious is the act of thrusting the foot into a sheathing shoe. These unconscious visions live with us day to day."

Aigremont deals with this more bluntly: "Sexual foot and shoe symbolism is very wide-spread and age-old in origin. The shoe is the symbol of the vulva and female organs, while the foot is the symbol of the penis (there are innumerable corroborations of this in ethnographic and folklore studies). One 'thrusts' the foot into the shoe or boot or slipper. These kinds of footwear have an opening, a hole, sometimes surrounded by fur or similar trimming, and this hole is filled with a human foot or flesh. The entering of the foot into the shoe simulates the entering of the penis into the vulva."

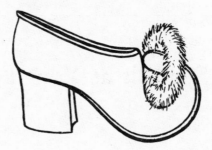

In this sixteenth-century shoe, the effect of sexual mating is obvious.

These insights begin to show why most footwear is designed and worn essentially as podoerotic art. The shoe has an ulterior sexual mission to fulfill. This is why, whenever footwear design is lackluster or passive, it loses much of its sales appeal or appeals only to sex-passive customers, such as the elderly or infirm or the psychosexually inhibited. "The modern shoe," writes Rudofsky, "is among the articles of dress whose improvement is retarded by the fact that it is an erotic implement."

One of America's top designers whose name is a prestigious label in some of the most expensive and fashionable women's shoes told me, "We like to dignify our designs by calling them fashion. But let's face it. The prime element we build into a woman's shoe is sex. If it lacks sex appeal, not only does it miss the mark of fashion, but it doesn't sell worth a damn. Shoes aren't merely sex symbols. They're sex motivators because they help give a woman the look, the poise, the carriage, that conveys a sensual language. Women know this well by intuition and experience."

Thus a kind of libido is deliberately infused into the shoes of women, men, teen-agers, and even children. This is the "law" applying to any covering of an erogenous part of the anatomy: that the covering in itself must express the sensuality of what it's supposed to be concealing.

Dr. Wilhelm Stekel, the noted psychiatrist who for years worked closely with Freud, declares, "The attractiveness of the foot and shoe

. . . is so extraordinarily common that these parts of the body (and their clothing) could easily be reckoned among the so-called secondary sexual characteristics. Throughout literature, there are innumerable eulogies of the foot and shoe."

Over countless centuries the shoemaker has been a fond and favored character of poets, philosophers, storytellers, artists, composers, and balladeers. He has been romanticized by Shakespeare, Pliny, Byron, Elizabeth and Robert Browning, Plutarch, John Heywood, Chekov, Emerson, Rabelais, Dickens, Cervantes, Chaucer, Horace, Plato, Gorki, Socrates, Stendhal, Aristophanes, and countless others.

Why the shoemaker? Why not the tailor or tinker, the silversmith or carpenter, the mason or milliner? It's not because of the shoemaker but because of the *shoe*. We're not in awe of the jeweler but the jewel. Historically, the shoe has been associated with the romantic and the erotic, with fertility, marriage, and sex matings. The universal custom of the bride tossing her shoe to the bridesmaids, or shoes tied to the departing carriage or car of the bridal couple, is rife with sexual inferences.

In France, for example, the bride forever preserves her wedding shoes to assure a lifetime of compatible and productive physical union. An old Anglo-Saxon toast to the groom at the wedding went, "May you fit her as this old shoe has fit me," a reference to the sexual mating. In several parts of the world the groom unties the bride's shoe at the wedding, a ritual suggesting the initial "opening up" to prepare the bride for defloration.

The romantic and sexual magic of the shoe flourishes in many forms. In Sicily, young women sleep with a shoe under their pillow to improve their chances of getting a husband. In rural Greece the women believe that a lost lover can be retrieved by burning an old shoe. In Spain and Mexico, admiring women toss a slipper into the bullring to applaud the matador. He picks up the shoes gently as kittens, kisses them, and tosses them back into the crowd.

Are these merely innocent romanticisms or quaint customs? Hardly. Phallic-yoni associations are interwoven throughout most of these customs, as though the shoe has some mystical aphrodisiac powers that will convert mating dreams into realities. Hidden behind the seemingly innocent romanticisms is always the inference that the shoe, because it's the special covering of an erotic organ, connotes something wicked, obscene, ithyphallic.

Jacob Nacht, in his *Symbolism of the Shoe*, writes, "Our first source of information concerning the shoe is in the Bible. Here the shoe partakes the character of the profane, symbolizing the Earth in contrast to the Holy. 'Put off thy shoes from thy feet, for the place whereon thy standest is holy ground' is the command of Moses (Exodus 3: 5). The Levites, whose function it was to carry the vessels of the Tabernacle, were required to take off their shoes while performing this holy service."

Renbourn adds to this: "In biblical language, the word foot was linked with female sexuality. And by the hair of the foot may have been meant the pubic hair."

The universal "sinfulness" and unchastity of the shoe is observed by the Moslems before entering their mosques, the Buddhists before entering their temples, the Japanese before entering thir homes. This is no mere gesture of respect or religious homage. It stems from the age-old phallic-yoni association of foot and shoe that makes the shoe "profane." Observers cite that when foreign men are required to remove their shoes under these circumstances, they feel "a sense of emasculation in their stocking feet." This is confirmed by psychiatrists and others who relate many instances where men associate public exposure of their feet with feelings of castration or emasculation. In the case of women, however, the removal of shoes often evokes feelings of shame.

The suggestive wickedness connected with the shoe can be seen in a simple example—a woman kicking off her shoes with abandon in the company of others. This impulsive gesture is quite unlike the quiet removal of the shoes in the darkness of a theater. Men interpret this as receptivity to intimate action. And in this action, all women know the signals they're sending.

Recently, in Chicago, a man accused by a woman of attempted sexual assault was acquitted by the court. The man testified, "I met her at a party and she agreed to let me drive her home. At her place we had a couple of drinks. Then suddenly she kicked off her shoes, kind of carefree like, and started dancing around. When she sat down she rubbed her feet and toes against me. I figured that with the kicking off of her shoes and the rubbing of her feet against me—well, what could be more of an open invitation?"

Said the judge, "When a woman kicks off her shoes in the private company of a man, it's a suggestive act of undressing. The defendant was right in interpreting this as a sexual invitation."

SHOE-SEX BEGINS EARLY

Men and women can wear many articles of clothing that look so much alike that they're almost interchangeable: pants, shirts, blouses, hose, coats, robes, sweaters, even skirts. But the shoes usually have a positive sexual identity with distinct differences in design to establish the "separation of the sexes." At root is the separation of the phallic symbolism of the male shoe and the yoni symbolism of the female shoe.

Starting only a few weeks or months after the birth of the infant, the shoe starts to play its early role in this separation of the sexes. Different colored bootees are bought for boys and girls, as though the parents are raising a flag over the crib to signify sex gender. There's a tired but pertinent little anecdote about one tot asking another how he could be sure the infant in the crib was his baby brother. "Oh, that's easy," came the reply. "See—blue bootees." Thus it may well be that very small children often make their first discoveries about sexual differences more by shoes than by anatomy.

At about age three or four, the child will begin wearing specially designed "boy" or "girl" shoe styles. These distinctions remain fixed throughout a lifetime. There is no practical reason why boys and girls, or men and women, should wear shoes with pronounced styling differences. The *only* reason is sexual, an insignia to designate the separation of the sexes.

Several years ago, John B. Reinhardt, former president of Trimfoot Company, a leading maker of baby shoes, told a large audience of shoe manufacturers, "What is fashion if it isn't sex attraction? It gets off to an early start with baby shoes when mothers seek to establish the sex status of their little children with footwear."

Fashion has always been a reliable barometer of a person's sex drive or sexual awareness. For example, juveniles don't become fashion-conscious until they become sex-conscious. In recent decades this sexual awareness has beeen advancing to earlier ages at a rapid rate because of changes in the biological clock. For instance, British and American scientists report that menstruation now begins with American and European girls at about age twelve. A century or more ago it started at ages fifteen to seventeen. The same quickening of sexual maturity has occurred with boys.

How does this relate to footwear, and especially the sexual link with it? In very definite ways. For instance, a generation or two ago, it wasn't until the child was eleven or twelve years old that he could start making his own decisions in selecting the shoe styles he wanted. Now studies reveal that today's children are making their own shoe-buying decisions and selections as early as age five. The pre-teen girl of eight or nine is insisting on her "heels" like her big sister wears. The pre-teen boy is equally demanding about getting into "man" shoes.

It's no coincidence that this early fashion awareness in footwear is paralleling the earlier age of sexual maturity. These young children are using their shoes to establish their sexual identity and signify their readiness to launch into "serious" boy-girl relationships. This is why the young, especially the teen-agers, buy the most exaggerated shoe styles, and also the most pairs (double the average for mature adults).

Young people, like the libido-driven young in the whole animal kingdom, are by their sexually restive natures constantly sending out mating calls. Footwear fashion is one of the loudest and most stimulating of these sex signals. Says St. Louis psychologist Nathan Kohn, "Feet and shoes have always been phallic symbols, and eroticism is expressed, for example, in high heels and 'naked' sandals. Why do people buy fewer shoes after marriage than before? Because shoes play a role in attracting the opposite sex."

This active association between sex-awareness and fashion-awareness holds sway right through the middle years. But when the advanced years arrive and the libido loses much of its aggressive drive, interest in fashion diminishes in importance. The shoe styles become more conservative, the heels lower, and fewer pairs are bought. Thus, you can get a fairly reliable "libido intensity reading" of a person by the kinds of shoes he or she wears.

Shoes are designed to focus attention on the erotic foot, to further sensualize it. "To a woman, a shoe is not so much a covering as an adornment," says noted shoe designer Herman Delman, who has tailored footwear for many of the world's most glamorous women. "In fact, in many cases it would be more accurate to call it an *uncovering* rather than a covering for the foot. It's one of the basic secrets of fashion in footwear that to beautify a foot, undress it."

This is why so many women's shoes are deliberately designed with a subtly "undressed" look via the silhouette, low-cut sides, cutouts, open toes and backs, the clinging fit, the sandalized strippings, the shell or low-cut fronts to show toe cleavage, etc. Even the names given to these fashions have clear-cut sexual inferences, such as "nude" shoes, or the "naked look," or an "opened-up look," or "sexy" or "bitchy" or "hooker" or "frenchy" shoes.

About ten years ago I appeared on a panel at a footwear fashion seminar conducted by DuPont at Wilmington, Delaware. On the same panel was Gypsy Rose Lee, who had reigned long as a burlesque queen. I recall her telling the audience:

"A near-naked woman and near-naked shoes have the same thing in common—the illusion that the best parts are hidden. It's that near-naked look that brings a male audience to a pitch. The first thing I ever considered with every costume I wore on stage was: Are the shoes sexy? If they weren't, the rest of the costume didn't mean a damn because when everything was stripped, all that was left was the G-string and the shoes. You and the shoes were now the whole show. I can recall regulars in the front rows who nearly went out of their minds looking not at me but at my sexy shoes."

The shoe, like the body, also has its "erogenous" zones or parts. Each part of the shoe serves its own erotic purpose, contributing to the erogenous whole. For example, the high heel has no utilitarian purpose whatever, its sole mission being sex-lure. The pointed toe (an almost universal toe shape) has strictly phallic and erotic roots. The human urge for tight-fitting shoes, as we'll soon see, is entirely sexual in motive. The selection of particular materials or colors in shoes is impelled, consciously or subconsciously, by psychosexual forces. The shapes, styles or types of shoes, along with their decorative features, evoke sexual images, each in their own way.

You'll see much of this unfold in upcoming chapters. You'll see how footwear fashions fall into distinct "sexual" categories for men and women—categories such as sexy, sexless, neuter, bisexual, masculine, eunuch, peacock, machismo. You'll see how the shoes people wear reveal their psychosexual personalities. And you'll see the shoe unmasked to reveal its true purpose as an article of sexual expression and communication and an instrument of erotic persuasion.

But first, however, let's see some of the unusual features about the foot that make it an erotic organ.

4

The Foot's "Sexual Nerves"

University of Houston psychologist James L. McCary states, "Erogenous zones are those parts of the body possessing a great concentration of nerve ends (sometimes termed 'sexual nerves') that, when stimulated, cause sexual arousal."

The human foot is rich with such "sexual nerves." The foot is a primary sense organ and hence by nature a sensual one. Kinsey cites the soles and toes "as areas which may be erotically sensitive under tactile stimulation." This tactile sensitivity of the foot may actually be greater than for any other part of the body, including the fingertips.

The sole and toe tips are more constantly in contact with the immediate physical environment than is any other part of the body. Every moment of standing or walking involves sensory contact with the ground. Even when a person is seated the foot is instinctively maintaining this contact with subconscious "pawing" gestures, a tactile pedic probing. Nature equipped the soles and toe tips, as with the paws of animals, with an abundance of sensory spots—thousands of sensitive nerve endings per square inch—denser than found in almost any other part of the body. These sensory areas have an unusual capacity and urge for sensually communicative uses.

Let's put this to a test. If you hang on a crossbar by your hands, feet dangling in the air, you feel a sense of helplessness. Having temporarily lost that vital pedic sensory contact with the ground, you're "out of touch" with the real world. You're more than immobilized. You are to a large extent "desensitized." You suddenly realize your great dependency on this ground contact as a vital channel of communication between the real world and your body and brain.

You feel safe and secure with your feet on the ground and your body weight planted firmly on them. But when you're in a rapidly descending elevator, the weight is "lifted" off your feet and you get a "funny feeling." That feeling is due to loss of ground contact, your security anchor.

Why is a cat, in a fall from a height, always able to land on its feet? And the same with many insects? This is because the tactile sense in their feet is so vital that foot contact with the ground is proof of their "return to reality." The cat lands on its feet because during the fall, the absence of accustomed tactile sensations in the feet automatically sets off a reflex action, the so-called flight posture, that assures a four-square landing on the feet.

The feet of the blind are extremely important vibratory aids to their sense of surroundings and direction, and to their stability. How do *you* walk in the dark if there's nothing to see or grasp and touch with your hands? Suddenly you're much more aware of the tactile capacities and importance of your soles and toes, especially if you're barefoot. You find yourself totally dependent on them. You find yourself "pressing" more with them.

The professional tightrope walker cultivates this pedic sensory potential to its fullest (he wears special soft-sole slippers) because his performance, even his life, depends on it. The professional dancer is instinctively "foot-grasping" with almost every step. A baby, during its first months of learning to walk, relies heavily on its plantar-sensory capacities to foot-feel its way along. Your own footing is much more secure and "aware" in thin- or soft-sole footwear than in thick- or hard-sole shoes.

Touch is the oldest of all senses, known as "the mother of all senses." It's also the most "sexual" of all the senses. It's the first sense to develop in the embryo. In fact, the *Dictionary of the Russian Language* declares that all the senses are simply variations of the basic touch sense: "In reality, all the five senses can be reduced to one—the sense of touch. The tongue and palate touch-sense the food; the ear, sound waves; the nose, emanations; the eyes, rays of light."

FOOTSIE–THE SEXUAL SPORT

Anthropologist Mantegazza says that "love is but a higher form of the sense of touch." The sensory foot has always known this, which is why it's an eager participant in the universal sexual game of footsie.

Psychologists and others speak of "skin eroticism" and "muscle eroticism." Erotic sensations can be aroused by the touch of earth, grass, wind, air, sun, sand, water. Such a sensation is experienced when you remove your shoes and stockings on a warm day and walk barefoot on the grass or sand, or dip your feet into a cool pool. The exhilaration is strongly sensual. The "barefoot feeling" is an expression of skin or muscle eroticism. It's particularly effective on the feet because of their highly sensory nature. Similar experiences of skin or muscle eroticism are found, for example, with the snug pressure of soft and supple leather against the foot.

Like the hand, the foot is a touching, grasping, feeling organ. The instinctive use of the foot for sexual touch purposes exists with most species of animals. The same urge, with the same motivation, is implanted in the human foot. The use of the foot in touching others with sensual or erotic intent is found in all cultures.

In German, for instance, the word *füssen* or *füsseln* means "to foot it; to make sexual advances with one's feet under the table." Our own expression of "playing footsie" means the same. Incidentally, Fredericks of Hollywood, an apparel chain, advertises sexy "Play Footsies" shoes for women. In Ovid's classic manual, *The Art of Love*, written nearly two thousand years ago, he advises the lover, "At the dinner table he will lose no opportunity for establishing secret contact between hands and feet." One of the most memorable and voluptuous scenes was in the film, "Divorce, Italian Style." The scene, which ends the movie, shows the bikini-clad bride on the honeymoon yacht, passionately kissing her husband, while at the same time her foot and toes are caressing the body of the hot-eyed young pilot of the yacht.

Among encounter and sensitivity groups, including Esalen, the use of the foot for intimate touching has become increasingly popular as its exhilarating erotic experience is being discovered. The foot touch is used in the same way as the hand touch, except that it can evoke a much more sensuous reaction. The experience of sole to sole and toetips to toetips in manipulative fashion is often electric in its erotic communication.

Not long ago a "novelty" item was introduced on the market, available in department, variety, and other stores, as well as via mail order. It was a rubber bath mat for use by men. The mat, which came in a variety of sizes, was covered with raised, foam rubber "breasts," including nipples and lifelike coloring. To the surprise of the stores, the "novelty" rose to a high tide of sales. Customers dubbed the mats with their own labels, such as "Tit Mats," "Mama Mats," "Bubby Bubbles," and others. One store reported a couple of men customers who ordered custom-made, wall-to-wall mats for their bathrooms.

One woman bought a large-sized mat and confided with a despairing sigh, "My husband has lost his sexual zing. Maybe this will do the trick—especially if I can get him into the habit of taking a bathroom walk before coming to bed."

Amusing, yes. But for many men this fantasy afoot has been no toy but an erotic reality. The combination of the foot's sexual nerves and the mind's sexual illusions has enabled the "Tit Mat" to render a gratifying podosexual and psychosexual service for many men.

Some years ago, a very popular "sex sport" among young people on the beaches of the Caribbean developed. Boy and girl lay on the sand, the soles of the feet and toes pressing in touch-grasp movements. Older couples soon adopted the "game" until the beach was strewn with "sole mates" undulating with the pleasure of their newfound sensation. It isn't unusual to see it on beaches today.

"The foot has always been considered a focus of sexual attraction," writes Rudofsky. "At least this is true in European countries where touching the coveted person's foot is an ancient form of courting. Traditionally practiced at a table as a sort of counterpoint to dinner conversation, it serves as a secret feeler between prospective lovers, a pedal variant of holding hands. . . . It seems that as a transmitter of emotions, the foot is vastly superior to the hand."

Frottage, from the French word "rub," means the sexual pleasure derived from or evoked by having the body rubbed, massaged, or press-touched. Freud and others believe this desire is linked closely with the sexual nature of most creatures. Almost every animal enjoys being stroked, petted, or otherwise having its skin pleasantly stimulated. Almost everyone enjoys the sensation of body pressure against a person of the opposite sex, as in dancing, hugging, embracing, etc.

Foot *frottage*—a rubbing, fondling, caressing or manipulation, especially of or by a person of the opposite sex—is one of the most common forms of the touching urge. The motive isn't therapeutic but erotic. A similar pleasure is experienced mutually by rubbing or pressing the feet or toes, shoes off, against the body of a person of the opposite sex. These *frotteurs* (and they number in the millions) obtain a sensual response from this.

Many women respond sensually to manual massage or manipulation of their feet by a male. I know of one woman who several times a year visited a podiatrist solely to have her feet "professionally" massaged. Each time she unfailingly had an orgasm in the process, enduring the greatest restraint to avoid revealing her ecstactic spell to the doctor.

An article on "The Sensuous Foot" in the January 1975 issue of *Penthouse Forum* magazine cites a case of how pedic sexual enlightenment can often occur by coincidence:

"One couple tuned in to footplay quite by accident. They returned home from work one night complaining that their feet ached. They stripped, filled the tub with warm water, and sat side by side on the edge of the bathtub soaking their feet. It was soothing, relaxing and, much to their surprise, strangely erotic.

" 'We then massaged each other's feet simultaneously with cocoa butter,' she explained, 'and it was so thrilling we made passionate love right there in the bathtub!'

"Foot care sessions became an evening ritual. They bought two battery-run vibrators and lolled on the bed, running the vibrators over each other's toes, soles and up the ankles. 'Initially,' she recalled, 'these sessions were merely a novel and stimulating prelude to ordinary lovemaking. . . . But after a month or so of this kind of pampering, our feet became really healthy and even beautiful.

" 'We began to suck on each other's feet without fear of germs. It has made our sex life much more interesting and added a special intimacy to our relationship.' "

Many thousands of women use an ordinary vacuum cleaner to "massage" their feet. While many of these women find this a refreshing relief for tired or hot feet, a surprising number of women do it as a form of what one psychiatrist calls "pedic masturbation" because of the erotic sensation derived from it.

The same psychiatrist reported such a case that he called "not untypical." The woman, in her mid-thirties, came to him saying that she had become "sexually frigid" toward her husband, and that this was threatening their marriage.

She said, "It seems that I always feel, well, sexually drained when my husband wants sex. I just can't muster up the feeling for it with him."

She said she loved her husband, and there was no other man in her life. The psychiatrist persistently posed questions to learn the reason for what she called her "sexual fatigue." Finally she confessed. Almost every day she was using the vacuum cleaner to "massage" her feet. At first she had used it simply to refresh her tired feet. Then she discovered that the suction effect over her soles, toes, and feet so sexually aroused her that "I've been having one or more orgasms from the sensation almost every day. At night in bed, I just don't have the strength or desire for more sex. Also, and I feel really ashamed to say this, this sexual thing with the vacuum on my feet gives me more satisfaction than sex with my husband."

FOOT-TICKLED TO PASSION

Another graphic example of the foot's "sexual nerves" is found in the foot's sensory-rich sole and its response, often erotic and sensual, to tickling. The noted psychologist Albert Moll states that the sole of the foot has a sensory quality "whose stimulation gives rise, directly or indirectly, to voluptuous sensations." As everyone knows, foot-tickling can drive some into flights of ecstasy and others to madness.

Essentially, however, the response to foot-tickling is sexual. Says Aigremont, "The tickling of the soles of the feet has been used by many preparatory to coitus. It serves as a foreplay center so that it might prolong the sexual enjoyment as much as possible."

Foot-tickling as an erotic stimulus is age-old and universal. "The sophisticated lover," says Renbourn, "knows that many women get intense erotic pleasure when the feet are gently stroked—like having the ear lobes nibbled." Paintings of foot-tickling can be seen in the Louvre as well as in the Museum of Pius Clementia in Rome. They're also commonly found in China, Japan, India and Southeast Asia. Egyptian Queen Hatshepsut (1600 B.C.) used to prepare for her lovers with exquisite podocosmetic care. First the skin of her feet was rubbed and scented with oil of ani until it glowed as though coated with gold. Then as she reclined on a luxurious lounge, palace eunuchs tickled the bottoms of her feet with peacock feathers "to bring her to a pitch of sexual readiness."

A short while ago a wealthy New York socialite visited her psychiatrist and asked whether she should try to "break the habit."

"What habit?" he asked.

She explained that two or three times a week she thoroughly rubbed the soles and toes of her feet with dog food. Then she summoned her two Pomeranians and they eagerly licked the scent of the food from her feet.

"It drives me to a sexual frenzy—the tickling sensation on my feet," she confessed. "It brings me to orgasm almost every time. Or sometimes I masturbate while the dogs are licking my feet. Doctor, is there, well, something wrong with that? With me?"

"Why not go the straight route with a man?" he asked.

"Oh, I enjoy sex with men, all right. But this foot-tickling and foot-licking thing is something special, something extra. If I asked a man to do that—well, wouldn't he think me mad or something?"

The doctor pondered the matter a moment, then said, "Why not ask the man? It might work, especially if you make it mutual."

She called a month later. "Doctor," she said excitedly, "please excuse the pun, but we're tickled to death. My lover and I, we're doing it to each other, and following it with real sex. It's given sex a whole new feeling for me."

The Russians, especially among the nobility and aristocracy, were devotees of sexual foot-tickling. They had learned it from the Tartar tribes. Foot-tickling for sexual arousal was used in the Muscovite palaces and courts for centuries. Many of the Czarinas (Catherine the Great, Anna Ivanovna, Elizabeth, Anna Leopoldovna, and others) were ardent participants. In fact, the practice was so popular that eunuchs and women were employed as full-time foot-ticklers. They developed this unique skill so well that their occupations brought prestige and good pay.

Anna Leopoldovna had no fewer than six ticklers at her feet, though more were employed to serve the other ladies of the court. The foot-tickling was usually done in the private boudoirs. While the ticklers performed their task they also told bawdy stories and sang obscene ballads, thus creating a sort of orgiastic atmosphere. All this, of course, was to work the ladies up to an erotic pitch so that they could meet their husbands or lovers in a sex-impassioned mood. It wasn't uncommon for these women to experience orgasms while being foot-tickled.

A few years ago, while I was visiting Russia and studying their footwear industry there, the director of a large shoe plant employing some seven thousand showed me a private collection of historical shoes from different parts of the world. In a corner was a vase containing several long, brilliantly covered feathers, and also slender artist's brushes with exquisitely soft bristles. As I touched them I recognized that they were ladies' foot ticklers.

The director smiled and said, "Ah, you seem to know what they are. Well, as old as they are, they are not out of date. They are prized by some of our Russian women today. Perhaps you would be surprised to know that the wife of one of our highest party officials, and some of her friends of equal standing, are known to. . . ." His voice faded and the subject was abruptly changed. Later, in Hungary and Czechoslovakia, I saw similar foot ticklers.

Yes, the foot is rich with its own "sexual nerves." It is no mere coincidence, as cited earlier, that the foot possesses such an abundance of sensory spots. This is clearly evident by the common erotic responses to such acts as foot-tickling, foot-massaging, foot-biting, toe-sucking, foot-kissing, etc. Sensual response to such actions is inevitable because first, we are dealing with a naturally erogenous part, and second, because all such actions involve touch, the most "sexual" of all the senses.

5

Oriental Podoerotomania

One of the most powerfully persuasive examples of the foot's natural eroticism and the shoe's sexual symbolism is found in the remarkable phenomenon of Chinese footbinding. Perhaps nothing in history so convincingly demonstrates the reality of the foot's "sexual nerves" and the role of the foot and shoe in the realm of human sexuality.

For nearly one thousand years some five billion Chinese were immersed in a sex orgy with the female foot. Not a mere cosmetic fascination nor a romance, but an uninhibited orgy that plunged hundreds of millions of Chinese men, mandarins to peasants, into ecstasies of sexual passion.

Throughout history, as well as today, most of the world has had a distorted and naïve view of the ancient Chinese custom of footbinding. The bound foot of females—known affectionately by Orientals as the lotus foot or lily foot—has always been regarded by the outside world as a barbarous and senseless custom, a cruel and frivolous tradition passed down through centuries by the whim of some early Chinese empress.

But the truth is something else entirely. The Chinese regarded the bound foot as the most erotic and desired portion of the entire female anatomy, and reflecting the very personality of the woman herself. The tens of millions of Chinese women who had their feet bound were the social and sexual aristocracy of the species, virtually a reigning clan of goddesses with sensual powers not bestowed upon ordinary women, that is, those with unbound feet. For most men, the thought of sexual intercourse without prior passionate lovemaking with the lotus foot, usually left the male as unresponsive as a stone. All other parts of the female body were of lesser erogenous importance. The bound foot vied with the vagina itself as the organ of ultimate sexual ecstasy. Lin Yu-tang declared that the custom was "sexual in its nature, its origin being undoubtedly in the courts of licentious kings."

For a thousand years the pornography of China centered on the lotus foot. When Chinese men had orgiastic dreams, the lotus foot was the erotic focal point. An act of voyeurism had no sane purpose unless there could be a vision of the bound foot. Much of the eroticism that prevailed in China for generations—in paintings, sculpture, poetry, literature, and ballads—focused on the lotus foot and the hedonistic and sexual images it aroused.

To regard Chinese footbinding as simply a "strange and barbarous custom" is to lose sight entirely of the sexual realities that comprised the momentum for this awesome force and instilled it with aphrodisiac powers that intoxicated an entire culture. Some provocative questions arise:

> Why this passionate love affair with the bound female foot? Why not, instead, the hands or arms, the breasts or neck or shoulders or hair?
>
> What gave this exotic custom its thousand-year staying power?
>
> If the practice was merely a curious fetish, how could a "fetish" afflict five billion Chinese (plus others) for nearly one thousand years?
>
> What was found so erotic about the bound foot that it could drive men—noblemen, intellectuals, clergymen, merchants, scholars, scientists, artists, rustics, and warriors—to such frenzied states of sexual passion?

It's easy to say or think that Chinese footbinding was a madness, a senseless atrocity. But, as we'll see in later chapters, body deformation and pedic sadomasochism is hardly an exclusive characteristic of the Chinese. It has always existed in most cultures, the American included. The human species prefers itself a little bent out of natural shape; it prefers illusion to reality, especially where the illusion enhances the erotic appeal.

The foot and its accomplice, the shoe, have played a major role in body deformation to increase sexual attraction. The Chinese simply carried this idea to exotic extreme. Long before the footbinding custom was launched in the early part of the eleventh century, the Chinese had always been admirers of the small, feminine foot, an admiration they shared with many cultures. There was a common saying, "A tiny foot can atone for three-fourths of a woman's ugliness." The small, dainty foot was extolled by the poets of Confucius' time 2,500 years ago. Such a foot was regarded as a mark of grace, cultural breeding and even intelligence.

But the Chinese, a highly imaginative people and especially aware of erotic sensitivities, simply added an ingenious new dimension to the small foot by devising the footbinding practice that gave the female foot—in fact, the whole female person—a sensual image of unprecedented intensity.

THE MAKING OF A LOTUS FOOT

The Chinese completely redesigned the foot. They shrank it and reshaped it to make it, in the eyes of the Oriental male, the most sexually charming and arousing sight in all nature. By a skillful binding process that started in early childhood, the four lesser toes were curled under the ball as far as they could go. The big toe, because it's the main digit and vital to balance and propulsion in walking, remained unfettered.

However, the main thrust was to bring the forefoot and heel as close together as possible by gradually bending the foot as one would a crossbow. In fact, these were called "bowed feet." The large heel bone, which normally is in a semihorizontal position, was pushed forward so that it was resting on end in a vertical position, much like the effect or look of a high-heeled shoe. This process ultimately reduced the foot to less than half its natural length and width and shrank it to the foot size of a small child.

But this resulted in some other important changes. The instep and arch now formed a very high and graceful curve. Also, the extreme contraction of the foot, heel to ball, created a deep cleft in the sole under the arch. The sole is normally covered with a thick layer of fascia or ligamentlike tissue. But because the bound foot was little used for walking, this fascia became very soft and fleshy. Thus this soft, fleshy cleavage, to the Chinese male, was the equivalent of the labia. Moreover, it was commonly used as a vaginal simulation by the male in pre-coital lovemaking. This form of podo-penis stimulation aroused the most intense kind of sexual excitement for male and female alike.

Chinese men appraised the subtle variations of the bound feet of different females just as American men make selective distinctions in bosoms, legs, or torsos. One self-styled authority on the lotus foot, Fang Hsün, several centuries ago listed in minute detail fifty-eight varieties of these feet. The three most admired qualities were plumpness

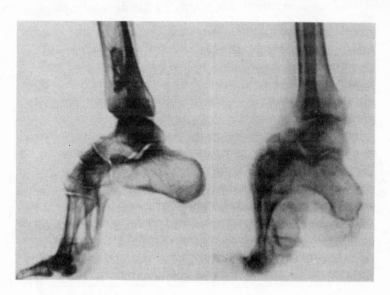

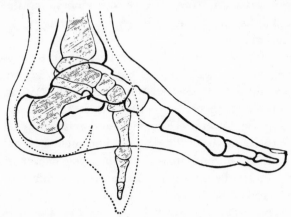

The bound, or lotus, foot of an adult Chinese woman, in an X-ray photograph and in a skeletal outline, contrasting it with a normal foot. The bowed effect is identical to the look and position of a foot in a high-heeled shoe.

(signifying voluptuousness), softness (for femininity), and fineness (the mark of refinement).

The binding process usually began between the ages of five and seven. The bandages were tightened as the age increased. At the young starting age the bones and joints of the foot are only semiformed, hence malleable (final ossification doesn't set in until about age eighteen). Thus these young feet were easy to reshape, though with much discomfort to the child. This was endured because many of the child's peers, plus relatives and other older women around her, also had bound feet. The knowledge that when she grew up she would be regarded as a beautiful and desirable woman because of her lotus feet and willow walk also helped her accept any distress. After a while, the growing girl developed a good degree of immunity to discomfort; the hurt stopped hurting.

The binding process itself was a true cosmetic art. The binding was done by the child's mother, nurse, older sister, or other relative. But by the early teen years the girl had learned the skill sufficiently to do it herself. The bandage, about two inches wide and ten feet long, was so wrapped as to bend the four smaller toes inward and under the foot. This "bowing" greatly shortened the foot and created an exaggeratedly high arch and instep. There were special small and tight shoes to help hold the foot in contraction during this "molding" process. The finished product was a lotus foot scarcely four inches long and two inches wide, more doll-like than human. It required four to six years to bring about this final change.

For centuries, an estimated 40–50 percent of Chinese girls and women had bound feet. Higher percentages were found in the cities and among the higher social and economic classes (where the lotus foot prevailed almost 100 percent). It existed also about 100 percent among prostitutes, concubines, and mistresses, where a lotus foot was essential to the calling itself. The incidence of bound feet was much smaller in rural areas, or among the poorer classes where this luxury couldn't be afforded because every member of the family was needed to toil in the fields.

Yet, it was the greatest sacrifice and pride of a poor, large family to assign one of its girls to the luxury of a lotus-foot life where she would be treated by family, relatives and friends as something akin to royalty. To *not* have bound feet wasn't only a social stigma but often a serious obstacle to courtship or marriage to a favored male. The prospective bride's shoe was exhibited before the young man's family, and was one of the deciding features that determined the price of the bride's purchase or dowry.

Women with "natural," or unbound, feet were commonly derided with such names as "duckfoot," "lotus boat," "goosefoot," or "demon with huge feet." Missionary nuns and priests, despite their opposition to the practice of footbinding, found themselves stymied in combating the practice, since a Chinese woman with normal feet was often condemned to a husbandless and childless life.

Even a few Chinese men had bound feet. Most were the "adopted" boys of adult homosexuals, who imposed the same footbinding ritual on the boys to create the lotus foot that was the dominant symbol of sexual desirability. Chinese homosexuals, transvestites, and professional female impersonators, while not actually having bound feet, delighted in simulating the lotus foot by tightly strapping their feet and squeezing them into small, lotuslike shoes and imitating the sensuous willow walk. The male lotus foot had as much erotic appeal for the homosexual and transvestite as the female lotus foot held for the heterosexual male. (Transvestites in all parts of the world delight in squeezing their feet into women's high-heeled shoes to impersonate the look of the female foot and gait.)

While footbinding remained largely indigenous to China, it was also practiced, though to a much lesser degree, among women in Korea, Japan, Indonesia, Mongolia, Tibet and other Asian countries. Even some non-Chinese living in China adopted the custom. Professor Francis L. K. Hsu, writing in 1953, reported that in a former Jewish colony in Honan, the Jews lived liked the Chinese and adopted many of their customs, "and their elderly women, like their Chinese sisters, had bound feet."

HOW IT BEGAN

There are various legends as to the origin of the footbinding custom. The most popular, though it has never been authenticated, is that the eleventh-century Empress Taki was born with a club foot, small and deformed. So that she would suffer no embarrassment, an edict was issued decreeing that for a woman to be a true aristocrat as well as feminine and desirable, her foot would have to be small and uniquely shaped like the foot of the empress. This could be accomplished only by the forced method of footbinding, which succeeded only if started in childhood. So all families desiring to have their girl children achieve the decreed ideal had the feet of these children bound.

Another legend has it that footbinding was deliberately designed by jealous and chauvinistic husbands as a form of fetters to keep their women indoors, away from temptations. A popular couplet of the day: "Why must the foot be bound? To prevent barbarous running around." However, Chinese history reveals no evidence of female seclusion as part of the culture. Moreover, the husband would be off to a hopelessly late start in trying to bind the feet of adult females.

The most accepted version among scholars of the bound-foot custom is that the practice started around the eleventh century. The reigning emperor maintained a large staff of exotic female dancers for the entertainment of himself and the palace residents. The dancers, in accord with Chinese custom, all had small, dainty feet, and they often danced on an exotic arrangement of strewn lotus flowers. These dancers were considered among the artistic elite. The small foot, already the symbol of femininity and grace, soon became associated with female sensuality—much as certain modern film personalities had voluptuous traits that won them status as sex symbols.

Chinese girls, seeking to emulate the small-foot ideal of these envied court dancers, and usually encouraged by their families, began to bind and deform their feet to acquire the tiny size and equally tiny steps that distinguished the dancers. The practice spread rapidly, accelerated by the fact that men were increasingly attracted to these bound-foot women with their doll-like feet and mincing, hobbled steps. It became a mass movement, ingrained in the culture, and gave rise to a whole new dimension in human sexuality.

The court dancers, and even the art of dancing by females, had now virtually disappeared, for who could dance in bound feet? But the names "lotus foot" and "lily foot," referring to the earlier court dancing on lilies and lotus flowers, prevails to this day, always associated with podosexuality. In India, for example, among the Tachikawa Buddhists, the lotus (*padme*) is the symbol for the vulva.

CHINESE PODOSEX

Over succeeding centuries the lotus foot became the most aphrodisiacal stimulant ever to arouse a people to such mass sensual frenzy in all history. To Chinese men it was erotic dynamite. Howard S. Levy, in his book, *Chinese Footbinding*, a modern masterwork on the subject, writes, "For genteel lovers, the tiny foot provided endless amusement. The woman enhanced her attractiveness by allowing it to protrude slightly beyond the skirt. She stimulated her partner by extending the feet daintily outside the loving bird coverlets. With pretending pique, she kicked the lover's foot with her own, while he conveyed intimacy by touching her foot surreptitiously. He also wrote a character on the foot, holding it in his palm. On other occasions he rubbed it in his palm in amorous play. The smell of the unwashed foot had its charms for some, who referred to it as a 'fragrant bed aroma.'"

The scenting of the lotus foot was a very important part of the personal toilet. There were numerous fragrances, each to stimulate a particular mood or for a special occasion. Levy reports the words of one Chinese lover: "Every night I smell her feet, placing the tip of my nose by the smell, which is like no identifiable aroma of perfume. I only regret that I cannot swallow down the white chestnut with one mouthful. But I can still place it in my mouth and chew the plantar [sole]. Much of it has already been 'swallowed'; the use of my tongue is, naturally, subsidiary."

If the idea of erotically intoxicating foot odors seems curious or even offensive to Westerners, it must be kept in mind that what we call offensive "foot odors" are the result of the chemical reaction of foot perspiration with shoe leathers and other shoe materials and chemicals. But the unencumbered and clean bare foot has an odor no different than that of the body in general. The Chinese lotus foot was covered with only a delicate clothlike slipper so that the foot itself gave off no offensive odor. Further, there was little contact of this foot with the ground. Lastly, the foot, and often the dainty shoe, were perfumed. Thus the Chinese male found the kissing and caressing of this lotus foot as sensually arousing as a Western male does from kissing the mouth, breasts, or neck of a woman.

Dr. J.J. Matignon, a French physician who lived and practiced in China for some thirty years around the turn of the century, recorded many of his observations on the footbinding custom. Referring to the sexual fascination of the lotus foot, he wrote, "My attraction has been drawn by a number of pornographic engravings, of which the Chinese are very fond. In all these lascivious scenes we see the male voluptuously fondling the woman's foot. When a Celestial takes into his hand a woman's foot, especially if it is very small, the effect on him is precisely the same as provoked in a European by the palpation of a young and firm bosom. All the Celestials I have interrogated on this point have replied unanimously, 'Oh, a little foot! You Europeans cannot understand how exquisite, how sweet, how exciting it is!' The contact of the genital organ with the little foot produces in the male an indescribable degree of voluptuous feeling, and women skilled in love know that to arouse the ardor of their lovers a better method than all Chinese aphrodisiacs is to take the penis between the feet."

The distinctive gait caused by the lotus foot was, to the Chinese male, as sexually exciting as the foot itself. In fact, the foot and the gait were usually inseparable as an erotic combination. The steps, like the feet, were tiny and delicate. The lotus-foot woman usually walked only with the support of a long staff to keep her balance, or with the aid of another person to support her. Even then she walked as little as possible. The gait itself was as fragile as a weed in the breeze, and was aptly called a "willow walk."

Looking back, today we may feel pity for those foot-fettered Chinese women and their labored, "unnatural" gait. But hold your pity. The very same fettered feet and mincing walk have been duplicated by women the world over for thousands of years: by the ancient Greeks and their pedestaled *korthornos;* by the women of Europe a few centuries past who struggled along on eighteen-inch-high chopines; by modern Asians who walk on their platformed *gétas;* and by our own modern women who walk in their three-inch heels and five-inch platform shoes. Women have always had an affinity for fragile foundations and willowy walking, and men have always responded erotically to the sight of it.

Chinese men believed implicitly that the lotus foot, because it altered the posture and the whole manner of walking, had a magical erotic effect on the entire female body, especially on the voluptuousness of the thighs and the coital powers of the genitals. The lotus foot supposedly created a sensual softness and more rounded contours of the thighs, and imbued the vagina with unusual sexual energies because of increased circulation and nerve sensitivity in the pubic area. Nageo Ryuzo, a sociologist and forty-year resident of China, declares that wealthy Chinese men sought lotus-foot concubines because sexual intercourse with them was likened to coitus with a virgin.

(Note: The same "theory," applying to the wearing of high-heeled shoes, persists among some men in America, South America and Europe today. That is, they believe that the habitual wearing of high heels alters a woman's posture and anatomy (which it does), and this in turn causes physiological and anatomical changes in the genitals and genital area that heightens sexual sensitivity and makes copulation more exciting.)

Dr. Chang Hui-sheng, a modern Taiwanese physician and a student of the lotus-foot era, states, "Footbinding had a physical influence on a woman's body. Her swaying walk attracted male attention. When the foot-bound woman went walking, the lower part of her body was in a state of tension. This caused the skin and flesh of her legs and also the skin and flesh of her vagina to become tighter. The woman's buttocks, as a result of walking, became larger and more attractive sexually to the male. We thus can see why men formerly liked to marry women with bound feet."

When Sun Mu-han, a nineteenth-century ambassador to Russia, was interviewed by the Shanghai press on the Chinese footbinding custom, he replied, "The smaller the woman's foot, the more wondrous become the folds of the vagina. There was a saying: the smaller the foot the more intense the sex urge. Therefore, marriage in Ta-t'ung, where binding is most effective, often takes place earlier than elsewhere. Women in other districts can produce these folds artificially, but the only way is by footbinding, which concentrates development in one place. There consequently developed layer after layer (of folds within the vagina). Those who have personally experienced this (in sexual intercourse) feel a supernatural exaltation. So the system of footbinding is really not oppressive."

Ku Hung-ming, a Chinese intellectual and writer of the late nineteenth century, declared that footbinding caused the blood to flow upwards and produced more voluptuous buttocks. He contended that European women who wore high heels achieved the same effect.

For a huge legion of Chinese (and not a few non-Chinese) men, sex without involvement of lotus-foot lovemaking was as unthinkable as sex without involvement of the genital organs. One nineteenth-century writer on Chinese culture stated, "Lotus and sex have a reciprocal effect on one another. Lotus depends on sex for its form, while sex depends on lotus for its use. If lotus playing doesn't culminate in sex, its delight is inexhaustible. If sex doesn't include the lotus, there is no way in which to reach the extremes of pleasure. The two are vital to one another, and each profits accordingly. There is a strange mystery between them."

Levy speaks of the mass attitude of the Chinese toward the lotus foot: "The tiny foot had the beauty of the entire body; it was glistening and white like the skin, arched like the eyebrows, pointed like jade fingers, rounded like the breasts, small like the mouth, red [with shoes worn] like the lips, and mysterious like the private parts. Its odor was superior to that from the armpits, legs or glands, and it also had a seductive power." One devotee expressed it, "When I loved a woman, I went all the way and wished I could swallow her up. But only the tiny feet could be placed in my mouth."

The small, bound foot created a deep crevice in the soft, fleshy sole under the high arch. Chinese men likened this to the vagina, and also to the cleavage of the bosom and buttocks. They derived ecstatic pleasure in fondling and caressing this area with fingers, mouth, tongue, and penis. Lotus lovers rubbed, chewed, licked, and sucked the foot, often leaving tooth marks. The women experienced an intense sexual arousal from this. It wasn't uncommon for the woman to bathe her feet in a basin of tea, then for the man to drink from it as though it were a love potion.

A prominent Chinese essayist wrote, "The pleasure of grasping the golden lotus is not inferior to that of sexual intercourse; in other words, one aids the other. The woman's foot is probably more mysterious than her private parts. . . . With the possible exception of having sexual intercourse with her husband, she is never willing to let a man remove the binding, inspect the foot, and rub it. So the man looks at the tiny foot with more interest than the natural one. His curiosity is intensely aroused; if one day he can really see it, his mad, intoxicating joy knows no bounds."

In his book, Levy refers to one of the countless lotus-foot love scenes. The lotus foot, he relates, "formed an essential prelude to the sex act, and its manipulation excited and stimulated beyond measure. The eye rejoiced in the tiny footstep and in the undulating motion of the buttocks which it caused; the ear thrilled to the whispering walk, while the nose inhaled a fragrant aroma from the perfumed sole and delighted in smelling the bared flesh at closer range. The ways of grasping the foot in one's palms were both profuse and varied; ascending the heights of ecstasy the lover transferred the foot from palm to mouth. Play included kissing, sucking and inserting the foot in the mouth until it filled both cheeks, either nibbling at it or chewing it vigorously, and adoringly placing it against one's cheeks, chest, knees or virile member. The devotee willingly washed his beloved's feet, trimmed her toenails, and even ate watermelon seeds and almonds placed between the toes."

The fondling of the penis with the lotus foot sent men mad with orgiastic ecstasy. Women practiced this art, developing it with expert skill, and also delighting in the tactic. Dr. Matignon describes this practice among the prostitutes: "Touching the genital organs by the tiny feet provokes in the male thrills of an indescribable voluptuousness. And the great lovers know that in order to awaken the ardor especially of their old clients, is to take the rod between their two feet, which is worth more than all the aphrodisiacs of the Chinese pharmacopoeia and kitchen."

This technique of podophallic manipulation is hardly restricted to the Chinese. It has long been used by more sophisticated lovers in India, Japan, and elsewhere. And experienced prostitutes in Europe and America service not a few clients who request this podosexual massage in preference to manual manipulation.

Many elaborate "sex manuals" were published and sold, all dealing with the techniques of lotus lovemaking. So sophisticated did these skills become that special manuals were written exclusively for men, for women, for prostitutes and concubines, even for the young as preparatory sex education. For men, the manuals gave detailed instructions on ways to hold, fondle, massage and caress the lotus foot. Men who acquired such advanced techniques were much admired by women and men alike. The manuals for women offered guidance for the many uses of the lotus foot—everything from coquettish foreplay to manipulation of the penis with the feet. Some women so developed this erotic artistry that they could clasp the penis between their feet and gymnastically lead it directly into the vagina without manual assistance.

Some women "masturbated" by rubbing or stroking their own lotus feet. For others, the orgasm reached its peak of ecstasy if the lover grasped her feet during the orgasm. It wasn't unusual for two women (lesbians or heterosexuals) to engage in simulated intercourse by each inserting the big toe into the vagina of the other, much like a dildo. The big toe of the lotus foot was of exaggerated size or length in comparison with the rest of the lotus foot, and the toe itself was a quite mobile member.

Levy cites the case of a woman who "delighted in urging her female boudoir companions to use their tiny feet instead of the male member, and was not satisfied unless she changed partners seven or eight times during the course of the evening." Completely heterosexual men applied the simulated act of fellatio on the big toe of the lotus foot with the same skill and eagerness of a homosexual. In fact, one Chinese authority of the seventeenth century gave his "official" blessing, stating, "While oral sex with the virile member of the lotus foot imitates a homosexual act, the male lotus lover need feel no more guilt about this than the woman who performs the same act on his penis."

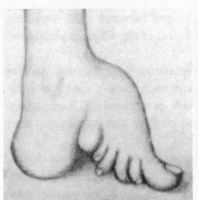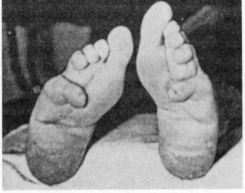

Two sensual characteristics of the traditional lotus foot were the exaggerated big toe, a simulated phallus, and the deep, fleshy crevice under the arch, viewed—and used—as a "second vagina."

There were "lotus societies" all over China—clubs for males interested in advancing the art of lotus lovemaking, or in exchanging experiences or techniques, or in viewing all forms of lotus "pornography." One of these societies published a manual of eighteen different positions of coitus accompanied by the manipulation of the lotus foot. Detailed instructions and illustrations appeared under such titles as, "Grasping Twin Bowed Shoes Behind Your Back"; "A Penetrating Grasp with Left and Right"; "Encircling Twin Lotuses"; "Twin Peaks Fixed at the Waist"; "Lovebird on One Foot"; "Lifting the Left One, Holding the Right One"; "Heavenly Hooks in Palms"; "Head Inserted in Lotus Petals"; "Upside-Down Lovers"; "Two Dragons Playing with a Pearl."

Because the lotus foot was the main sexual focus, it was inevitable that codes of modesty would surround it. A Chinese woman would feel less embarrassed exposing her genitals than her lotus foot. That privilege was reserved solely for her husband or lover. Even to talk to a Chinese man about his wife's feet was considered the gravest indecency. "The golden lotus," writes Levy, "was regarded as an exclusive possession of her husband. Even close relatives avoided the woman's tiny feet; their being rubbed by a man was considered as an act of ultimate intimacy. If one other than her husband rubbed her feet or stole her shoes, the properly reared woman felt extreme embarrassment and shame."

Dr. Matignon adds to this: "The beauty of a Chinese woman resides largely in her feet. A foot which is not deformed is a dishonor. For the husband the foot is more interesting than the face. Only the husband may see his wife's foot naked. A Chinese woman is as reticent to show her feet to a man as a European woman her breasts. I have often had to treat Chinese women with lotus feet for wounds or excoriations. They exhibited the prudishness of schoolgirls, blushed, turning their backs to unfasten the bandages, then concealed the foot in a cloth, leaving only the affected part uncovered. Modesty is a question of convention. Chinese have it in their feet."

The mystery that surrounded the lotus foot intensified its sensual appeal. The foot was washed and bound in the strictest privacy. The Chinese voyeur was the Peeping Tom who sought more than anything to catch a glimpse of the naked lotus foot, or a woman removing or putting on her wrappings. It wasn't uncommon for Chinese Christians in confessionals to ask absolution for their "sin" of having looked at a woman's foot with evil thoughts.

The footwear designed for the lotus foot often consisted of genuine works of tapestry or embroidery art. The lotus shoe wasn't really a shoe in the ordinary sense; that is, hard sole, leather upper, heels, the usual shoe styles. It was more a doll-like shoe to cover an adult foot barely three or four inches long and little more than a thumb's length in width. The sole of the shoe was very soft and padded. The upper was cloth that covered the whole foot and ankle like a bootee, for modesty's sake. The cloth was silk or satin, brightly colored and elaborately decorated. There was often a drapelike collar around the top. The shoes were made by artisans or were home-sewn with care as great as a seamstress would take with a couture gown.

A typical lotus-foot shoe was rarely more than four inches long.

There were many different styles, each for a special occasion. There were even special sleeping or "bed shoes" of bright color to contrast with the pale skin, designed for erotic arousal of the bedmate, like a sexy nightgown. The shoes were kept immaculately clean and new-looking, and usually were fragrantly scented, as were the feet. Each kind of shoe had its own special erotic scent to suit the occasion. Greater care was given to footwear than to any other article of clothing. The shoes, after all, were the covering for the sexual focal point of the entire body.

The romantic custom of drinking from a woman's slipper or shoe is found in many countries. But Chinese men drank from the lotus shoe as though they were consuming some forbidden nectar with great aphrodisiac powers. Because the lotus shoe was cloth and fragile, the drinking was done from a dainty cup placed in the heel pocket of the shoe. Says Levy, "The Yüan and Ming dynasties made a love fetish of the tiny foot, and the shoes became symbols of passionate love and an integral part of the drinking games."

When today we speak of sexy shoes, none, no matter how sensuously designed or worn, can compare with the erotic image and effect of the lotus shoe. Today, in all countries there are shoe fetishists who experience erotic fantasies about women's shoes. But in China, the large majority of adult males were lotus shoe fetishists. Theirs was a constant love affair with the lotus shoe as it was with the lotus foot.

END OF AN ERA

Throughout the long reign of the footbinding custom many attempts were made to outlaw the practice, to no avail. To the Chinese, the ban of the lotus foot was the equivalent of banning sex itself. The first full-scale effort was launched by the Manchu conquerors of the seventeenth century. But so strong was the resistance that the movement was abandoned. Christian missionaries for a while in the eighteenth and nineteenth centuries forbade footbound girls and women to enter their schools and churches. But whole families stayed away. The schools and churches, with no alternative but to remain virtually empty, succumbed and permitted the footbound to enter.

Leaders in some provinces imposed severe penalties, including beheading, on parents who bound their children's feet. But even these extremes proved futile. Chinese and non-Chinese moralists and reformers attacked the footbinding practice as "serving the lewd and lascivious desires of men" and leading them to temptation and sin. Zealous reform societies were organized, spreading extensive propaganda. Still there was little effect. All the Chinese Adams and Eves had too long enjoyed the taste of the forbidden fruit.

Nevertheless, the persistent voices of protest gathered volume and influence. When the first government of modern China assumed control in 1902, an imperial decree was imposed over the whole nation that no child anywhere was to have the feet bound. Slowly the footbinding custom diminished, though with sadness and reluctance by Chinese men (and many of the women, as well), for it was as though an entire nation had been castrated and left sexually impotent.

Even so, the custom persisted in an underground fashion. In 1933, the Village Administration Bureau of Shansi Province found that there were 323,000 girls under fifteen in Shansi alone with bound feet, and more than a million women. Journalist Edgar Snow, in his *Red Star over China* (1935), reported an unusual reversal of the protest movement against bound feet in the 1930s. When the Kuomintang army captured a village, the girls with natural or unbound feet were often killed or conscripted into a labor force or slavery. Their "liberated" feet were supposed to signify proof of Communist partisanship and the new "liberal" movement. On the other hand, girls with bound feet were permitted to go free, and often were given special treatment by the soldiers. Dr. S.J. Shulman, serving with the U.S. armed forces in western China near the end of World War II, reported seeing several middle-aged Chinese women with bound feet.

This national intoxication with the human foot will certainly prevail as one of the strangest and most prolonged erotic love affairs in all history. For most of the rest of the world it was easy to succumb to the belief that footbinding was simply a bizzare fetish, a mad eccentricity. Such a concept, however, is completely out of touch with reality. Consider these facts:

How could a "fetish" take mass possession of some five billion people?
How could a mass fetish prevail for nearly one thousand years?
How could a fetish linked to the Chinese culture spread its influence so that the footbinding custom was adopted by many persons in surrounding countries, or by non-Chinese people who lived in China?

One Chinese statesman of a couple of centuries ago, in reply to criticisms of some foreign observers regarding the footbinding custom, remarked, "If China were now the greatest power in the world, wouldn't every foreign woman today be inclined to footbinding?"

That's certainly something to ponder. Had the world been exposed to the same cultural, psychosexual, and direct sexual influences of footbinding, a good share of its people might well have succumbed to it. But perhaps more important are the questions: Did the Chinese make a sexual and psychosexual discovery that had been (and largely continues to be) generally unknown to most of the rest of the world—the discovery of the inherent erotic nature of the human foot and its sexual covering, the shoe? Or did the Chinese simply carry to extremes an anatomical and sexual attraction which, in more moderate form, has always been universally recognized and accepted?

But how can one condone such an obvious bizarre form of body deformation? Ironically, while the Western world has deplored as "unnatural" the ancient Chinese custom of footbinding as an erotic force, most of the world's people, especially its women, have always practiced their own forms of body or foot deformation, and for the same erotic and sex-attraction purposes.

If the Chinese concentrated their deformation on the foot, American, European, and other women (and often men) have for centuries been doing the same with tight shoes, the wearing of styles that have no kinship with natural foot shape, high heels that force alterations in the whole anatomy, stiff-soled shoes that prevent natural foot function, laced shoes and boots that impede circulation, and platform soles that can jeopardize human life itself.

The human desire for sex attraction is so deeply embedded that the human species is willing to undergo almost any form of "unnatural" and even agonizing ordeal for erotic and sexual goals. And the foot and shoe have always been in the forefront of this universal psychosexual urge to reshape the human form.

6

Thank Your Foot for Sex

Even with the dramatic evidence of the thousand-year footbinding tradition of the Chinese, along with other podosexual evidence we've presented so far, the question may still persist in your mind: If the foot is truly an erotic organ and the shoe is really its sexual covering, what makes it so? By what biological or other reasons can the foot lay legitimate claim to its sexual nature and its close connection with human sexuality?

Let's start with what will seem to be an incredulous statement. The foot is largely responsible for most of the erogenous features of the human body and also for the distinctive postures of human copulation that are unique in all nature. In short, you can thank your foot for human-type sex, and for much of what we regard as the sexually appealing features of the human body.

Podogeny or podogenesis is the study of the evolutionary development of the foot. In tracing this evolution, science has unveiled a startling reality: the one organ most responsible for man's emergence from his anthropoidal ancestry to his present human form, is the *foot*. More bluntly, had the foot not evolved into the unique structure and design it now is, we'd still be living in trees or caves, and the scope of our sex lives would be as limited as that of the animals.

Man owes much, perhaps all, of his human character to his foot. The foot is the most "human" and specialized part of the entire human anatomy. Any of man's other organs or parts—hand, visceral organs, spine, central nervous system, brain, heart, pelvis, limbs, genitals, etc.—can be matched by corresponding parts in other animals, except for differences in refinements. But there is no other foot in all nature that can begin to resemble the human foot; no other foot that has that distinctive combination of straight-ahead big toe, ground-touching heel, and raised arch. It is this foot that has been largely responsible for making man himself an anatomical and erotogenic phenomenon in nature.

"The important feature about earliest man," writes Duke University anthropologist Weston La Barre, "was not so much his brains but his feet." To this the noted British surgeon F. Wood Jones adds, "If 'missing links' are to be traced with complete success, the foot, far more than the skull, or the teeth, or the shins, will mark them as Monkey or Man..It is in the grade of the evolution of the foot that the stages of the missing link will be most plainly presented to the future paleontologist."

But how could such a "minor" organ or part like the foot bear such enormous influence on our evolution, our anatomy, even our sexuality? It was a chain reaction, with the foot serving as the catalyst that revolutionized the whole manner of gait, and consequently the whole posture and anatomical structure. Writes Dudley J. Morton, the eminent orthopedic surgeon and authority of foot anthropology:

"Alterations in structure for terrestrial bipedalism appeared first in the feet and gradually extended upward to different parts of the body. . . . The course of human evolution was characterized by progressive adaptations for erect terrestrial bipedalism."

It is a biological and physiological law among all living organisms that a change in one part brings functional and anatomical changes elsewhere in the body. The foot launched man into humanhood. The ability of man to become the only creature to stand and walk upright by virtue of his unique foot did much more than free his hands and encourage development of his brain and intelligence. In radically changing his entire anatomy it gave birth to a whole new group of erogenous zones and sex-appeal features. Sexually, he was to become unlike any other living creature.

Even the common frontal or face-to-face position in human copulation, standing or lying down—a coital position distinctive among all terrestrial creatures—is due largely to the foot, which enabled us to assume our upright posture and striding bipedalism. It also made possible a variety of other copulative positions which can be called exclusively

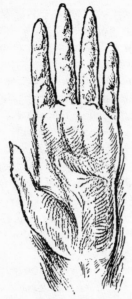

Chimpanzee's Hand.

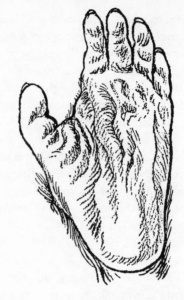

Chimpanzee's Foot.

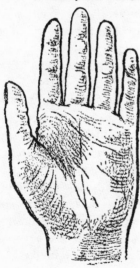

Human Hand.

Human Foot.

The chimpanzee hand and the human hand are very much alike, as are the chimp hand and foot, both with opposing "thumbs." But note the enormous differences between the human hand and human foot, and the chimp foot and human foot. The human foot, anatomically and functionally, is unique in all nature.

human. Summed up, the human foot contributed importantly to the enormous versatility that distinguishes human sex and sexuality.

The foot and hand have a common evolutionary ancestry. Both once were "paws," fore and aft, when man's early predecessors were quadrupeds. Because of this common origin, the hand and foot today have very similar sensory and tactile traits. Both are highly sensitive; both have the same instinctual touch-feel urges involved in the whole process of sexual arousal.

This close hand-foot association is seen also in the anatomy of the foot of apes and the hand of man. Both have long, prehensile fingers or fingerlike toes. Both have the opposing thumb or big toe. This reveals their common origins and the virtual interchangeability of human hand and ape foot. Thus, if hands and fingers play a direct role in erotic touching, the foot and toes have the same natural urge and role and, moreover, are frequently sexual participants in this way.

The human baby serves as a model for this common ancestry of hand and foot. Note how the baby instinctively spreads its toes fanlike, revealing the original fingerlike prehension of the toes. The baby pos-

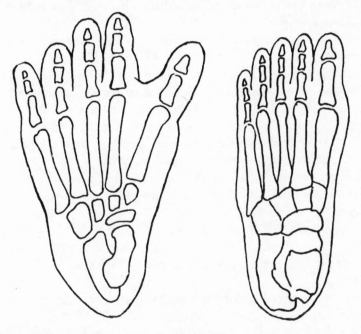

Our anthropoidal ancestry is seen clearly in the foot of a nine-week-old fetus, left, compared with the adult foot.

sesses enormous toe-grip strength, some twenty times more than that of a shoe-wearing adult in proportion to size and weight. This powerful toe-grasp ability is a carryover from earlier evolutionary days. It's also an instinctual touch-feel capacity, a persistent urge within the foot (as with the hand), and is part of the foot's innate sensual nature.

The most recent fossil findings date *Homo erectus* back between three and four million years. However, man didn't start walking upright because his brain had developed sufficiently to teach or inspire him to do so. His intelligence and manual skills didn't precede his bipedal posture and gait. To the contrary, as anthropologists point out, it was his upright posture, by grace of his "new" foot, that lifted him up into humanhood. Up to then, his brain size had developed very slowly. Once the body acquired its upright posture, the brain rapidly doubled in size and man's intelligence capacity virtually exploded in contrast to its former level.

The fact that the foot is responsible for the development of man's huge brain size and is the mother of man's intelligence comes as a surprise to most people because, anatomically, the brain seems so remote from the foot. Yet, this is corroborated by almost all qualified investigators. Some examples:

"The foot was developed before the brain," declares the celebrated British anthropologist and anatomist, Sir Arthur Keith.

"With the adaptive change in the human foot," says George T. Pack, New York surgeon, "there was a current enlargement of the brain box and its contents, resulting in an increased capacity to think."

Morton states, "The potentiality of human intelligence was started on its road to realization with the beginning of terrestrial bipedalism. . . . The earliest changes in the prehuman body frame were manifested first in man's feet, and then in the leg bones and pelvis. . . . An increase in the size of the cranium would have been subsequent to humanoid changes in the feet, legs and pelvis."

Anthropologist Le Gros Clark writes, "In the process of human evolution the expansion and elaboration of the brain followed, and were conditioned by, the perfection of the limbs for an erect mode of progression."

It is a demonstrated biological principle that the smaller the species, the more brain weight to body size. For example, the ratio of brain weight to body size is $1:27$ in a small songbird, $1:28$ in a mouse, $1:800$ in the ostrich, $1:40,000$ in the whale. On this biological basis, man should have a 1:300 ratio—about the same as for a large dog or a full-grown sheep, and his brain should weigh about the same, approximately 130 to 200 grams.

But man is the *only* creature to break this biological principle. His

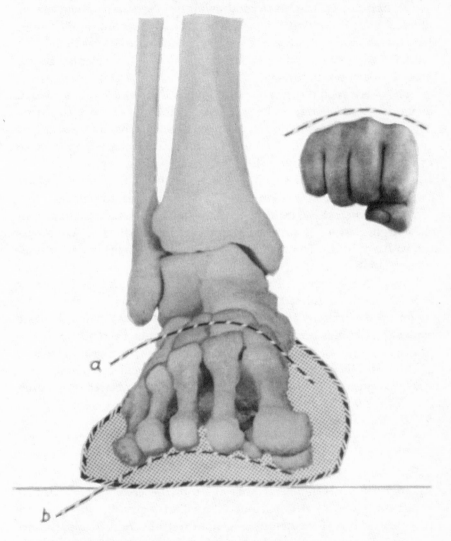

A dramatic demonstration of the common evolutionary ancestry of the human hand and foot. The metatarsal arch at the ball of the foot (a = top, b = bottom) is remarkably similar to a clenched fist. (*Myodynamics Laboratory, University of Rochester*)

brain-to-body size is over seven times what it ought to be, and it weighs a phenomenal 1,400 grams. In a newborn baby, fully one-seventh of its total weight is brain.

But the foot, which made possible the upright posture and bipedal gait in humans, went even beyond giving us a whole new concept of physical body or "figure," along with its many new erotogenic features. It was responsible also for our modern standards of facial beauty, or what we regard as "handsome" features, which, of course, play an important role in sex attraction.

The oldest skull that can be called human had room for only twenty ounces of brain. Later, Stone Age men had acquired more than two pounds of brain. Modern man's brain weighs three pounds. This rapid and huge enlargement of the human brain radically changed the shape of the head and redesigned all of its features—brow, eyes, ears, teeth, jaw, chin, lips, cheeks, and nose. As noted by anthropologist Franz Weidenreich, an authority on bipedal evolution, "brachycephalization" (roundheadedness) is one of the finishing human touches resulting from the upright posture, in turn resulting from man's distinctive foot. Weston La Barre adds, "The vertical body precedes, both in time and causation, the globular skull in man."

What does all this tell us? That almost every physical feature in humans that is considered erotogenic or sex-appealing, whether in the figure or the face, owes its character to the foot. Without the foot evolving as it did, our sex-appeal qualities would be reduced to the brutish features of the gorilla (whose sex life and sex-game activities are miniature compared with humans). Also, without that human foot our brain power and intelligence would again do no better than match those of the gorilla, our closest counterpart.

We are human in every sense because of the foot.

HUMAN SEX APPEAL EMERGES

Another rapid development resulting from the erect posture was an important group of new anatomical features, especially in regard to the female. Most of the human erogenous features are unique in the entire animal world, and it is largely man's erotogeneity that has given his sexuality and sex life such enormous scope. Animal sex is relatively plain and limited sex. Human sex is far more complex and versatile. And the foot helped to make it so.

We commonly speak of man's evolutionary progress having greatly accelerated once his hands were made free. But the hands of apes and monkeys, as well as those of other animals (squirrels and beavers, for example) have always been largely free. Yet this in no way helped to make them more intelligent or humanlike. The human hand (or fore-paw) has shown very little change compared with the revolutionary changes of the foot. For example, a strong adult tossing a fifty-pound weight from one hand to the other will tire after a few throws. But a small child "tosses" his fifty pounds of body weight from one foot to the other some twenty thousand or more times a day, yet neither he nor his feet tire.

"The human stock," writes Morton, "transferred completely the function of locomotion to the lower extremities; the upper extremities thus became entirely free for manipulative purposes. The physical requirements were fulfilled which permitted the subsequent advances in human progress. The combination of ground life and erect bipedalism was the essential proviso for that progress. The anthropoids, by remaining in the trees where the function and locomotion continued to impose its major demands upon the upper extremities, were deprived of both of the factors which were basic to human progress. The inevitable result is their total barrenness of intellectual or cultural progress."

The "shame" or self-consciousness about exposure of the genitals supposedly came suddenly to Adam and Eve when the forbidden apple was bitten. But Freud takes a much more scientific and pragmatic view of this genital self-awareness. He cites that the attraction of scents and odors, so important as a sexual stimulant among animals, insects, and man's antecedents, was supplanted by the sense of sight in humans —and that the many sexual and psychosexual consequences were the result of man acquiring the upright posture and gait.

According to Freud, in early man the role of odor as a sexual stimulant "was taken over by visual excitations, which, in contrast to the intermittent olfactory stimuli, were able to maintain a permanent effect. . . . The diminution of the olfactory stimuli seems itself to be a consequence of man's raising himself from the ground, of his assumption of an upright gait; this made his genitals, which were previously concealed, visible and in need of protection, and so provoked feelings of shame in him.

"The fateful process of civilization would then have set in with man's adoption of an erect posture. From that point, the chain of events

would have proceeded, through the devaluation of the olfactory stimuli
. . . when visual stimuli were paramount and the genitals became visible, and thence to the continuity of sexual excitation, the founding of
the family, and so to the threshold of human civilization."

Thus, Freud declares, not only did the upright posture and gait
significantly alter our sexual and psychosexual perspectives, but it was
also essentially responsible for the distinctive human feature of year-
round sex, for the formation of the family as the prime unit of society,
and for the founding of civilization itself.

Because of the upright posture and gait, the human sexual equipment, including the female breasts, was now clearly visible. According
to Freud, humans now felt a need to hide this equipment from the view
of others—either out of modesty, or to create a magnetic sensual mystery, or both. This was the beginning of our sex mores and our psychosexual inhibitions and fantasies. Says Freud:

"Thus, we should find that the deepest root of the sexual repres-
sion which advances along with civilization is the organic defense of
the new form of life achieved with man's erect gait against his earlier
animal existence."

Again the significant sequence: first the prime and original catalyst, the new and unique design of the human foot, which made possible
the upright posture and gait. This in turn exposed our genitals to view,
which set a new form of sexual excitation in motion, which in turn
resulted in a whole series of changes in our attitudes and practices involving sex and sexuality.

Three remarkable phenomena occurred as man separated from his
anthropoid cousins and started to reach for a new identity on the evolutionary and sexual ladder.

1) His thumblike big toe gradually moved in toward the other toes
until it pointed straight ahead and was parallel with the other toes. This
new position of the big toe served as a push-off and enabled him to take
a full stride.

2) His heel, instead of being raised up off the ground so that all
the weight was on the ball and toes, pawlike, came to rest on the ground
to help bear and balance the body weight of his erect posture. He thus
became the first and only creature to use his heel in standing and walking.

3) He developed a long, springy arch along the inner border of the
foot, as well as three lesser arches inside the foot. These were the body's

"shock absorbers" for his standing, walking, running, jumping.

These three changes in the foot are believed by anthropologists and others to be the most significant changes in the course of man's anatomical evolution. They played a primary role in earning his crown as *Homo sapiens, Homo erectus,* and *Homo sexualis.*

They made him the only full-time, erect-posture biped in all nature.

They freed his forepaws for countless sophisticated tasks and skills, and were no longer needed to support body weight or for locomotion.

They made possible the accelerated and enormous development of his brain and the emergence of human intelligence.

They helped to redesign his entire anatomy and thereby introduce a whole new set of sexual and erogenous features that were nonexistent or inconsequential in his earlier semibiped or quadruped form.

They even changed his coital postures, enabling him to shift from the conventional and limited animal positions to the distinctively human forms that are unique in all nature.

"Man's foot is all his own and it is unlike any other foot," writes Frederic Wood Jones. "It is the most distinct human part of the whole of his anatomical makeup. It is a human specialization; it is his hallmark, and so long as man has been man, it is by his feet that he will be known from all other members of the animal kingdom. It is his feet that will confer upon him his only real distinction and provide his only valid claim to human status."

We take our erect, bipedal stance and walk for granted, rarely realizing how truly distinctive it is in all nature. University of Virginia physiologist Dr. S.W. Britton created a stir some years ago with a paper presented before the august National Academy of Sciences in Washington, D.C. He showed how he had conducted experiments, using a tilted table or seesaw board to which animals and humans could be strapped and tilted in any direction, horizontal to vertical. In the vertical, or head-up, position his various animals had struggled, sunk into comas and died because their circulatory systems were unable to cope with gravity and keep their brains and central nervous systems adequately supplied with blood. Rabbits, for example, succumbed in less than twenty minutes after being tilted in the vertical position.

Only humans were able to retain this upright position. Apes, for instance, can sustain the erect posture only spasmodically for very brief periods. The very large share of their ground standing is on all fours, or locomoting via a "knuckle-walking" gait. Only man can stand or walk erect fourteen or fifteen hours a day, longer if necessary. La Barre writes, "In skull, backbone, thighbone, heel and pelvis, and in everything having to do with full and free standing on his own two feet—man stands alone, because he alone stands."

Yet, even today as a full-fledged erect biped, man must still struggle to prevent himself from reverting to the old anthropoid slouch. Tests conducted at Columbia University show that it takes eighteen percent more physical energy to stand up straight than to slouch. Thus, when a person habitually slouches in standing or walking, he's more than exhibiting poor or careless posture. He's subconsciously reverting to his anthropoidal ancestry. And it's no coincidence that from a standpoint of personal sex appeal, we associate the erect posture with youth, vigor, and virility, and the slouched posture with senility, debility, and a feeble libido. The erect human gait is an erogenous feature of its own. Writing in the *Journal of the American Podiatry Association*, Dr. J.R.D. Rice states, "The entire problem of posture has a deep-seated sexual significance."

How has this unique human foot been responsible for "sexualizing" the human body; that is, creating many of the erogenous features that we regard as sexy about the human figure, especially the female's? For example:

> The large, softly contoured shape of the lower limbs is due to the rich musculature that evolved to support body weight and leverage in walking. In humans, the lower limbs represent about a third of total body weight, far more than for any other biped, or as represented by the rear legs of any quadruped. The foot was responsible for the size and contours of the erogenous thighs.
>
> Since earliest civilization the human male has always been erotically responsive to "pretty legs" and "trim ankles" on the female. Anthropologists and naturalists cite that we are the only species for whom leg-appeal has direct erotic value. The thirteen leg muscles responsible for leg and ankle shape are attached to the foot. They developed as they have *because* of the foot. Foot position affects leg shape. If a woman stands on the balls of her feet, or in high heels, the leg takes on contours and muscle undulations that don't exist when the foot is flat on the ground. Without this altered foot position or high-heeled pose, the "million-dollar legs" of a Betty Grable or Marlene Dietrich would have been priced at markdown values.

The buttocks—their global shape and pendulumlike movements in walking—are an erotic feature of the human form, especially in the female. The highly developed gluteal muscles, which give prominent shape and mobility to the buttocks, are the consequence of the erect posture and bipedal gait, both made possible by the design of the foot. Says La Barre, "The large human buttocks are a bipedal specialization, for the buttocks of other primates are small in size. . . . The pelvis in man is also more massive, since the entire weight is supported on only two legs."

The graceful S-shape of the spinal column (further accentuated by high heels) is part of the curvaceousness in the erotic arsenal of the human figure. This architecture evolved because of the upright posture balanced on two arched feet. The apes have a short, S-shaped thighbone and a straight spine. Conversely, man has a long, straight thighbone and an S-shaped spine, the result of his erect posture. In fact, a baby reveals its early origins by its straight back-

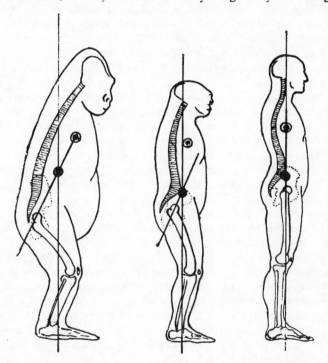

Gorilla, Neanderthal man, and modern man. The solid black circle is the center of gravity, and the circle above is the center of body weight. The more stooped the posture, the more angled is the line. Only in man is it straight. Note the consequent differences in anatomical shape—legs, thighs, spine, buttocks, neck, and face.

bone. The S-shape curve begins to develop as he starts to walk and assume the erect posture.

The broad beam of the female pelvis and hips, along with its contoured profile and sensuous undulations, is an anatomical design unique in nature, and made possible by the foot and erect posture. This posture required a shift in the body center and line of gravity. This caused the pelvis to widen considerably to provide a strong anchor for the new torso muscles needed to hold the body erect. From this came our broad, mobile hips and large, protruding buttocks.

The female bosom, prominent and visible as part of the frontal anatomy, and made voluptuously mobile by the bipedal gait, developed because of the foot which made the upright posture possible. No other animal in its natural or wild environment has the prominent breast. Only the human female has this unique specialization. (Note: Domesticated milch animals such as the cow have the permanent breast, but only because man, by domesticating these animals, made it possible. These same animals, in their natural or wild environment, do not have a prominent breast.)

The flat or slightly rounded abdomen, also a part of the frontal anatomy, is another erogenous zone that became so because of the posture and foot.

The "long leggy look" traditionally associated with sex-appeal in the female is the result of the upright posture gracefully balanced on two feet. (One reason for the perennial popularity of the high-heeled shoe is that it accentuates the long leggy look.)

Even the long, graceful neck of humans is traceable to their erect posture and distinctive foot. The apes are almost neckless because of the huge, thick neck muscles that are needed to hold up the head in the semierect stance or gait. But man's head is supported by gravity so that it "rests" on the body, thus eliminating the need for powerful muscles to support it. Thus the neck became long, slender and graceful, and acquired erotogenic traits of its own.

The distinctive human gait, while not itself an erogenous zone, is nevertheless one of the most sexual of physical attributes, particularly in the female. This gait form owes its sensual character entirely to the unusual design of the foot.

Lastly, as cited earlier, the human foot that changed the whole architecture of the body, made possible the distinctive human form of frontal or face-to-face copulation, along with many of its versatile variations.

The human foot, then, is the "mother" of most of the erogenous features of the body and its unusual coital methods. Imagine for a moment that this foot hadn't evolved as it did. There would be an instantaneous plunge down the evolutionary ladder, coming to roost on some low anthropoidal rung. Most of what we now consider the erogenous zones or parts would be non-existent. Most of what we now consider attractive about the human figure or face would also be non-existent. Human sex or sexuality as we understand it now would be completely denied to us.

The conclusion is inevitable. The foot, as the catalyst and progenitor of so much of our human sexuality, therefore has a *natural* kinship with our sexual and psychosexual makeup. Its age-old biological and physical link to the evolution of human sexuality gives the foot legitimate claim to its own erotic nature. This may well explain much of the long human history of our erotic affinity for the foot and its covering, the shoe.

7

The Foot You Never Knew

The human foot is constantly being examined, X-rayed, written about, talked about, complained about, doctored, washed and anointed, dressed and undressed, praised and damned. Yet, despite all this attention, the foot is seldom *really* seen or *really* understood. Its true nature is one of the best-kept sexual secrets of the human anatomy.

The doctors see the foot chiefly as an ailing and complaining organ in need of relief or "correction"—a complex arrangement of bones, joints, ligaments, muscles and arches. The view is as impersonal as that of a pathologist approaching a cadaver for autopsy.

The shoemen in their stores fit shoes to more than three million pairs of feet a day. Most become immune from pedic overexposure. Most are so shoe-obsessed that they see little else. This is illustrated by the American shoeman who, while visiting Rome, had an audience with the Pope. Returning home, a fellow shoeman asked about his papal visit. Came the reply, "He was wearing a 10 David (D) red velvet pump with blue embroidery on the vamp."

As a result of this constant looking yet overlooking, much of the true nature of the foot, especially its remarkable sensory, erotic and communicative characteristics, escapes the vast majority. They see the foot, like the infant first discovering its genitals, only as a curious and unusual piece of anatomy. Thus we've made a sort of eunuch out of the foot, when in truth it is a virile, sensual organ that plays an active sexual role in our lives.

THE FLOW OF SENSUAL VIBES

Sense, sensory, sensual. These are deeply interwoven in the foot. It's through the foot, serving as a "computerized" sensory distribution center and courier, that we establish and maintain our physical awareness and reality of the earth beneath us. "The foot is an important link between a person and the earth," says orthopedic surgeon Philip Lewin. The earth is constantly emitting vibrations and electromagnetic pulsations, a kind of communicative "life force" flowing up and through our bodies. Thus the foot, as a primary sensory receptor, is a constantly vibrating organ.

Within the electromagnetic field surrounding it, the foot serves as an in-and-out communications center between the earth and the body and brain. Our prefix *ped-* or *pod-* is from the Greek "foot." From this comes *pedo*, meaning ground, soil, earth; and *pedogenesis*, meaning soil formation, earth origin. Our word "sole" comes from the Latin *solum*, meaning soil or ground. Thus, as a kind of radar-sonic base, the foot is ceaselessly picking up and transmitting those electromagnetic emanations throughout the body. Some investigators believe that this little-known but vital function of the foot even serves to "extract" energy from the earth, similar to the way a plant root extracts moisture from the ground for nourishment. These two-way ground-to-foot vibrations may thus be an important energizing power helping to serve the body's life forces.

Radiesthesia is the strange ability of humans to detect electromagnetic energy. As James Beal of NASA's Space Flight Center puts it, "We are all tuned in." Each cell in the body is a tiny, complex electrical system that picks up magnetic impulses not only from the atmosphere but especially from the ground. Hence the tactile hypersensitivity of the toe tips and sole of the foot is no coincidence, but is apparently part of our natural equipment to "pick up" these electromagnetic forces and convey them through the body.

The Pavlov Institute of Physiology at Leningrad has shown that the sensory receptors for pressure (deep touch), which are present around muscles, joints, ligaments, tendons, and the Pacinian corpuscles, possess very definite resonance properties—that is, response to vibrations and sound—and generate what the Institute calls a "bioelectric activity" in these corpuscles. It's no coincidence that the feet, therefore, contain one-fourth of all the bones and joints in the body, a share far out of proportion to the size of the feet. But then, it's only logical that the foot would have such a multiplicity of parts to provide the vital resonance and vibratory apparatus necessary for conveying "bioelectric activity" and the flow of electromagnetic messages to the central nervous system and brain.

A variety of electric "foot vibrators" can be purchased in stores. They provide soothing relief for tired feet by their vibratory massage action. But it's no secret that some women derive intense sexual sensations from the vibratory action against the soles of their feet, in the same way as some women can achieve orgasm from foot tickling or foot massage.

In one popular male stud house patronized by well-to-do women in Los Angeles, the stud first massages the woman's feet with a scented lubricant. This is followed by an electric vibrator against the lubricated feet. One house stud describes it: "The feeling of that vibrator can drive many of them near out of their minds. The blood and nerve sensation seems to rush from their feet right up to their crotch and set it afire."

This supersensory sole and the foot itself have a primal association with the earth's life force. Because we're so dependent on the sensory awareness of this foot for physical communication, mobility and even life survival itself, in all cultures we find such expressions as "a good foot is as a good eye"; or we speak of a "firm footing," or "getting off on the right foot," or "standing firmly on one's own feet." Conversely, the depletion of the life forces is expressed in such terms as "one foot in the grave," or of one being "on one's last legs," or "dragging one's feet."

THE FERTILE FOOT

The earth-foot association is so closely linked with podosexuality and podophallicism that in virtually all societies throughout history the foot is believed to have magical fertility powers. This is traced to the foot's intimate and constant contact with Mother Earth and the foot's sexual nerves. The soil is the maternal source of all life. The foot is a dominant phallic symbol. Thus emerges the historical concept of a "mating" between Mother Earth and the phallic foot, the male-female union.

The foot connects the individual with the earth. The earth is gross, earthy, reproductive. This is why the mythical deities or spirits of fertility, wantonness, lechery, and sensuality are usually portrayed as having the feet of animals (horses, donkeys, steers, bulls, geese, goats, etc.). Some examples are Hecate, Freya, Satan, Lilith, and the Queen of Sheba.

Karl Menninger makes this observation: "In many parts of the world the foot, especially the foot of a woman, has been and still is used as a symbol of fecundity. This symbolism is very ancient. By virtue of the fact that the foot established a connection between the fecund and life-giving earth and the gods or heroes (goddesses, heroines, saints), these deities and persons were credited with possessing a fecundating and healing power which enabled them to render fecund or to heal or strengthen those who won their favor. Woman was supposed to derive her procreative power from contact with the earth, the mother of all things, thus her foot became the symbol of the fecundating principle. . . . After a while, the fructifying power was possessed not only by her foot but even by the footprints, the sandals and shoes of kings, queens, saints, etc."

This ancient foot-fertility association is far more than legend. The foot-earth contact is so deeply interwoven with the sense of physical reality around and beneath us that it's vital to the awareness of the physical reality of our everyday lives. Dr. Philip Brachman, writing in the *Journal of the American Podiatry Association*, states, "The sensory organs of the soles of the foot are particularly important in maintaining effective balance. When these sensations are lost because of extreme cold or heat, or because of some pathology that does not allow the soles of the feet to retain their sense of touch, standing balance is also impaired or lost entirely."

A few years ago a married woman about thirty years old was becoming increasingly despondent. She had long wanted a child but had been unable to conceive. She derived little satisfaction from sex and thought that might be the cause. She went the full medical route—family doctor, gynecologist, psychiatrist. This changed nothing.

One evening she was in a serious car accident. Her leg and hip were badly fractured. She spent the next several months recovering, and unable to walk. Gradually she started walking again, but this time in flat-heeled shoes—quite different from the very high heels she'd worn constantly since she was a teen-ager.

Then almost miraculously, she began feeling an intense desire for sex. She couldn't understand this new excitement and passion. Her husband, of course, was delighted. And soon she learned that she was pregnant. She explained to her gynecologist:

"It was the strangest feeling. When I started walking again after all those months, it was a new sensation. It seemed that for the first time I was actually *feeling* the ground under my feet. I had never felt that before, as though the soles of my feet were without any feeling at all. Now I suddenly felt alive, as though I had just discovered a whole new sense of touch. And it seemed to go through my whole body like electricity—a kind of, well, sexual electricity."

What "miracle" happened? During all those years of constantly wearing high heels, the soles of her feet had developed very thick calluses. Also, the toes had become curled back so that there was no toe-grip touch in her step. Between the calluses and the toes the sensory powers of the soles and toes had been destroyed. She had "lost touch" with the physical realities of earth contact.

During her many months of immobilization the calluses had disappeared. Her soles were sensitively soft and natural again. Also, the flat-heeled shoes permittted her toes to stretch out and resume ground contact. She had fully regained the ground contact that gave her the new touch sensation which, as she explained, spread through her like "sexual electricity." She had reawakened those sexual nerves in her soles and toes.

History is rife with foot-fertility customs and legends. For example, the ancient Romans paid tribute to Mars, the god of spring, with foot-stomping fertility dances at weddings and spring plantings. These were called Mars Gradivus—Mars meaning "the stepper" and Gradivus, "reproduction." Bacchus was assigned the foot of a bull, signifying phallic virility and fertility powers.

In Silesia and Prussia, on the Eve of St. Andreas, German patron saint of lovers, young unmarried girls rub their feet against the bed-post (itself a phallic symbol), believing this will bring a husband and fertile years to follow. For centuries it has been the custom among barren Swiss women to make a secret trip to certain hot springs or spas to bathe their feet as a cure for infertility. In many parts of Europe it is believed that the footprints of dwarves on the soil is the certain sign of a fertile harvest.

An old and persistent superstition in some European countries (and in Colonial America) is that female barrenness is caused by a witch's curse. The only way to guard against this evil is to drive a nail into the imagined footprint left on the threshold by the witch's step, and she will discontinue her visits. The nail into the phallic foot is a symbolic castration that nullifies her powers over fertility.

Even the shoe, because of its association with the foot, has had legendary connection to fertility (which may be the reason why the old woman who lived in the shoe had so many children). In Germany, the bride who puts on her husband's shoe or slipper can expect to have easy labor with her first child. In Bohemia, hens are believed to lay more and bigger eggs when given peas out of a shoe on the eves of holy days.

Why this persistent and universal association of the foot with birth and fertility? Its roots are several: the foot's age-old phallic symbolism; the mating principle of phallic foot and Mother Earth; the life-force powers emanating from the electromagnetic vibrations of the earth; the sole's rich sensory and sensual nature; and the inherent erotic character of the foot itself. Thus, as with many customs and legends, there often exists an underlayer of validity to the beliefs.

THE MYSTICAL MARVELS INSIDE THE FOOT

Leonardo da Vinci referred to the foot as "a masterpiece of engineering and a work of art." His appreciative eye saw the amazing architecture of the foot's twenty-six bones, covered by nineteen foot muscles, plus another thirteen leg muscles attached to the foot; he saw nearly fifty ligaments criss-crossing like a vast network of elastic hinges; and 4 arches, two lengthwise and two across; plus a half mile of tiny blood vessels weaving like miniscule rivers to nourish the whole area; and another half mile of tiny nerves entwined and vibrating throughout the entire structure and giving it remarkable sensory and tactile capacities; and hundreds of thousands of sweat glands with matching skin pores to make the foot a kind of breathing organ.

Over a lifetime this foot will flex, stretch and contract some 300 million times, yet remain functionally intact. With every step it will bear weight of 125 to 200 pounds, a cumulative total of some 1,000 tons a day, and 25 million tons over a lifetime. And in that span it will carry the average person anywhere from 150,000 to 250,000 miles.

Why did nature build the human foot with such a multiplicity of parts and complexity of architecture? Why not a simple, compact structure like a horse's hoof? Because nature's design and plan for the human foot went much beyond mere standing or walking or body support. It imparted unusual sensory capacities to give the foot extremely sensitive touch-feel ability. It imbued it with communicative powers to enable it to function almost as a sixth sense. It established two-way links with the central nervous system and brain, and with the body's emotional and psychic apparatus.

And, significantly, nature allied the foot with the body's sexual and psychosexual forces by giving the foot its own special kind of sex-response, or sexual nerves, thus imbuing it with an erotic character of its own. The foot would be not only an erogenous part of us, but would be an active partner, consciously or subconsciously, in human sexuality itself.

You look at your toes and visualize them as five short, stubby projections packed together. But you're not seeing the real toes in their *natural* state. Habitual shoe wearing has largely immobilized them. For example, among natives in regions where shoes are never worn, the toes have extraordinary strength and dexterity, capable of fanning out like fingers and performing all kinds of nimble, grasping, touching-feeling functions. They're used to climb trees, to hold tools or utensils, to pick up objects, to weave, etc.

Dr. Dudley J. Morton, in extensive foot examinations of African natives, found only a tiny percentage with foot ills or defects, mostly infections such as from parasites (this compares with an 80 percent foot defectiveness among shoe-wearing Americans and Europeans, as confirmed by numerous surveys). Dr. S.J. Shulman, in his study and foot examinations of several thousand non-shoe-wearing people in China and India, reported that not a single corn, bunion or ingrown nail was found. He states:

"Almost everyone examined showed a marked spacing between the first and second toes such as found on young babies. . . . People who have never worn shoes acquire very few defects, and even those few are painless and non-debilitating. The range of their foot motions is remarkably great. . . . These figures prove that restrictive footgear causes most of the ailments of the human foot."

There are numerous instances where armless persons have learned to develop and use their toes to write, paint, use a typewriter, sew, shave, use fork and knife, hold a cup, and many other functions ordinarily done by the hand and fingers. Those are your *real* toes. For example, Carl Unthan, born without arms, wasn't satisfied just to learn how to feed and dress himself with his feet. He learned to play the violin with his toes and so excelled at it that he had the honor of performing with the great Johann Strauss.

The thumb, a marvelous manual device, accounts for about 45 percent of the useful work done by the hand. The big toe serves an equally vital function for the foot—to maintain body balance, as a lever in gait, etc. It is so vital to postural stability and human locomotion that this may be a major reason for its age-old phallic symbolism as a life-force part of the anatomy. For example, innumerable cases are medically reported where loss of the big toe is often psychologically equated with feelings of castration or emasculation. And, significantly, in sexual foreplay the big toe (but never the thumb) is not infrequently sucked in simulated fellatio—a quite understandable gesture considering the natural erotic and sensory character of the foot and toes.

A well-developed, contoured arch has long been viewed as a sex-attraction feature and also a mark of "superior breeding." It signified that its owner was not of the laboring class where daily toil was supposed to weaken and flatten the arches. The myth of the "aristocratic" arch still persists, even in America.

There's an irony about this. An abnormal condition known as "pes cavus" is characterized by an extremely high arch and bowed instep. It is frequently due to a shortening of the calf muscles and a tightening of the muscles on the bottom of the feet, a bowstring action that bends the arch. Yet, this anatomical defect actually contributes to the foot's cosmetic and sensual appeal. Standing in high-heeled shoes creates the same visual effect.

In the 1920s, the director of an exclusive and expensive finishing school for girls in Connecticut was brought to court by one of the parents for teaching the girls "the barbarous custom of Chinese footbinding." In court, the director, a stern matriarch, admitted that her girls were instructed in the "art" of mildly binding their feet at night with linen tapes to shorten the distance between heel and ball and thereby accentuate the curve of the arch and instep.

She firmly declared, "But it is no barbarous custom. Anyone knows that every well-bred woman has a high, graceful arch, and that every well-bred gentleman considers this a mark of good breeding in a woman. It's my responsibility to develop such traits in these young women."

The long, inside arch has since time immemorial been regarded as an erotic feature of the foot, especially in women. Even this arch may have a subtle sexual reference point. Our word "fornication" comes from the Latin *fornix*, meaning the arch of the vaulted chamber of ancient Roman brothels, or the arch of the aqueducts under which prostitutes and their clients "fornicated."

Conversely, flat feet detract from the foot's cosmetic and sensual appeal—and sometimes even diminish the sex-attractiveness of the person. We associate the arched foot with a youthful, springy step, which in turn we relate to an active libido. In reverse, we associate the flattened arch with a labored, shuffling gait, with infirmity and senility, and limited or lost libido.

Well, what can we now call a "normal" foot? The doctors define it as one that's structurally and functionally sound. If you applied that definition to a "normal" person, you'd have no real insight into the *real* person. So with the *real* foot.

But now, what about the shoe, the traditional covering for the foot? Throughout history and continuing to the present day, the human race has insisted on doing unbelievable things with footwear to sexualize and eroticize it. But this has been virtually inevitable. For if the foot is erotic by nature, it's only natural that its covering, the shoe, would be designed and used primarily for sex-attraction purposes, as we'll now see in the chapters ahead.

8

Our Sex Motives for Wearing Shoes

We wear shoes chiefly for sex-attraction purposes—to send out sex signals, consciously or subconsciously. And we select particular styles of shoes to convey particular kinds of sex messages. But whether these messages are positive and aggressive, or negative and passive, they reflect psychosexual attitudes about ourselves or about what we want to transmit to others. In short, your psychosexual personality and general personal image is mirrored in the shoes you wear.

Moreover, people "read" us by our shoes. A survey conducted a few years ago by the Research Institute of America revealed that eighty percent of executives, when hiring salesmen, use the salesman's personal appearance as a yardstick of the man's reliability and sales ability. Four out of every five executives said they looked at the salesman's shoes—whether the shoes were shined or had runover heels, etc. But they also observed the *style* of the shoes. Peacock styles registered negative. Staid or overly plain shoes suggested non-aggressive salesmen. Avant garde styles indicated the man might be a swinger or playboy type. The best marks were given to stylish "masculine" shoes.

At the University of Nevada, tests given to students in a psychology course involved identifying the occupations and personalities of persons, showing pictures only of faces and shoes. The students acquired the skill of identification with a high degree of accuracy: business executive, housewife, playboy or swinger, sportswriter, actor, wealthy lawyer, salesman, maid, call girl, factory worker, secretary, etc. A similar test was run in *Life* magazine (December 4, 1950), with readers asked to identify faces and shoes with occupations and personalities. This brought a heavy reader response and a high degree of correct matching, as was reported in the December 25, 1950 issue.

"The shoe appears to be a particularly expressive item in the identification of roles and statuses," writes Marilyn J. Horn. This means a need not only to be well-shod but fashionably shod. Being fashion-attuned indicates that the person is active, young-minded, self-aware and sex-aware. This is illustrated by the example of the psychiatrist interviewing a lady patient. "Now," he said, "tell me about the dream you had." She answered, "Well, I dreamed I was walking down the street with nothing on but my shoes."

"And you felt embarrassed?" said the psychiatrist.

"Dreadfully so," she replied. "They were last year's shoes."

But can sex attraction really be the primary shoe-wearing reason? How about such motives as modesty or protection or status? Aren't they equally important? Not even close, according to an almost unanimous consensus of authorities. Let's take a closer look at these motives.

MODESTY

No serious student of clothing history and psychology believes that modesty plays any important role in wearing clothes or shoes. One investigator, J. Clovis Hirning, expresses the consensus: "Most authorities agree that . . . the concealment function, or modesty role, of dress was secondary and not involved as a motive for wearing clothes."

Footwear and clothing aren't worn to conceal the body out of modesty, but to attract sexual attention by concealing it. As Montaigne remarked, "There are certain things that are hidden in order to be shown." Fashion is a ceaseless conflict between the desire to look dressed and undressed, a constant struggle between the put-on and take-off. Sociologist Marilyn J. Horn, in her book, *The Second Skin*, declares, "Herein lies the paradox of clothing: that it is used not to cover but to attract. . . . The origin of clothes swings from the theory of modesty to the opposite extreme—exhibitionism."

In Western cultures particularly there has been a "modesty" about public exposure of the naked foot. But this modesty is hypocritical. We dress or cover erogenous parts not to conceal them but to draw attention to them. This is why most shoes are essentially sexual coverings. And it's the reason why footwear fashion is podoerotic art.

The human species is one of the very few with a year-round sexual appetite. To keep this appetite stimulated we use a false lure called modesty, which fashion cleverly designs to magnetize attention to what it pretends to hide. This is why women, who are endowed with far more erogenous zones than men, wear fewer, lighter, tighter fitting, and more sensual and opened-up footwear and clothing than men. Nature itself even endowed women with more fatty tissue to protectively equip them for this kind of body exposure. True modesty, therefore, plays only a very minimal role in the wearing of footwear and clothing.

PROTECTION

J.C. Flugel, whose work, *The Psychology of Clothes*, is rated as a masterwork in its field, says, "The primacy of 'protection' as a motive for clothing has few if any advocates."

There are certain exceptions, such as dressing for cold weather, or for special kinds of work. But contradictions arise even here. Why does the Eskimo, whose prime concern is survival, decorate his boots with colored beads or trim them with ornamental fur or carved embossings? Why does the nurse demand current fashion in her duty shoes? Why do we wear clothing in warm or hot weather when protection against cold is no longer valid?

But aren't shoes needed for foot protection against hard pavements, or as protection against rocky terrain or infection? No, not for the natural foot. The bare feet of natives in many parts of the world are constantly on hard-packed or rocky ground. Yet their unprotected feet have developed their own protective features and are in perfect health.

During World War II, Dr. S.J. Shulman made foot examinations of some four thousand Chinese who had never worn shoes. Included were scores of Shanghai rickshaw men. He reported that virtually one hundred percent of the rickshaw men had remarkably strong and healthy feet and well-developed arches. Yet most of them had for years been averaging distances of fifteen to twenty miles a day—barefoot or in soft-soled slippers, over *cobblestone streets.*

Havelock Ellis concludes it clearly: "Clothing was intended not to conceal or even protect the body, but to render it sexually attractive." So also with the foot and footwear.

STATUS

A group of men (or women) standing naked side by side in a shower room have no identity or status. They're of a single caste. We fear sterile nudity not because of modesty, but because it strips us of identity and status and leaves us a nonentity in a herd. Only clothing saves us from anonymity. So we select certain types of footwear and clothing to express our personalities and give us a psychosexual identity. "The clothes you wear," says Dr. Joyce Brothers, "can often reveal what you want people to think of you."

Even in a democracy where everyone wants to *be* equal, few want to *look* equal. Thus shoes and clothing have always been used to indicate economic status, social position, occupation or profession, rank or caste or class, age, sex, and geographical or cultural origins.

But even the status motive for wearing particular styles or types of footwear and clothing is impelled largely by sex-attraction reasons. By our shoes and clothing we try to convey a favorable image. But favorable image to whom? And for what purpose? If we're making an impression on the opposite sex it's obviously for sex-attraction reasons. If the impression is being made on members of our own sex, the basic reason is also psychosexual: the "look" of success, importance, vigor, youth, etc. In either case we're transmitting the message that the libido is alive and well and the fires of virility are still burning. Status appeal is essentially sex appeal.

SEX ATTRACTION

The motive of body decoration for sex attraction is stronger than the other three motives combined. "Dress is used in all societies for the purpose of sex attraction," declares Robert Riley. John Taylor, editor of England's *Tailor & Cutter* and spokesman for men's fashions, states, "Sex is itself the basic motivation of all clothing design, whether the application be direct or indirect."

It isn't enough for humans to be equipped with erogenous organs or parts. It has been necessary to decorate these parts to further enhance their erotogeneity. Thus, way back in mankind's earliest civilized beginnings we invented fashion. The foot, being an erotic organ, also needed a sexualized covering, which is why footwear was one of the first forms of clothing. Ever since, the human race has had a perpetual love affair with fashionable footwear.

Dr. Renbourn writes, "Women and the young of both sexes dress up and follow fashion for what I would call the Narcissistic Principle: the actual pleasure or enjoyment, a psychological condition, arising from the contemplation of one's body in the mirror, or the exhibition of the clothing that covers it. Women wear their delicate high-heeled shoes, or their boots, not for comfort, but mainly to give themselves narcissistic pleasure—and hope that men (and women) will turn and stare with admiration."

The "clothes" of animals and humans serve the same purpose of sex attraction. The only difference is that the plumage of animals is natural while the plumage of humans is artificial. There has never been a society, no matter how primitive, where complete nakedness existed. Even in tribal societies that are stripped down to penis sheath and G-string, special clothing or decorations are donned for ceremonial dances whose purpose is to excite erotically the opposite sex. This confirms Burton's view in his *Anatomy of Melancholy:* "The greatest provocations of lust are from our apparel."

Only when and where there is social interaction—especially where *new* social contacts are in prospect—do people "dress." Hermits are oblivious to their appearance. There is little dress-awareness in rural areas, or when city people go to isolated places. Thus, people dress to impress other people, for status, identity, and particularly for sex attraction. Consciously and subconsciously, we select our shoes and clothes to transmit sex-appealing messages of the kind and degree we want.

"Mankind," writes clothing historian Lawrence Langer, "striving to rise above the call of the flesh, became one of the most erotic of all living creatures because of his clothing." This dressing up of an undressed body to heighten sex appeal is illustrated by the young American GI who, seeing his first bare-bosomed native on a South Seas island, gasped: "Boy, wouldn't she really be something in a tight sweater!"

The footwear and clothing industries from time to time blow their trumpets about "functional" fashion. This is absurd. Not only has fashion never been functional, but it was never so intended. What could possibly be functional about snug or tight shoes, high heels, platform

soles, backless shoes, pointed toes, strippy sandals, and shoe ornaments?
They make no functional sense. But they do make sex sense. Fashion is
essentially an aphrodisiac. Ben Franklin summed it up simply with an
astute observation: "She who paints her Face thinks of her Tail."

The eroticism of footwear serves as a substitute for the eroticism
of the foot. And so Goethe was inspired to remark, "We exclaim,
'What a beautiful little foot!' when we have merely seen a pretty
shoe." We use fashion to cover nature's bare facts, artificial aids to sustain illusions. Deceit becomes a necessary truth of all fashion. This applies particularly to erogenous parts of the anatomy including the
foot. Says Havelock Ellis, "The boots and shoes under civilized conditions much more frequently constitute the sexual symbol than do the
feet themselves; this is not surprising since in ordinary life the feet are
not often seen."

Footwear often contributes to sex attractions far beyond the locus
of the foot by eroticizing the legs, the hips and buttocks, the posture
and carriage, the gait. The shoe has sensualizing effects on the whole
person. A marriage counselor recently reported about a marriage that
was on the brink of collapse. The couple's sex relations had grown infrequent and cold. The husband had begun seeking the company of
other women, and the wife didn't seem to particularly care. She told
the counselor, "My husband just doesn't inspire me any more." He
complained, "I may as well be making love to a robot."

Then suddenly, when the counselor felt that reconciliation was impossible because several of the suggested remedies had failed, the couple
resumed marital and sex relations with an almost unprecedented ardor.
What happened? The husband explained to the counselor:

"It was an accident, a happy coincidence. One summer evening we
were out together. It was so warm that Cele wasn't wearing stockings.
When we got home and undressed for bed, she took off all her clothes
except the high-heeled, thin-strapped sandals she was wearing. And she
was walking around naked with those sexy shoes on. Suddenly, in my
eyes and mind, she was the sexiest woman in the world. My blood
went crazy—and I was making love to her with a passion I hadn't felt
almost since our honeymoon."

The wife added, "It's just like old times now. And I don't mind that
Howard wants me to walk around naked in those high-heeled sandals

before we go to bed. In fact, that's the only kind of shoes I buy now—the sexier the better."

Unusual? Not at all. Remember Gypsy Rose Lee's comment about the men in the front rows watching her strip routine, "who nearly went out of their minds looking not at me but at my sexy shoes." The sensuous magic isn't solely because of sexy shoes, but what those shoes, in the minds of many men, do to sensualize the look of the whole woman.

"Shoes may produce pleasure rather than mere passive comfort," says Renbourn. "Pleasure is a sort of emotional state which may depend on the impact of the particular part of the body upon the mind. . . . The sight of the foot or its shoe; the sound of a man's step or the click of high heels; the natural or cosmetic smell of clothing or leather excites, in many people, an active state of erotic pleasure. If comfort is sensory, pleasure is more sensuous."

SEXUAL IMAGES VIA ADVERTISING

One of the first and oldest commercial advertisements dates back about two thousand years. It used the foot to sell sex. In a recent excavation in the old Turkish city of Ephesus, a stone-paved street was found. At the entrance was a slab of marble with a carved footprint, and carved beside it the nude form of a curvaceous beauty. A message to male passersby was inscribed on the slab, informing them that if they were in search of sexual pleasure, they could follow the footprint and it would lead them to voluptuous girls for hire in a particular house on the left-hand side of the street.

There was really nothing unusual about this. The foot has always had a symbolic role in language. In Aztec writing, footprints were used to indicate roads. In Egyptian hieroglyphics, the foot and leg indicated the letter "B."

Today, about $350 million a year is spent in the United States to advertise footwear. For decades most of this advertising was dull and unimaginative, consisting of such tired clichés as, "For Your Walking Comfort," "Fashion Afoot," "Step into Spring," "Superb Craftsmanship," and a variety of other phrases as inspiring as a yawn. Shoemen either divorced themselves puritanically from the erotic realities associated with the foot and footwear, or they never realized that the association existed in the first place.

In recent years, however, they've begun to emerge from the darkness of commercial chastity and discover what men and women have known for centuries: that most shoes are purchased for sex-attraction reasons. So today they're putting more romance and sensual reality into their advertising.

For example, a couple of years ago a manufacturer of women's fashion shoes tried an experiment. He selected four of the prettiest shoes from his line. He advertised them in two test campaigns, one in Philadelphia, the other in Chicago. The same newspaper space and advertising budget was assigned to both.

The Chicago ads were headlined, "Walk into Spring in Elegant Fashion." The shoes were pictured and captioned with prices, descriptions, available sizes, etc. The Philadelphia ads, however, were headlined, "Make It a Sexy Spring with These Sensuous Fashions." Sales in Philadelphia were five to one over Chicago.

Many of today's shoe brands pose under Italian names to make them more exotic—names like Cellini, Italiano, Da Vina, Pallizzio, Tappani, Bandolino, Andiamo, Rossini, De Angelo, Medici, D'Antonio, Capezio, Paparelli, Boccaccio, Amalfi, and countless others. Almost none is an Italian shoe designed or made in Italy. It makes no difference. What's important is that American (and most other) women associate Italian shoes and names with something seductive, flirtatious and libidinous.

Some American shoe manufacturers are even trying to inject some sensual suggestiveness (as done with cosmetics) into their own brand names, such as Sofkiss, Pussycat, Caressa, Tramps, Risque, Pedi Bares, Foot Loose, Miss Hugable, Gay Shoes, Feather Bed, Angel Touch, and Hugtite. While these are mere toe-dipping into the erotic pool, at least they're a starting breakaway from some still-existing brands that seem as though they were concocted by the Daughters of the American Revolution—names like Arch Relief, Balanced Posture, Betty Brown, Tred-Flex, Life Stride, Red Cross, Style-Eez, Lady Style, Enna Jettick, Foot Defender, Sorority Debs, Cobblers, Cushion Walk, and Naturalizer.

Some of the men's shoe manufacturers are also emerging from the utilitarian darkness into the sexual light with their advertising. For instance, Bare Foot Gear advertises, "Here's sensuality in sports shoes."

Crosby Square shoes are labeled "Super-Stud." After Six Formal Wear says of its patent leather dancing pumps with a grosgrain instep bow, "If you wear these shoes in the office, be prepared for a whispering campaign."

A magazine ad by Weinbrenner Shoe Company is headlined with the verse: "Elizabeth, the Virgin Queen, at love was no beginner; Sir Walter really turned her on with his bump-toe Weinbrenner." Volare, importer of Italian shoes, has a "V" insignia stamped on the back of the heel of its men's shoes. One of its ads shows a rear view of one of its shoes, and beside it a huge-bosomed female with exaggerated décolletage. The headline of the ad: "Two Great Italian V's." A Bostonian Shoe ad shows an embracing couple cropped at the hips. The man is wearing slacks and shoes, but not a thread of clothing is on the girl. The headline: "Wouldn't You Like to Be in His Shoes?" A magazine ad prepared by The Sanders Company Advertising, El Paso, Texas, shows a small picture of a pair of cowboy boots—but above it a large photo of a sexy, bare-bosomed girl. The headline: "Have I Got a Pair for You."

Converse sneakers' ad shows a bikini-clad girl running her bare foot up her escort's leg under the table as they sip cocktails on a beach patio. The ad headline: "For guys who want to keep playing after the game is over." Viner Brothers' ad in *Playboy* shows a nude girl (cut off at the hips) with feet slipped into a pair of men's loafers, and saying, "My Playmate wears nothing but Viner casuals." International Shoe Company's "Trujuns" brand pronounces in print, "The kind of gear that turns her on—Saturday or anyday."

The women's shoe ads are also moving more openly onto the sex scene. Desco Shoe's Shennanigans line advertises, "Girls who get into Shennanigans have more fun." American Girl promotes its slingback styles with platform soles as "Bare Backs and Soft Bottoms." Williams Shoe Manufacturing Company says of its imported boots, "Here Come the Sexy Europeans." B. Altman advertises its sandals as "The Strippers." Jordan Marsh promotes its cushion-soled shoes: "Don't love me just for my body. Love me for my sole." A Sbicca ad shows a woman in a shoe store rejecting a particular style, with the salesman turning to the manager and saying, "She wants something sexier."

In the March 1973 issue of *Cosmopolitan*, Joyce Shoe Company, in a four-page, four-color ad showed ten totally naked paired-off young men and women (backside view) in an Eden-like garden with shoes strewn about on the grass. The ad copy was to the point: "Joyce Shoes —find your own good reason to take them off."

Toulouse, a high-fashion shoe store in Cedarhurst, New York, prepared an illustrated ad to be placed in a concert bill at the Nassau Coliseum. It read: "Many people never take off the shoes they buy at Toulouse." Coliseum officials refused it, saying, "It seems obvious that the legs wearing the shoes were in a position of copulation."

In 1973, Linda Lovelace, much-discussed star of the movie *Deep Throat*, made her television debut in a series of commercials for M&J, a West Coast chain of shoe stores. Dressed seductively and wearing platform shoes, she cooed, "I'm Linda Lovelace, and I know what you want." The theme of the whole commercial series was, "For men who know what they want."

The shoe people are beginning to discover that sex is more than an after-hours activity, but is immersed in the product they sell and in the motives of why people buy and wear shoes. If they, like the cosmetics people, recognize that the reality of fashion is sensual illusion, they may well see the per capita consumption of footwear take a giant stride. The shoe designers have always created podoerotic art, which is what consumers admire. Now the manufacturers and retailers may awaken to podoerotic advertising, which is what consumers respond to.

9

The Podoerotic Artists

You often hear it said, "Who thinks up all those crazy shoe styles?"
But there are no crazy shoe styles. Shoes aren't designed to satisfy a
designer's whim. They're designed to sell. To sell they must be sexually
communicative and express a silent podosexual and psychosexual language spoken by each individual.

Each year, the American footwear industry introduces about
250,000 shoe styles, which are merely different arrangements of patterns, shapes, colors, materials, heel heights, and ornaments. These are
sifted down from as many as two million preliminary sketches or ideas,
most of which never get into the final lines. About 90 percent of this
torrential flow of footwear fashions is directed into one channel: to
sensually turn on the buying public.

Does it succeed? Unfailingly. The average American man or
woman admits to having a "closetful" of shoes, yet continues to buy
more. From a utilitarian standpoint, only a couple of pairs per person
a year would suffice. But fashion is always rearing its sexy head and,
like the persuasive serpent, gets the public to bite and buy an average of
over five pairs per capita. This is exactly the way the public wants it.
Those "crazy" shoe styles the public buys are simply helping to satisfy
an insatiable appetite for podoerotic aphrodisiacs.

The designers, however, can never "decree" a fashion or force the
public to buy anything against its will. Pointed toes, for example, were
introduced in the late 1940s, and were rejected by the public. But

less than a decade later, as a new lifestyle and social mood emerged, pointed toes became enormously popular. Actually, designers create or innovate very little. Their prime function is simply to reflect the changing moods and lifestyles of contemporary society.

What's meant by a "new look" in fashion is simply a new page on the sex-appeal calendar. The human species can't sustain the same moods or mores for long. That's why we have fashion "cycles." Jean Cocteau expressed it: "Art produces ugly things which frequently become beautiful with time. Fashion produces beautiful things which always become ugly with time." Thus the changes occur because the "old" fashion has run out of lure power and fresh stimulants are needed.

Clothing designers have the entire body to work with. They can alter fashion to periodically highlight one body part and subordinate another. But the shoe designers are restricted to a single, small erogenous zone. Yet they're forever doing wondrous things with it via the shifts in heel heights, shoe shapes, open or closed fronts and backs, thin or thick soles, square or round or bumpy or pointed toes, the ingenious mixtures of colors or materials, and the exotic effects of ornamentation. And through their podoerotic art they sustain the sensual interest in the shoe and the erotic organ it covers.

But the shoe also contributes importantly to the fashion shifts or erogenous interest in the whole body. If the buttocks is the "new" focal point of fashion, it's vital for the heel to be high to accentuate the posterior illusion. If the contemporary erogenous look is a long, slender silhouette, then the shoe must have a slim look with pointed toes, high thin heels, and sleek lines.

There seems to exist a mysterious kind of biological and social phenomenon that periodically causes a pronounced shift in our footwear and clothing fashions. With approximately every decade there's an abrupt change in society's "sex temperature." This brings a change in the focal points of fashion, and a corresponding shift in the kind of special treatments given to footwear styles. The sex temperatures of these decades alternate, hot and cool, with surprising regularity.

For example, the roaring twenties were followed by the Depression thirties and an abrupt sobering up of society and fashion alike. The forties were an upheaval of war followed by postwar boom, a decade of great turbulence. Then came the calm fifties, the Eisenhower years, imposing a layer of relative tranquility. The sixties, true to schedule, exploded into many forms of social protest and violence, plus the prolonged war. The seventies have again brought a more sober and sombre mood over the nation.

A look at the footwear and apparel fashions of each of these decades reveals a clear reflection of the times and lifestyles and their alternating shifts in emotional and sexual temperatures. Compare the fashions of the hot twenties and the cool thirties, or the cool fifties with the hot sixties. Compare the moods, mores and sex temperatures of those decades. The contrasts are sharp and dramatic—and so were the fashions. Good fashion designers, therefore, are largely social weather forecasters. Their success depends on their ability to sense changes in the libido turbulence and sexual wind currents.

It goes further. Most nations or cultures fall within certain ranges on the sex thermometer and these ranges largely determine the shoe styles they wear. Take, for example, Latin countries like Italy, Spain, Mexico, the West Indies, and the nations of South and Central America. Their footwear has an exotic character, an open sensuality about the styling and even the way it's worn. The shoes are more colorful, flamboyant and dramatic. The styles reflect the peoples of warm, vibrant, emotional, and esthetic temperament. Latin countries have always stressed machismo in the males, sensuality in the females. It's no coincidence that a large share of the innovative footwear styles we import come from Italy, Spain, and other "warm" countries. These peoples have a libido association with their footwear. One dramatic example typifies this.

Immediately after World War II, Italy, among other European nations, was in desperate economic straits. Many of the people had no shoes, or those they owned were in fragile condition. America dispatched a couple of shiploads of good American shoes—sturdy and with sound utilitarian styling. Suddenly the Italian government was embarrassed. Expressing deep regret, it said it would have to return the shoes or have them routed elsewhere. Why? The people, despite their critical need, would not wear them. Those sturdy but sexless American shoes ran so counter to the more exotic tastes of their culture that they preferred to go shoeless.

By contrast, take such "cold" countries or cultures as Britain, Germany, Russia, the Scandinavian countries. Their native footwear styles are comparatively dull, sterile, unimaginative, reflecting a more reserved temperament and a definitely lower level on the sociosexual thermometer. The styles echo a kind of emotional inhibition. In fact, differences in sex temperatures and consequently in footwear styles can be seen even in the same country. In Canada, for example, the shoe styles worn in French Quebec are much more exotic and colorful than those worn in British Ontario.

What about footwear styling in America? Traditionally it has leaned more toward the "cold" than the "warm" cultures. However, America consists of a polyglot population, an intermix of various cultures. The ethnic groups (which are large and influential) retain their distinctive styling preferences, while the more "Anglicized" Americans continue to lean toward traditional or classic styling.

Who are the designers who create our huge annual outpouring of footwear styles? Most shoes in the United States and throughout the world are designed by men. Definitely this isn't because men have more designing talent than women. Partly it's due to tradition. But a large share is due to the simple truth that men, heterosexual men, have a psychosexual desire to dress and undress women head to toe. If women dress chiefly to be attractive to men, then the male designer feels it is both his right and duty to design and select the clothes and footwear they wear to please *him*. And most women seem to prefer it this way.

These male shoe designers aren't misogynists with an innate desire to punish women through the foot. They are podoerotic fantasists who delight in converting their illusions of pedic beauty into sensuous realities. I recall an interview and discussion I had in the 1950s with Andre Perugia, who for more than two decades was regarded as the greatest of European shoe designers. He told me:

"Almost every woman is not only conscious of her feet, but *sex*-conscious about them. She knows that a beautiful foot is part of a beautiful woman. But because the foot is concealed so much of the time, it is up to the shoe to create the sensual illusion for the foot. And that is the true secret of creative shoe design—not only to sustain the foot's natural sensuality, but to add to its sensual powers."

Shoe design isn't some esoteric or whimsical phenomenon. It's a specialized art form. But these artists must deal with commercial realities. A creation may be praised for its beauty and originality, but if it doesn't sell, its beauty and originality are damned. And it doesn't sell unless it incorporates sensually appealing features. The shoe designer, therefore, is not a mere artist but a specialized one—a podoerotic artist.

ALL SHOE STYLES HAVE SEXUAL ROOTS

Every existing basic shoe style has sexual roots. Just as a homing pigeon, once released, instinctively flies to its natural destination, so every shoe style evolves with sensual features to fulfill its natural mission as a conveyor of sex attraction.

Our word "shoe" evolved from the old Anglo-Saxon *sceo,* meaning "to cover." Various dialects altered the word to "schewis" then "shooys," and finally to "shoes." However, with the advent of civilization, the original idea of a "covering" wasn't intended in a protective but in a *sexual* sense. It was the covering for an erogenous part, the same way as clothing is used as a covering, to add body mystery and enhance sex attraction. And each basic shoe style is simply a particular kind of covering or sensual illusion for the erotic organ beneath.

Now, ironically, of the millions of "new" shoe styles that emerge each decade, all are founded on only eight basic shoe designs: the boot, oxford, sandal, moccasin, pump, mule, monk strap, and clog. What's more, the newest of these eight basic designs from which all of our shoe styles are developed is over three hundred years old. The astounding thing is the seemingly endless ingenuity of shoe designers to produce millions of different looks or versions of these eight basic styles and thus sustain a constant freshness about footwear fashions.

And now for a little shock: all these eight basic styles were designed originally by and for men. There has never been one of these originals designed by or for a woman.

On first glance it may appear that surely there must be more than eight basic shoe styles. However, anything outside of these basic eight is only an adaptation or variation. For example, most lace-up shoes are simply offshoots of the oxford; shoes with instep straps are merely pumps with straps attached; a slingback is part of a pump or sandal; a men's slip-on style is actually a pump; platforms or thick-soled shoes are essentially clogs; backless shoes on high heels are updated versions of the ancient mule.

However, if all basic shoe styles were originally designed by and for the man, the woman picked up where he left off and really showed him what ingenuity could do. Moreover, she had a great advantage because the female foot has much more inherent eroticism. So she took his proud creations, feminized them, and gave his footwear designs sensual powers that far surpassed his own. His eyes have followed her dressed feet ever since.

Let's take a brief look at how these eight designs began—and especially how they were either sex-motivated at their point of origin, or acquired sexual features as they evolved.

The Oxford. This low-cut, instep-laced style originated at Oxford, England, in 1640, and is the "youngest" of the eight basic styles. But its real popularity began when it was adopted by the fops and dandies among the university students in 1740 (the oxford didn't appear in the United States until 1898).

The oxford was designed to serve as a kind of foot corset. This reduced the "spread" of the foot, making it appear smaller and trimmer, just as a corset created the illusion of a small, youthful waist and hips. In fact, it was the laced corset that inspired the oxford. Both had the same motive: to make a particular part of the anatomy look smaller, slimmer, more youthful and curvaceous.

The Sandal. This has always been one of the sexiest of shoe styles, especially in the more feminine, fragile versions balanced on high heels. The style itself dates back at least 6,000 years. Its word root is from *sanis*, meaning a board of leather to which a simple thong was attached to hold it onto the foot. Sometimes a tiny, irritable pebble or grains of sand would wedge between the board and the foot. The Latin word for a small, sharp pebble is *scrupulus*. The Romans compared the pricking of one's conscience with having a pebble in one's sandal—which gave birth to our own word "scruple."

Men and women lost no time converting that early simple sandal into works of seductive art and erotic symbolism. They added many straps of different widths, colors and materials, criss-crossing them, entwining them around foot, ankle and leg, decorating them with jewels and erotic insignia. It became then, even as today, one of the most sensuous of shoes, partly concealing and partly revealing the sinuous movements of the foot beneath. A reference in ancient Maccabean Jewry cites that the "lady Judith," before setting out on her perilous mission, "drew sandals upon her feet . . . to allure all men that should see her." In the Book of Judith, Holofernes admires her dress and jewels, but it was "her sandals that ravished his eyes."

The Boot. This style dates back about 4,500 years. Originally it was a shoe with a separate wrap-around legging. Later the legging was attached to the shoe and the result was the boot. When that happened, creative imagination went to work by decorating and flaring the upper part so that it resembled an ornamental bucket. In fact, the French called it *butt,* meaning water bucket. This evolved into "boute," and finally "boot." In the nineteenth century, sailors coming ashore would stuff illicit merchandise into their bucketlike boots. That's how the word "bootlegger" originated.

But the boot was inevitably destined for erotic expression. Over the centuries it underwent countless variations of sensual treatment for men and women alike. The wide-top cavalier boot worn by the dandies of the seventeenth century was lavishly adorned with colorful lace overlapping the top edge. Military boots worn by soldiers and civilians alike became associated—today no less than yesterday—with strivings for masculine and machismo identification. The leg-hugging, knee-high (or higher) boots popularly worn by women in the late 1960s (as well as in centuries past) were blatantly sexual in look and intent. Psychiatrists commonly associate boots with sadomasochistic and psychosexual drives.

The Monk. This is a low-cut slip-on shoe with a high tongue and a wide strap across the instep, attached to a buckle or other fastener on the side. This style, long popular with men, was designed originally by an Alpine monk in the fifteenth century, and for a long time was worn mostly by monastics throughout Europe. But when adopted by the civilian population it soon became sexualized. The buckles became very ornate, and the shoe itself was richly decorated with color, stitching or embroidery, jewel implants, etc. Even the high tongue was twisted or curled to deliberately give it a phallic look. A further appeal was found in the "corseted" feeling of the wide strap pulled tightly across the instep, which helped the foot to look smaller, sleeker, and more sensual. Thus even the monks couldn't keep the monk style celibate.

The Moccasin. This is the oldest foot covering known to man. It has been traced back some 15,000 years. Its original form was a simple wrap-around of a piece of crudely tanned hide. But even the basic moccasin couldn't retain its simplicity for long.

The moccasins of all Indian tribes of both North and South America were, and still are, decorated with beads, fringes, shells, ornamental slashes and cutouts. Most of the earlier moccasins were soft-soled. The supple leather gave the foot a pleasant skin-to-skin tactile sensation. Few moccasins today are strictly utilitarian. They are "styled" with all kinds of decorative variations to give them more eye-appeal.

The Pump. This style, one of the most persistently popular, dates back many centuries. It started as a simple, low-cut slip-on or slipper worn mostly around the house. In the early days some careless and slovenly people wore these "slipshoes" outdoors. This was frowned upon and gave rise to our word "slipshod" for persons who dress or do things in an untidy or sloppy manner.

In 1836, elastic goring was invented in England. Attached around the shoe's topline or collar, it allowed the shoe to cling snugly to the foot for a more elegant look. Gradually, straps, buttons, buckles, bows and ornaments were added. Exotic leathers and fabrics were used. Higher and higher heels were attached to it, for both men and women. Soon the simple pump or slip-on shoe was foot-flattering and sensual in look.

The pump evolved into one of the most seductive of styles because its hugging fit accentuated the contours of the foot. The low-front shell pump deliberately showed a suggestive cleavage of the toes. The D'Orsay pump, low-cut on the sides, exposed the curve of the long arch and the sinuous movements of the foot. It was designed by Count Alfred Guillaume Gabriel D'Orsay, a Continental dandy during the first half of the nineteenth century. The women adopted it and further sensualized it. To this day, the delicate, high-heeled pump remains one of the sexiest of shoe designs—especially on the foot of a woman who can do seductive justice to it.

The Mule. This got its start as a simple, flat, backless slipper with the ancient Sumerians. They called it a *mulu*, meaning an indoor shoe or slipper. Many centuries later the Italians put a curvaceous heel under it. This sexualized both the foot and shoe by putting the foot on a pedestal and leaving the foot half dressed and half undressed. It continues to be popular throughout the world, and is often used as an evening shoe. Or it may have a slingback or halter strap that helps hold the shoe onto the foot. However, its half-open, half-closed look is designed on the same principle as the see-through blouse or dress.

The Clog. This is another design of ancient origin. It was the original platform shoe, and perhaps even the forerunner of the high heel.

In its original version it was a shoe that rested on a raised wooden base. Its purpose was to add height, hence importance and sex attraction, to the wearer.

In Japan it has been known for centuries as the *géta*, with its platform raised from two to twelve inches off the ground. The European version is called the sabot, a wooden shoe without a platform. In the early days of the Industrial Revolution in Europe, French and Belgian workers rebelled against the new machinery that threatened their jobs. So they threw their sabots into the machines to damage or stop them —which is how we got our word "sabotage."

Clogs have remained a universal fashion, the essential model for all platform shoes, and frequently appear on the fashion scene, popular especially with younger women for the sexy, long, leggy look they give.

It's impossible to divorce sex from shoes. The chastity belt was utilitarian in function but sexual in motive. So also with shoes. Because the foot is an erotic organ, its covering, the shoe, must be symbolically sexual in design and intent. The function of the shoe designer, therefore, is to create podoerotic art.

But erotic symbolism isn't expressed in all footwear in the same way. The sex-appeal features in shoe design must comply with the psychosexual personality of the individual. This is why there are so many different types and styles of shoes, each to fit the personality of the individual. This is why women's shoes can be classified as sexy, sexless, neuter, and bisexual; or men's shoes as sensuous, peacock, eunuch, masculine, and machismo. Over the next couple of chapters you should be able to determine which of these best reflects your own psychosexual personality.

Sexy, Sexless, Neuter, and Bisexual Shoes

All women's footwear belongs in one of four categories: sexy, sexless, neuter, and bisexual. Each of these types reflects or expresses a woman's psychosexual makeup and personality. Sometimes a woman will switch her natural character for a special occasion, and correspondingly switch her shoes. She may, for example, be a habitual neuter shoe wearer, but for a special evening on the town when she's in the mood to unleash some of her usual decorum, she'll wear sexy shoes. But the type of shoes she wears *habitually* is a reliable key to her true personality and psychosexual makeup.

What distinguishes each of these types of footwear? Who wears the different types? And what does each reveal about a woman?

SEXY SHOES

Sexy shoes beg to be admired with a sensuous admiration, not only for the shoe but for the whole person. A couple of centuries ago a certain style of French shoe was called the *venez y voir* or "come-hither" look. The back part had cutouts or peepholes surrounded by jewels, and the heel itself was colorfully ornamented. The style was designed to lure the male eye to follow a woman *after* she'd passed by (today's shoemen call this "back interest"). Women all over Europe embraced this saucy style and it had a long reign. Today the same "come-hither" look is seen in slingback or backless shoes on high heels, or with other ornate decorative features on the back part and heel. They convey the same follow-me message to the male eye.

Shoe manufacturers and retailers agilely side-step the use of such terms as sexy, bitchy, or hooker shoes in their advertising. They use more coy terms such as "naked" sandals or a "nude" look, which is simply bitchy by other names. Women wear sexy shoes for no other reason than because men find these styles, along with the women who wear them, sexually attractive. The late shoeman Harold R. Quimby put it succinctly in verse:

> There was a girl from Sandy Hook
> With ankles trim and neat.
> She wore red shoes with lots of straps
> To give the boys a treat.

But sexy shoes are hardly limited to hookers, call girls, strippers, or nymphomaniacs. They're seen every day on Main Street or in suburbia. Designer Herman Delman cites an example of this: "One of the most perfect ladies I know chooses a cutout, naked sandal in red, green, or some other bright color. You would definitely call them sexy shoes. But oddly enough, when this customer wears such creations on her feet, she still looks like a perfect lady." Class, therefore, is the ability to wear bitchy shoes and look like a lady instead of a hooker. And millions of women make the effort every day.

But while the shoe can add to the sexiness of the figure and person, it still takes the right figure and person to do full justice to the special features of a sexy shoe. When in the late 1950s a shoe retailer appeared on Groucho Marx's popular TV show, "You Bet Your Life," Groucho asked him, "What's the hottest thing today in women's shoes?" The retailer's response: "Brigitte Bardot."

What's a sexy shoe? Prominent shoe designer Beth Levine defines it as "a shoe that indicates the personality of the wearer and her sensuousness. It's what the shoe does to the instep, the arch. The pitch of the heel and the feel of the materials is important." Then she adds, "When shoes get sexy, business gets better."

The sensuality of a shoe differs in degrees. Sexy shoes are more subtly erotic, whereas the bitchy or hooker shoe is flagrantly sexual. Jayne Mansfield, sex symbol of the sixties, selected her wardrobe of over two hundred pairs of shoes with their sex-appeal value constantly in mind. For her it was sexy shoes, yes; bitchy shoes, no. "Shoes, like all adornment," she declared, "should suggest but never shriek sex."

Hollywood couturier-designer Don Loper comments, "Shoes are a dead give-away. Nothing is so attractive to a man as a well-turned ankle and a beautifully shod foot. The shoe is always the frame for one of woman's most alluring physical charms, her feet."

One of the world's most extensive shoe wardrobes was owned by Rita Lydig, a wealthy socialite and one of the most extravagant fashionables during the first quarter of the twentieth century. She owned hundreds of pairs of shoes, almost all of them outrightly sexy types, many designed exclusively for her. So large and unusual was this collection that in 1970 the New York Metropolitan Museum of Art presented a special exhibit of them. Mrs. Lydig left one memorable quote: "In my view, sex begins with the foot. That's where a woman begins to dress up, or down. A shoe without sex appeal is like a tree without leaves—barren."

Saul Steinberg, long one of the outstanding caricaturists on the contemporary scene, utilizes voluptuous fashions to characterize his female subjects. He comments, "The shoes are always sexually aggressive."

What particular features give a woman's shoe its sexy look and appeal? There are a number of them:

The Heel. The higher, slimmer, and more contoured the heel, the sexier. This makes the foot look smaller, the arch and instep curvier, the leg longer and shapelier, the hips and buttocks wigglier. Such heels sensualize the body lines and gait.

The Fit. Sexy shoes have a skin-tight fit which accentuates foot shape and the sinuous movements of the foot inside.

The Materials. Some materials, especially when snugly fitted, evoke both a sensual look by the viewer and a sensuous feel by the wearer. Some leathers in particular have this quality, such as kidskin, calfskin, lizard, snakeskin, certain fabrics, and the suggestive see-through look of clear vinyl.

The Colors. Certain colors lend sensual effects to footwear, particularly bright and bold ones. They shout to be heard in a sexual sense.

Toe Shape. The pointed or tapered toe is an undisputed phallic symbol. Square or round or stubby toe shapes, no matter how much in fashion, desexualize a woman's shoe and foot. That's why most women's shoes most of the time in most parts of the world have always been a pointed shape. They slenderize and sexualize the foot look.

No mistaking the intent of this thigh-high lattice boot.

Seminakedness. Sexy shoes are frequently seductive semicoverings. Examples: stripping sandals, open-back pumps, wrap-around ankle straps, low-cut shell pumps, D'Orsay pumps with low-cut sides, mules, cutouts over the vamp, deep-cut throatlines that expose toe cleavage. The look is half-dressed, half-undressed.

The idea of cleavage or décolleté associated with the bosom has a common parallel with the shoe and foot. The throatline of the shoe is the silhouette of the vamp's edge just below the instep. There are many different types of throatlines on women's shoes but, significantly, *never* on men's shoes. It's no coincidence that on the shoe these décolleté effects are known as throatlines. On the shoe, as on the dress, the shape of the throatline can be low-cut or high-cut, V-shaped, round, or square. A sexy dress exposes bosom cleavage. A sexy shoe exposes toe cleavage.

One of the sexiest types of footwear worn by women is the knee-high (or higher), leg-clinging boot. Note, for example, how most majorettes or cheerleaders at college or professional football games wear high, leg-hugging boots with their mini-skirts or hot pants. With the girls constantly kicking up their legs, the whole idea is to convey an eye-catching, sexy image—and the boots are vital to this image.

When fashion designer Kenneth Jay Lane recently saw a movie rerun of Greta Garbo wearing high, leg-clinging boots, he said he started "thinking dirty." This reaction is far more common among males than realized. During the boot boom in the late 1960s, hundreds of thousands of men made an erotic pastime of watching booted girls pass on the street. Women have always known or sensed this male response, which is one reason for the long life of the boot style.

The madam of one large and expensive Atlanta brothel insists that her girls wear high-heeled, leg-clinging boots of knee height or higher while on the premises. A local underground newspaper quotes her: "There's nothing, not even booze, that warms up a waiting customer with anticipated pleasure better than watching near-naked girls prance around in those sexy boots. Some of the men have admitted shooting off in their pants just at the sight of it."

Leathem writes, "There is always an interesting sexual conflict that arises when anyone (particularly of the male sex) sees an extremely feminine woman who has adopted certain malelike items to her dress. . . . Boots enhance a woman's *sensuality*, not her beauty. Any booted woman, haughtily looking as though she had a whip, caters directly to masochistic fantasies—the higher the boot and the higher the heel, the more eroticism emanating from this female. She is sadistic, her victims are masochistic, and her whole bearing and manner elicit the kind of sexual tension associated with pleasure-pain."

It's no coincidence that the mass popularity of high, leg-hugging boots for women in the late 1960s paralleled the launching of the women's liberation movement, whose initial symptoms centered less on emancipation than on a subconscious vengeance regarding the chauvinistic male. Perhaps no article of clothing expressed the new, emerging female aggression more than these erotic boot fashions. And many men derived a secret masochistic, masturbative pleasure from it all.

Who wears sexy shoes? Any woman who wants to look seductive and sex-appealing. Said Jayne Mansfield, "I choose my shoes with the same care as I choose my cosmetics—because shoes are a point of attraction to my feet. European men consider a woman's feet part of her sexual attraction more than American men do. Perhaps that's because American women don't emphasize their feet as one of their most potent physical charms."

A woman wearing sexy shoes is certainly trying to convey a sexual message. She wants to be noticed and admired as a feminine and sensuous woman. Her shoes transmit her feelings and attitudes, saying silently what she may be too inhibited to say openly. For centuries women have been sending these sexual signals via their shoes and men have been accurately decoding them.

SEXLESS SHOES

Sexless shoes are known by such names as "sensible," or "comfort," or "orthopedic" shoes; or, in the trade, as "old ladies' running shoes."

What's a sexless shoe? In women's shoes it's a drab, somber, lackluster look—low or flat heel, usually a mannish oxford or tie shoe, rounded or slightly bulbous toe, fitting high around the foot like an old-fashioned lace collar, usually black or some other dull color, devoid of ornamentation, dowdily utilitarian. It has neither personality nor femininity. Just as a nerve is removed from a tooth to deaden it, so these shoes are castrated by removal of all sensuous features to desex them.

There are certain extremes of the sexless shoe. One example is the so-called "space," or "contour," shoes. The custom-molded types sell for up to $100 a pair. Comfort, yes. But the same can be said of snowshoes. Treadeasy Shoe Company advertises its own version: "They're

The EARTH® shoe, the heel on a lower plane than the sole. A comfortable but totally desexed style. (*EARTH® shoes*)

ugly—but they feel beautiful." The space shoe is usually laced on the side, has a flat heel, a toe broad enough to match a cow's smile, is colorless, and strictly utilitarian. It was probably designed by God in one of His moments of wrath.

A more recent version of this, with variations, is known as the EARTH® shoe, whose overnight popularity has spawned more than fifty competitors under different brand names. The shoe features what is called a "negative heel"—the plane of the heel lower than that of the sole.

Stylewise, the EARTH® shoe, along with its imitators, has the esthetic appeal of a bullfrog. But while they're sexless in look they've been reported to have a stimulating sensual effect on some wearers. One podiatrist told me:

"I've already had at least two of my women patients tell me that since wearing these shoes a while they've begun to feel more 'sexually alive,' as one woman expressed it. I have no idea of why or how it happens, but I do find it strange that these shoe styles, devoid of any sex appeal in appearance, can have any sexual effect on the wearer."

But there's really no mystery to this effect, especially where the foot has acquired a "pes cavus" condition—a kind of contracted, bowed foot with toes bent back. The soles and toes of such feet have lost much of their natural ground contact so vital to touch response. But when the foot is housed in a flat-plane shoe, the whole sole of the foot and the toes reestablish full-scale earth contact. The foot's sexual nerves are reactivated with the impact of this reborn sense of touch, which sets off a stimulating neural reflex through the body.

Who wears sexless shoes? Mostly sexually turned-off women: the elderly or infirm; women of certain religious callings or members of service organizations such as Salvation Army lassies, Mennonites and Amish, etc.; or women with serious foot ills. Then there are those women with psychosexual inhibitions or neurotic problems, who use their desexed shoes as a pedic chastity belt. Or butch-type lesbians who deliberately masculinize their appearance.

There are also those women who proudly rebel against being "slaves of fashion" by wearing anti-sex-appeal footwear and clothing. And still another group, mostly young, who succumb to what clothing historian James Laver calls "slob fashion"—those who wear dirty, frayed sneakers, clumsy work-style boots, shabby sandals, go barefoot, or adopt a senile fashion called the "granny" shoe.

It's not unusual to hear men ridicule "silly" fashions and tell their wives they ought to wear "sensible" shoes. Yet, if they saw their mistresses with sensible shoes they'd squawk like wounded roosters. And there are the doctors who are constantly crusading for women's sensible shoes. But the shoes their wives wear are almost never sensible.

The very term "sensible shoes" repels most women. Few will submit to voluntary desexualization. Harry Golden's *Your Entitl'* sums it up: "A woman says goodbye to youth when she starts to wear sensible shoes. When comfort becomes so important that she climbs down from stiltlike heels, she is out of the charmed circle of youth. Romance flickers out except for movies and perhaps a remark to Mrs. Kohn that the new clerk in Spiegel's delicatessen looks a little bit like Tony Curtis."

Certainly all women who wear sexless shoes aren't desexed. They only look that way. A few years ago, Nordstrom's of Seattle, one of the nation's largest shoe stores, received a letter from a woman customer. It read: "I received the shoes you sent me and they are fine. For ten years my feet hurt me. The last couple of years my feet have been so tender and sore I couldn't even sleep with my husband. After wearing your comfort shoes for only two months, I now find I can sleep with anyone."

Eleanor Roosevelt was a consistent wearer of sexless shoes, which was her "style." In the early 1950s she had special shoes made for her by a Brockton, Massachusetts, orthopedic shoemaker, A. Fikany. This wasn't because her feet troubled her, but because, as she explained in one of her syndicated "My Day" columns, "sensible shoes make comfort sense." After one of her visits to Boston, where Fikany came to take the foot measurements to make her shoes, Fikany told me, "Mrs. Roosevelt always makes it a point to tell me, 'I'm not interested in style but in fit and comfort.' "

I took a look at one custom-made pair of drab, low-heeled oxfords he was ready to send to her and said wryly, "You can't tell whether these are for Franklin or Eleanor."

He smiled and replied, "Once I made a pair for her in a dressier style. Nothing fancy, but just a bit more touch of fashion and a little higher heel than the usual flat ones. She sent them back with a short note that said, 'These are for dancing, not walking.' I've learned that for Mrs. Roosevelt, the simpler and plainer, the better."

But can't shoes have sex-appeal fashion and be comfortable, too? It's very unlikely. Fashion and comfort have rarely slept in the same bed. How many times have you heard a woman humbly apologize for wearing desexed, sensible shoes? "I bought them only because they're so comfortable"—trying to explain away her self-conscious, dowdy look. Illusion is the real difference between the sexy and sexless shoe. The illusion of the sexy shoe is in its erotic communication and suggestiveness. The sexless shoe is stripped of illusion and sexual promise. It seeks no sexual communication and receives none.

NEUTER SHOES

Neuter shoes are neither sexy nor sexless; neither fashionable nor unfashionable; neither sex-attractive nor sex-detractive. They have a eunuchlike quality—a glimmer of promise, but on closer examination found wanting. In the trade they're known by such names as "mama" and "dumb" shoes. More liberally they're called "conservative" fashion.

A neuter shoe usually has a low or medium heel, a semirounded toe, and is closed up rather than open. The color is subdued, the material conventional, and the ornamentation, if any, is minimal. There is a look of restrained propriety about it, as if to say, "My foot is decently dressed."

Neuter shoes reflect a quiescent or semiactive libido. When a woman, especially a married one with a growing family, passes age forty or so, she often gets into the habit of wearing neuter-type shoes. Her concern is to dress "nicely" as she thinks a middle-aged wife and mother should. She's no longer sending sex signals to other men. Yet, let that same woman become widowed or divorced and again on the alert for a new man or husband, and she quickly exchanges her neuter shoes for sexier ones. Thus the shoes she wears don't so much reflect her sexual capacities as her sexual communication and awareness.

In countries where political and social emphasis is given to the equality of the sexes, neuter (or sometimes sexless or bisexual) shoes are an important part of the somewhat uniform dress of men and women. Russia and modern China are two prominent examples. For more than half a century, Russia has clothed its people in neuter shoes and apparel (though its ambassadors and consuls constantly smuggle in sexy European shoes for their wives and mistresses). The Chinese have applied this sartorial neuterism even more rigidly. Sex is subordinated to a repressed role in the Communist socio-political systems. Both the Russians and Chinese know that the best way to defuse sex in a culture is to keep the shoes and clothes neuter or sexless.

Neuter shoes lack the aggression of sexy shoes, yet manage to stay outside the cold boundaries of sexless shoes. And they're worn by people of the same temperament or psychosexual attitudes—neither sexually aggressive nor sexually inert. They are passive styles for psychosexually passive persons.

BISEXUAL SHOES

There's an odd breed of footwear that can best be designated as bisexual or unisexual. It makes its appearance every now and then for a brief, faddish stay. We've seen this in recent years, especially with the young, in the "his and hers" look-alike styles; and also in the so-called "monster" fashions for women in the late 1960s and early 1970s. These latter shoes had a heavy look, with thick soles, broad and bulbous toes, low and chunky heels, and were made with rugged materials. Though flamboyant in colors and decoration, they had virtually no male-female distinguishing features, and these styles were worn by young men and women alike.

Short men with small feet, who were having a difficult time finding these bisexual styles in their sizes in men's shoe stores, were advised in the February 1973 issue of *Gentlemen's Quarterly:* "The alternative then is to search through several reputable *women's* shoe establishments, where chunky, high-heeled, bump-toe shoes, styled exactly like currently fashionable men's footwear, are readily available." About the same time, young women were shopping in men's stores to buy men's rugged work boots, which had become another unisex fashion.

Bisexual shoes usually appear during periods of social rebellion. For example, bisexual shoes (and clothing) were prominently on the scene in the latter half of the 1960s with the explosive liberation of sex attitudes, social mores and political protest. These open defiances of the Establishment brought on a wave of unisex styles worn by boys and girls alike—long hair, jeans, leather jackets, sweat shirts, open-collar shirts, sneakers, flat sandals, heavy, chunky shoes, boots, etc. A bisexual look equated with freedom and equality, and the shoes and clothing were an important insignia of the "movement."

But this set no precedent. During and following the French Revo-

lution nearly two hundred years ago, many young Frenchwomen
called *marveilleuses,* and their male counterparts known as *incroyables*
(the incredibles), deliberately dressed in shabby disarray—long un-
combed hair, tight pants, tattered coats and jackets, clumsy rustic
boots (in the 1960s this was known as the "poor boy" look). Though
this social rebellion against the elders was short-lived, the flaunting of
the bisexual look was one important way to express defiance and protest.

Hardly anything desexualizes the look of a woman more than
unisex-style shoes—the heavy-look "monster" styles with thick soles,
rounded bump toes, thick heels, garish hardware, and heavy leathers.
The desexing effect stems not only from the rustic, utilitarian look of
the shoe, but from the thick soles that force a stompish, Frankenstein-
like walk that defeminizes the gait and desensualizes the whole woman.

A similar effect results when young men wear the same styles, especially the high platforms and high heels. These shoes tend to feminize
the gait because a natural masculine step and stride is impossible in
them.

Thus the wearing of these unisex styles desexed the look and walk
of women and feminized the appearance and gait of men. From this
emerged a provocative consequence—at least as a challenging possibility. Unisex or monster-type styles had their reign in the 1967–1974 period. During the same span the U.S. birth rate reached a record low,
and actually dipped below the zero population level.

In 1975, the unisex-monster-style cycle started its fade-out, replaced gradually by the incoming trend of more feminine styles for
women (dressier looks and higher, thinner heels), and more classic,
masculine styles for men. Also in 1975, for the first time in many years,
an *increase* in the birth rate occurred. The population experts expect
that this turnabout in the births curve will be sustained. The fashion
forecasters are at the same time predicting a steady return to more
feminine clothing and footwear for women.

Is this correlation between shoes and sex coincidental? If unisex
styles desexualize the look and gait of the person—that is, masculinize
the female and feminize the male—do these same styles have some subtle, psychological desexing effect on the woman, and on male-female
sex affinity? It's a tantalizing thought to ponder.

But bisexual footwear and clothing styles have always been doomed to a short life because they're unnatural to both male and female alike. "One of the greatest allurements would be lost," says Havelock Ellis, "and the extreme importance of clothing would disappear at once if the two sexes were to dress alike; such identity of dress, however, has never come about among any people."

Flugel states flatly, "The fundamental purpose of adopting a distinctive dress for the two sexes is to stimulate sexual interest." Dr. Hirning adds his own strong view: "The adornment theme in dress is to call attention to sex differences, to secondary sexual characteristics, and to sexual prowess. Dress has subserved the function of sexual arousal, of calling attention to emphasizing sex, and still does."

Even the writers of the Bible recognized the importance of differences in male and female attire: "The woman shall not wear that which pertaineth to the man, neither shall a man put on a woman's garments; for all that do so are abomination unto the Lord thy God [Deut. 22:5]." One of the criminal charges brought against the martyred Joan of Arc in 1431 was that she wore thigh-high leather boots—a style traditionally reserved for men, and hence she was held in violation of a sex taboo of the day.

One persistently popular bisexual shoe style is the "loafer" since its introduction from Norway to the United States in the middle 1930s. Worn by men and women alike, it is simply a version of the age-old moccasin. The loafer is devoid of either a male or female personality, and its unisex character makes it more of a mere foot covering than a genuine fashion.

From a utilitarian standpoint, there's no practical reason why men's and women's shoes should be styled differently. There's only one reason for a difference: to help establish sexual identity. Every basic shoe style ever created—the boot, sandal, pump, oxford, etc.—was soon given special treatments to masculinize or feminize it. Bisexuality in footwear exists, but wherever it has existed it has been either short-lived or minimally used. Like the eunuch, it exists in a lonely sexual limbo.

How would women's shoes in America divide into the sexy, sexless, neuter and bisexual categories? How would such a division compare with that in "warm" and "cold" cultures or countries? I've posed this question to scores of leading shoe designers, manufacturers, and retailers in America. Their estimates, intermixed with my own based on observations in some twenty different countries, are as follows:

	AMERICA	"WARM" CULTURES	"COLD" CULTURES
Sexy shoes	45%	75%	30%
Sexless shoes	10	5	20
Neuter shoes	40	15	40
Bisexual shoes	5	5	10
	100%	100%	100%

But what about the men? Do their shoes or shoe styles convey any erotic character and psychosexual messages? Definitely. Men's shoes are as sex-communicative as women's, but in different ways. In fact, some of the men's styles that have appeared through history have been among the most flagrantly lecherous articles of apparel ever worn. Let's now see the reality of this.

II

The Podosexual Male

The female foot is far more naturally erotic than the male foot. It is softer, more contoured, more sinuous in its movements, and expresses femininity. By contrast, the male foot has a heavier look because of more musculature, more hairiness, a thicker skin texture, is less delicately contoured. The male is subconsciously aware of these differences, and the contrast creates an erotic illusion about the female foot in comparison with his own. So he has sought to find ways to compensate for it. As a result, he has often adorned his feet in such ways as to make his shoes little short of frankly phallic symbols.

Unlike the males of other species, the human male is limited in erogenous characteristics. He has no brightly colored ring around his rectum, no bushy tail, no fine feathers, no magnificent wings, no thick and shiny fur, no spectacular antlers. Thus, to glorify his sterile physical person, he had to become an artificial peacock, using his clothing and body ornamentation to perform the sex-attraction functions which the males of other species achieve with their natural endowments.

Because men have fewer erogenous qualities than women, this has borne enormous influence on how men and women dress. Men, for example, use more and heavier apparel to create illusory effects of masculinity and virility. Women use less and lighter clothing to highlight their natural erogenous features. A study by Harvard University's School of Public Health found that the average adult male wears about 5 pounds of clothing as against only 1.8 pounds for the average woman.

Life magazine found the average man's clothes to weigh 7 pounds as compared with only 1.3 pounds for the average woman. A man and woman may take identical shoe sizes, but the man's shoe will be two or three times heavier and cover the whole foot. The woman's shoe will be light, delicate and opened up.

Thus, the way men dress their feet has erotogenic motives. They must artificially decorate them to give them some erotic personality. As a confirmation of this, you'll recall that all the eight basic shoe styles were originally created for and by men, none for or by women.

"Feet are awfully important in a woman's sizing up of a man," says men's wear designer and Coty Award nominee Don Robbie. "A shoe should be a slow come-on. The guy should just sit back, relax, perhaps move his feet a little—and let the shoes tell what's on his mind."

Hence the way a man dresses his feet reveals much about the man. In fact, his shoes are so associated with his psychosexual identity that virtually all male footwear can be assigned to one of five categories: the Sensuous, the Peacock, the Masculine, the Eunuch, and the Machismo. Let's take a brief look at each and the men who wear them.

THE SENSUOUS SHOE

There are visibly sensuous men just as there are visibly sensuous women. These are body-conscious and women-aware men; not in any lecherous or aggressive sense, but in subtly carnal, hedonistic ways. They use their clothes and footwear with meticulous selectivity to transmit this sensuality.

Sensuous shoes are mainly un-American. They're styled with a Continental flair, usually Italian, Spanish, or French, that is instantly understood and appreciated by European, South American, and Asian men, and universally by women—but only by a select group of American men. The shoes are lightweight, flexible, made of soft and supple leathers, with thin, close-edged soles, heels slightly higher than average but never extreme, the colors and materials a bit unusual but not garish, the fit snug, the styling slightly exotic yet contemporary.

The shoes themselves speak a hedonistic language. These men have highly tactile and sensitive feet and a thoroughly masculine yet sinuous gait (they're almost always magnificent dancers). They wear their sensuous shoes with complete confidence in their own masculinity. Says motivation analyst Dr. Ernest Dichter, "Only a man who feels per-

A contemporary sensuous shoe for men. Such shoes are lightweight, made of soft leather with thin soles, and are snug-fitting. The tassels on this example are phallic symbols.

fectly secure as a man can allow himself to wear anything with feminine overtones, for he is not threatened by it."

Former film heavy Adolphe Menjou owned over two hundred and fifty pairs of always fashionable shoes, which were constantly being replaced with new ones. He was a college classmate of George Gayou, who used to operate the huge annual National Shoe Fair in Chicago, which drew some 15,000 shoemen from all over the world. Menjou, at the invitation of Gayou, would occasionally make an appearance at the Fair. On one such occasion I met him. While we were having a drink together in Gayou's hotel suite and discussing shoes, Menjou told me:

"I have a reputation of being a ladies' man. I don't deny it. In fact, I work at it. But about this shoe thing—I've had women admire my shoes more than my clothes [he owned more than two hundred suits]. If you have an eye for women, you'd better have an eye for shoes. If the shoes have sex appeal, then the romance—please excuse the pun—is off on the right foot."

The sensuous male shoe, however, has often reached for extremes to

Boot with ornately laced top and extreme flare, popular with debonair men in seventeenth-century France. Known as the "bastard boot" because of its flagrant hedonism.

become outrightly sexy, even lecherous. About eight hundred years ago a particular male shoe style called the *poulaine* started as a mildly sensuous shoe. But over the next three hundred years it developed into perhaps the most blatantly sexual and pornographic shoe style ever worn. It was also known by such names as the *cracowe* and *pontaine*, depending on the country in which it was worn. It had an extremely long toe tip called a *liripipe* or *learup*, meaning a tippet or point of leather. It began with a turned-up toe extending about two inches and which was frankly phallic in design. Imaginative men quickly exploited its phallic possibilities. Soon the toe became longer and longer until it had to be stuffed with moss or wool or other filler to keep it erect.

Simulating an erect penis was precisely the purpose of the *poulaine*. The stuffed toe grew from a couple of inches to four and eight, and ultimately to fourteen or more. Some even had to be attached to the knee with a little chain to prevent tripping over it. This phallic extension flapped with lifelike mobility with each step. Some bolder men had these long tips designed and colored as a replica of an erect penis, precise in every detail. Sometimes a tiny bell was attached to the tip, tingling in walking to make sure that the *poulaine* was noticed. These were called "folly bells," signaling that the wearer was receptive to a little sexual frolic (similar bells were used later on codpieces).

The *poulaine* was introduced in Europe in the eleventh century by a French nobleman, Fulk Rechin of Anjou. Legend has it that he had this long-toed shoe designed to relieve pressure on an ingrown toenail, but no evidence has ever been found for this. He introduced it unabashedly as a sexually titillating fashion (he was a notorious dandy and roué of his day). The hornlike style which at first caused chuckles in the royal courts, won Fulk the nickname of "Cornadus"—the Horned One, which in modern Italian means a cuckold.

But such an ingenious work of erotic art as the *poulaine* was destined for bigger and better things. Imaginative men, encouraged by fascinated women, employed it with erotic creativity. The *poulaine*, for example, was used commonly at dinner parties in the courts and homes of the affluent for under-the-table titillation. The man's erect *poulaine* would reach across to lift the skirt hem of the female guest seated opposite him, making its way up as high as the lady would permit. By virtue of this pedic dildo, it wasn't unusual for these dinners to be accompanied by one or several orgasms between the soup and dessert courses.

Some women were known to use the *poulaine* for masturbation. The effect of the sexual imagery was even more physically pleasurable if the *poulaine* happened to belong to a lover. It was a common saying for a wife or mistress to remark sarcastically to a husband or lover who was unable to achieve an erection, "Your *poulaine* is more man than you."

From the beginning the church was shocked by the flagrant obscenity of the *poulaine*. The clergy at first tried to discourage the wearing of these shoes on the grounds that they hampered the saying of prayers when people were on their knees. This brought no results. The invective from pulpits all over Europe grew more intense, generation after generation. The condemned *poulaine* was decreed one of Satan's curses. For example, when the Black Plague swept Europe in the Middle Ages, killing almost a fourth of the population, numerous leading clergymen blamed it on God's displeasure with the wearing of the profane *poulaine*.

Censure reached the highest levels of church and state. In 1215, French Cardinal Curson forbade the wearing of these shoes by professors at the University of Paris. In the fourteenth century, Pope Urban V publicly cursed the fashion as "an exaggeration against good manners, a scoffing against God and Church, a worldly vanity, and a mad presumption."

The style soon seeped down to the commoners, where its bawdy uses stampeded through the populace. In 1367, France's King Charles IV decreed at Montpelier that no commoner thereafter would be permitted to wear *poulaines*. But the ever-popular "mad presumption" simply went underground and was worn everywhere at private parties, dinners, dances and other social events. Nevertheless, church and state persisted. Governments compromised with decrees that limited the length of the *poulaine* to six inches for commoners, but permitting lengths of up to twenty-four inches for the aristocracy and nobility, and no restrictions whatever for kings and princes. In 1463, England's King Edward IV finally enacted a stringent law limiting the toe length to two inches for everyone. Thus the "mad presumption" eventually shrunk to something akin to reality.

The 300-year reign of the *poulaine* finally ended in the late fifteenth century. But the long popularity of this phallic fantasy was so influential that it was responsible for the rise of another phallic illusion, the codpiece, which was adopted in the sixteenth century.

Flugel speaks of the infamous codpiece during Tudor times as being "embellished by padding in such a way as to simulate a perpetual erection." Our next stage, he continues, "may be taken from an earlier period, when the phallic symbol was found, not near the genital area itself, but on a remote part of the body, namely the feet. There was in the Middle Ages a tendency to fashion the long shoe, known as the *poulaine*, in the shape of a phallus, and this practice enjoyed a long popularity in spite of the storm of indignation which it aroused."

Thus it may well be that the term "cock of the walk" had its origin more with the *poulaine* than with the rooster.

The *poulaine*, however, was hardly a new idea in phallic footwear fashions for men. The exaggeratedly long toe is a design theme that

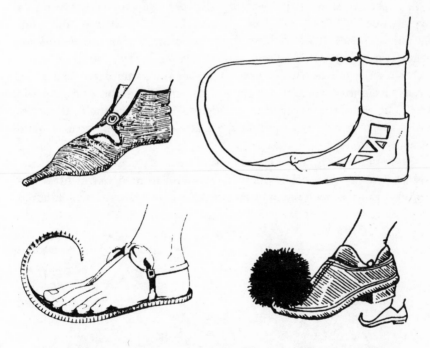

The *poulaine*, a male shoe style of the Middle Ages that flourished for over three hundred years, was blatantly sexual. The toe of the shoe grew so long that it had to be stuffed with moss to keep it erect; sometimes it was chained to the ankle. The design theme of the exaggerated toe traces back to ancient Egypt, lower left, and today persists in the *opanka*, the national shoe of Greece, lower right. The turned-up toe embedded in a furry pompon is a clear male-female symbol.

can be traced back at least three thousand years to Egypt, as well as to ancient China, Turkey, Persia, Mongolia, and elsewhere—and even today is worn in some parts of the world.

Why its persistent and universal popularity? Because the big toe itself is a universal phallic symbol. Thus, if the shoe covers this toe, then the toe of the shoe must be used as a substitute so that this important phallicism isn't lost. One archaeologist cites that the toes on the shoes of young princes and aristocrats of an ancient era were gradually lengthened as these adolescents matured—the lengthening conforming to the enlarging penis of emerging young adulthood. Thus their long-toed shoes symbolized the approaching readiness of the young males to assume sexual and reproductive roles.

Another version of the *poulaine*, the turned-up toe style worn as a native shoe, is found today in Turkey, Greece, Bulgaria, and other Balkan countries. It is a boldly phallic style theme. But it contains another feature of sexual symbolism—the large, furry pom-pom worn either on the toe tip or further behind on the vamp area. This is no casual decorative feature. Originally it symbolized the female pubic area. The erect, turned-up and extended toe curves around to direct its tip at the pompon, and signifies the male-female mating that is quite obvious to the eye.

Still another sensuous male shoe that made its mark in erotic pedic history was known as the "duckbill," which had its debut in fifteenth-century Europe, and retained its popularity for nearly two hundred

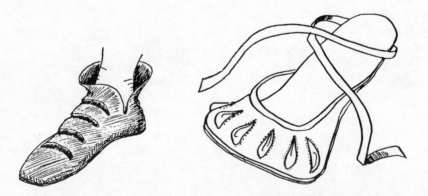

The fifteenth-century "duckbill." Multiple vaginalike slits opened and closed with each bend of the foot to reveal pink flesh or hose beneath.

The scarpine, or "bear's paw," first emerged in late fifteenth-century Germany and was later outlawed by the English as obscene. Each toe, separately pocketed, represented a phallic member.

years. This style was also known by such names as "cow mouth" and "bear's paw," and went the opposite direction of the *poulaine*. The toe was extremely wide, twelve inches or more. Legend has it that it was designed for King Henry VIII to relieve his swollen, gouty foot, but there has never been any verification of this. Actually, it was designed as a shoe with sexual overtones, and was frequently carried to obscene extremes.

However, instead of this style being used as a phallic symbol, it was translated into a female genital symbol. The expansive area of the upper of this broad-toe shoe provided a large "canvas" upon which to depict openly erotic suggestions. One popular treatment was to decorate the upper with vaginalike slashes in the leather over the vamp and toe. Sometimes the edges of these slits and cutouts were trimmed with fur or colored stitching to suggest a pubic effect. With each step these slits would open and show the pink skin or hose beneath. The opening and closing of these slashes left little to the imagination. (Even today, the slashed effects or teardrop cutouts often seen in women's modern shoe designs are a carry-over of this concept.)

Today's versions of men's sensuous shoes are more erotically subtle. For example, the exaggeratedly long, pointed-toe style known as the Winkle Picker enjoyed a sweeping popularity with young men throughout Europe and America in the 1950s. These were merely toned-down models of the *poulaine* and conveyed the same phallic symbolism.

Sensuous shoes, however, go beyond the foot imagery itself. They reflect the psychosexual personalities of the men who wear them. Not all men can do justice to these styles. A sensuous shoe worn by men who lack a sensuous body image loses much of its sensual identity. That's why other styles are created and worn—to give other men other ways to express their psychosexual makeup through the shoe styles they wear.

THE PEACOCK SHOE

Whereas the sensuous shoe is undisguised in its erotic intent, the peacock male and the peacock shoe are less sexually mature. The peacock shoe is conspicuous rather than aggressive. It has no special design, no full-fledged fashion commitment. It's styled solely to be flamboyant, brazen, ostentatious, a touch of rococo, ornately offbeat—whether by its shape, the thickness of its sole, the height of the heel, its bold hardware, fancy stitching, gaudy colors, or other decorative features. Stylistically, it's always to the extreme left.

Who wears peacock shoes? Insecure men who have a driving need for personal identity. This style, garish and pretentious, is a conspicuous look-at-me shoe. That's why they're worn mostly by the young and some ethnic or minority groups—because these men are vying for attention, admiration and status. Thus their peacock shoes are a kind of broadcasting station emitting loud messages by loud styles. They aren't so much interested in evoking sex initiative as they are sex visibility.

Shoes and shoe styles have always tended to be associated with a man's age. Society tacitly believes that the shoe styles (and clothing styles) worn should stay within a man's natural libido range. For example, Julius Caesar was criticized for "presumption" when in public he wore the high red boots usually associated with the peacock fashions of younger men. Thomas Jefferson was censored for abandoning the boot styles of his day to don stylish low-cuts popular with young men. He was charged with "frivolous dressing."

When, in the past couple of centuries, the female usurped the male's assumed priority right to his plumage, it was a stroke of virtual emasculation from which he is still trying to recover. What happend to defrock him after all those centuries of peacockery? The sudden shift to sartorial sterility occurred with the French Revolution at the end of the eighteenth century. It brought on what Flugel calls "The Great Male Renunciation." The sartorial splender that distinguished wealth and aristocracy from the commoners abruptly disappeared. One walked the streets in fine and fancy clothes and shoes at the risk of his life. The Revolution had launched a new social order whose banner was "liberty, equality and fraternity."

Men adopted attire that was austere and simple to conceal their identity. The Revolution had ordained that men would not only be equal but would look equal. Male attire and footwear became democratized and desexed. If the peacock wasn't dead, he was at best in a prolonged coma in Europe and America.

Male peacock styles of the 1970s feature platform soles, high heels, bump toes, and ornate patterns. (*Verde Shoe Co.*)

In the middle 1960s, the long-suppressed and deplumed male un-leashed his bonds and began a revival of the Peacock Era. It started with the young blades and the so-called Mod Look from London's Carnaby Street. It became a contagion of uninhibited fashion that caught fire with the young all over the world. Peacock styling was re-born, profligate and delightfully whimsical. It was the decade of re-bellious liberations—Youth Lib, Women's Lib, Gay Lib, Sex Lib, Black Lib—and Male Sartorial Lib.

Volare, the American importer of Italian men's shoes, was now ad-vertising, "If I have only one life to live, let me live it as a peacock." It was the message of the emancipated male who could again express his libido through his pedic plumage. But long-ingrained habits aren't easily changed. In the seventies the sudden burst subsided and the pea-cock was semisubdued. But the urge for peacockery is innate in the male, and is certain to reappear in the near future.

THE MASCULINE SHOE

The majority of over-thirty American men find it difficult or impossible to wear either sensuous or peacock shoes. European and other men are amused by this inhibition. A huge legion of American men confine themselves to a category of footwear best classified as "masculine." And, ironically, it's frequently a psychosexual defense for an insecure mas-culinity.

Masculine shoes are usually heavy in weight and look, semistiff, sturdy, colorless, subdued. These features, in the minds of their wear-ers, reflect masculinity. These styles are often called "classics"—wing-tip brogues, thick-soled cordovans, the loafer, moccasin-front patterns, grainy leathers, staidly laced fronts, moderate shapes and toes. The colors run the gamut from black to brown to black again, and maybe with a "sporty" white for summer.

Who wears "masculine" shoes? Men who tend to be conformist in personality, habits, attitudes, behavioral patterns. This covers a vast sweep of the adult male population—business executives, doctors and lawyers and other professionals, bankers, brokers, educators, scientists, white- and blue-collar workers, merchants, salesmen, etc. They live a psychosexual masquerade, the masculine costume smothering the pea-cock inside.

President John Kennedy had an affinity for smartly styled shoes and owned more than thirty-five pairs. He once, while a senator, confided to a shoe manufacturer from his home state of Massachusetts, "At times I find myself in a hell of a dilemma. I like fashionable shoes, sexy-looking shoes. But in my position I have to worry about my damned image. So the shoes have that semiconservative look that conflicts with my natural style. No wonder they say that politics is a Jekyll-and-Hyde game."

The masculine shoe has its own kind of "sexual expression" embedded in its character—its strained effort to convey sturdy manliness and active virility. Ironically, it's almost solely in America that the masculine shoe is so common and dominant. It may well suggest that American men, more than the men of other cultures, have greater need for masculine props of costume to distinguish them from the women who stole their sartorial plumage. Strangely, masculine shoes may well reflect a man who is least secure about his own masculinity.

THE EUNUCH SHOE

The eunuch shoe for men corresponds to the sexless shoe for women. It's a recessive, reactionary and inert article of clothing, the insignia of the sexual dropout. It's almost always black, with a plain toe or simple straight tip. It is usually laced, has a moderately rounded toe. It's devoid of any distinctive style or color or even the slightest ornamentation to give it some sexual identity. It's a totally sterile, desexed shoe.

There are millions of men who wear nothing else but this style, whether at work, at a picnic or ball, in the desert or on top of a mountain. The style never changes because the psychosexual state of the wearers is as fixed as a star. Who wears them? Among the wearers are clergymen, morticians, men obsessed with their work (scientists, educators, and many businessmen), many of the elderly, or the tens of thousands of middle-aged bachelors who live quietly, and usually celibately, alone.

These shoe styles (as well as the lifestyle) rarely change year in and out. These men, who make a shoe purchase less than once a year, repeatedly ask for the same style as though it was sacrosanct. The eunuch shoe is a bastard article, unnatural to the whole realm of clothing and footwear. When a shoe is desexed, it loses its justification for existence, and one may as well go barefoot.

These shoes reflect precisely what the wearer wishes to communicate—that he is a sexual recessive, a non-activist, sexually withdrawn.

His eunuch shoes are nevertheless conveying a sexual message, but in a reverse manner—a statement of voluntary excommunication from the natural concerns of sex attraction.

THE MACHISMO SHOE

This lacks the subtle eroticism of the sensuous shoe, the colorful imagination of the peacock shoe, the feigned boldness of the masculine shoe, or the recessive character of the eunuch shoe. Instead, the machismo shoe is one of the most savagely sex-ridden of all male footwear styles—chauvinistic, aggressive, sadistic. For macho-shoe wearers it isn't enough merely to be or appear masculine. They must stomp this impression into the minds of others, especially females.

The boot is the best-known form of machismo footwear. Knee-high or calf-high, heavy and leathery, usually with bold hardware such as clumpy buckles or shiny studs, frequently with wide and thick straps, heavy soles, and loud-clicking heels. These boots reflect a kind of swashbuckling personality, hostile and ruthless and challenging, which is precisely the image the wearers wish to transmit.

A classic example is the attire typically worn by motorcycle gangs —the heavy, studded, stomp-type boot matched by metal-studded leather jacket, leather pants, etc. All of it has a militant character with a portent of violence and sadism. Even the ordinary work boot has been adopted as a macho "style" unrelated to its utilitarian function. These are often worn by young men seeking to convey the rugged he-man look that suggests impending threat or challenge.

The cowboy boot also belongs to this group, though in modified form. It has its own machismo character, the cowboy and his boots representing an image of aggressive male thrust, of hardy toughness.

The same principle applies to all military-type boots. For example, young paratroopers will wear their heavy combat boots when off duty in town for machismo- motivated display. The history of military footwear emphasizes the heavy, savage boot, all part of the machismo image and attitude considered essential to the aggressive character of the occupation. Bismarck said, "The sight and sound of good Prussian boots on the march are a powerful military weapon by themselves." Hitler's goose-stepping soldiers with their heavy studded boots were their own threat of impending terror. General Patton was fond of saying, "A soldier in shoes is only a soldier. But in boots he becomes a warrior."

Three macho boots, ranging from an extreme example, with heavy straps across heavy leather to a modified yet still rugged boot to the cowboy boot, an American classic.

The machismo boot in any form, like its wearers, suggests a kind of psychosexual malevolence. Ironically, this footwear is sometimes worn by psychosexually passive men who wish to transmit a different image. But whether these boots are worn by psychosexually aggressive or passive men, the machismo or gladiator character of the boot itself feeds the undernourished sexual ego of the wearers.

THE LIBIDO THRUST OF MEN'S SHOES

The more vigorous and aggressive the male libido, the more sexually aggressive the shoe styles worn. It's virtually an immutable law. Different men give out sexual signals in different ways, which is why men's shoes fall into sexual categories to comply with the psychosexual communicative patterns of each male group. The shoes reflect particular kinds and degrees of libido—sensuous, peacock, masculine, eunuch or machismo—which men wish to convey to women especially, but also to other men.

But who are the pacesetters responsible for the trends in men's footwear (and clothing) fashions? In America, they consist of four groups: the blacks (along with other minority groups such as Puerto Ricans and Mexican-Americans); the theatrical or show business clan; the sporting crowd; and the homosexuals. But what about the young men? No. The young influence fads but rarely fashions. Fads have a limited staying power and radius of influence, while genuine fashions have a longer life and wider scope of influence.

Why these four groups? What do they have in common? Many years ago, Thorstein Veblen, in his classic work, *The Theory of the Leisure Class*, focused on the concept of "conspicuous leisure" and "conspicuous consumption." He demonstrated the innate desire in most of us to consume beyond necessity as a way to display visible prosperity, social importance or status, and personal identity. In short, it isn't enough merely to have the means of economic and social well-being. We also feel a need to be conspicuous about it. We do this in many ways, via our homes and the way we furnish them, the cars, the boats, the swimming pools, the schools we attend, the clubs we belong to, the titles we hold, the parties we give, the social circles we move in, the neighborhoods we live in, the trips we take, and countless other accoutrements that serve as economic and social insignia.

But our four fashion pacesetting groups usually don't have access to these same means of conspicuous consumption. Many of their members are nomadic, often unmarried, semimarried, or between marriages. They aren't tied to a particular place, or rooted to a particular job. Yet they're socially mobile. They're able to spend more on themselves. They visibly express their conspicuous consumption through expensive and showy cars, or as big spenders and lavish tippers. But their *main* expression is through their clothes. The more avant-garde or unusual their apparel, the more conspicuous. They now have a special identity.

In an article in *Phylon* magazine, "Men's Clothing and the Negro," Jack Schwartz writes that "when the black is denied access to many status symbols, he is forced to use contemporary devices to raise self-esteem, aid status symbolization and cushion the traumatic effects of a subordinated position. Clothing is one of these available devices." Blacks are innovators of peacock-type styles. Studies show that the average black male buys better quality and spends more for his shoes than the average white male, although his income is appreciably lower.

The show business or sporting crowd leans heavily toward avant-garde footwear with erotic styling—almost always sensuous or peacock, but rarely masculine, eunuch or machismo types. They were among the first to adopt the expensive and fashionable Continental imports. The genuine alligator shoe, very expensive (but now on the ecological ban list), was always a favorite of this group.

New York menswear designer Bill Miller comments on homosexuals as fashion pacesetters: "The fashion-conscious homosexual is generally a single man. He has all the time and money at his disposal to spend on doing the things he wants to do. Because homosexuals are single they tend to lead very active social lives. This requires that they have wardrobes to go with their many activities. The average man would like to dress as smartly as the homosexual, but does not have the homosexual's time or money to spend on his wardrobe, nor is his social life as hectic so that he really requires a large wardrobe."

Thus the singular lifestyles of these four groups motivate these men toward conspicuous dressing. Their shoes and clothing must be *unlike* those of the average adult male, having a visible splendor, and always in the front lines of fashion. These same styles, usually with modifications, will usually be adopted by the mass of men a couple or more seasons later.

What share of shoes in these various "sexual categories" are worn by adult men in America? How do the shoe-style choices of American men compare with men of other cultures? This is what we found from an extensive consensus of several hundred experienced shoemen:

STYLE CATEGORY	AMERICA	"WARM" CULTURES	"COLD" CULTURES
Sensuous	15%	40%	15%
Peacock	15	30	15
Masculine	50	10	45
Eunuch	10	5	20
Machismo	10	15	5
	100%	100%	100%

American men, especially in the over-thirty age group, still lean more toward the cold rather than the warm culture pattern in the selection of their shoe styles. They still display much psychosexual inhibition in their footwear. This fixation about conformity and an over-reaching for a "masculine" identity reveals an insecurity about the American's sexual self-image that doesn't burden most men of "warm" cultures.

12

The Sensuous Stilts

Men are still uncertain whether the greatest of all inventions was the wheel or the high heel. It's still debatable which of these innovations has had the greater influence on the course of human history.

The high heel makes no practical sense whatever. It has no functional or utilitarian value. It's an unnatural fixture on a shoe. It makes standing and walking precarious and tiring. It's a safety hazard. It's blamed for a host of pedic and bodily ills. It has been called silly and frivolous, and has for centuries been censured as a wicked device of the devil.

There's no logic for its existence. Yet it has persisted for centuries as one of the most ingenious and popular instruments ever created for the erotic stimulation of men and women alike. This is why men have always been more magnetized by women with high heels than high brows. Says Rudofsky, "Men are perfectly frank in admitting that high heels stimulate their sexual appetite. They seldom fail to express their predilection for them, and women, consequently, assign to stilted shoes all the magic of a love potion."

No other item of attire has such a positive phallic identity as the high heel. Women derive a sadomasochistic pleasure in wearing them. The masochism stems from the foot distress and deformation the woman usually endures—yet a pleasurable pain in knowing the sexual effects conveyed. The sadism lies in the phallicism of the heel itself, as though the woman has taken possession of the male's genital powers. In fact, some women and girls are known to use the high, thin heels of their shoes to masturbate.

Women have long used the spike or stiletto heel subconsciously to "stab" back at men in a male-dominated world. (An average woman walking on such heels exerts over two *tons* of weight per square inch on the bottom of the heel with every step.) At a recent psychiatry seminar in Boston, one psychiatrist reported a case of a young woman, a feminist, who had become obsessed with a repetitive dream of walking over men's erect penises in her high-heeled shoes. The doctor explained:

"She had heard of men speaking of the sexual fantasy of walking barefoot over 'acres' of women's breasts. The vision of this infuriated her. How could she retaliate? She concocted her own fantasy. She envisioned 'acres' of men lying naked side by side on their backs, each with a penis in firm erection. She then walked over these penises in her high heels. Her sadistic pleasure was in hearing the sound of each penis crunching beneath her heels, and the men screeching in pain.

"This became almost a nightly dream. Her problem, however, wasn't the dream, but the fact that it was accompanied by one to several nightly orgasms. She awoke mornings feeling drained of energy, fatigued, and unable to sustain a day's work. She had become victim of her own vengeful attitude against male chauvinism."

But the fantasy of sexual revenge via high heels can also work in reverse. In an article titled "The Real Nashville," by Patrick Anderson, in the *New York Times Magazine* of August 31, 1975, the author writes:

> "One of the all-time country music greats was once married to a woman who might in fairness be described as a shoe freak, in that she owned several hundred pairs of shoes, some of them rather expensive. Eventually, the marriage failed and her husband found himself forced to vacate the mansion that his songs and his singing had paid for. Embittered, as men can be at such moments, he hit upon a plan for revenge. On his last day at home, he took a claw hammer, sneaked into his wife's dressing room, and pulled the heel off every last shoe she owned."

The idea that a woman who owns many pairs of shoes is a "shoe freak" is naïve. There are thousands of women who own one hundred or more pairs of shoes and keep buying more. Is it a fetish? In most instances, no. But it *does* have definite sexual connotations, as we'll see later.

However, there's much more to this happening with the country music man than the apparent petulant act of spite or revenge. By removing the phallic heels from his wife's shoes, he was subconsciously desexing her, a symbolic act of surgical castration on the woman he now hated. As another possibility, he could have been a shoe fetishist and bought many of those high-heeled shoes for his wife himself—or she bought them in such large numbers at his urging to please him. As a shoe fetishist, he would equate the high heels with penises. His removal of the heels was the same as denying *his* penis to her forever.

Psychiatrists cite that many men derive a sadomasochistic pleasure in observing women in high heels. The sadism comes from viewing the insecurity and discomfort of women in these heels, forcing them to be more dependent upon masculine support. The male's masochistic pleasure lies in the subconscious thought of her lethal weaponry, and in the "transfer" of his own phallic power to the woman. (The shoe fetishist, as we'll see later, is driven to sexual ecstasy by this masochism associated with women's high-heeled shoes.)

When is a heel high? Heels are measured in eighth-inch heights. An $\frac{8}{8}$ heel is one inch; $1\frac{6}{8}$ is two inches; $2\frac{0}{8}$ is two and a half inches. Any heel $1\frac{5}{8}$ and up is considered a high heel. During any high-heel fashion era, more than half of women's fashion shoes will have heels two or more inches in height, and heels of three inches or more are quite common.

THE EROTIC MAGIC OF HIGH HEELS

The high heel goes much beyond sex symbolism. Consider the various erotic ways it adds new dimensions to the sensuousness and sex-attraction of a woman:

It gives more shapely contours to the ankle and leg, a sexier, leggier look.

It makes the foot look smaller, the arch and instep more femininely curved.

It causes postural changes that accentuate voluptuousness in the shape and movement of the lower limbs, the pelvis and buttocks, the abdomen and bosom, the curve of the back, the carriage.

It feminizes the gait by causing a shortening of the stride and a mincing step that suggests a degree of helpless bondage. This appeals to the chivalrous or machismo nature of many men.

It adds to the height of the wearer and provides a psychological and emotional uplift that enhances sexual attraction.

These sensuous stilts have a seductive effect on the foot itself. "The existence of high heels," says C. Willet Cunnington, in *Why Women Wear Clothes*, "is a proof that the foot is to be seen and admired." These heels increase the curve of the long arch by ten to fifteen degrees, and also add more contour to the instep. A three-inch heel will visually "shorten" a foot by as much as two inches—the equivalent of six full shoe sizes (a full size is one-third inch, a half size one-sixth inch).

Any woman can try it with a simple test. Stand in stocking feet and place a flat ruler behind the heel of one foot. Raise the heel a couple of inches off the floor while resting on the ball of that foot, and at the same time keeping the ruler in its original position. You'll now see a space, a "shortening," of one or two inches between the ruler and the back of the heel.

You'll recall that Kinsey reported on the natural reflex action of the foot and toes during sexual intercourse: "The whole foot may be extended until it falls in line with the rest of the lower leg, thereby assuming a position which is impossible in non-erotic situations for most persons who are not trained as ballet dancers."

Well, that's *exactly* the "sexual" position assumed by the foot in a high-heeled shoe. It simulates the reflex position of the foot during coitus, especially at the point of orgasm or ejaculation. So a tantalizing question arises: Do both men and women subconsciously recognize or intuitively sense this "sexualized" position of the foot in high-heeled shoes? And can this be one of the reasons for the sex-appeal of high heels?

The whole body posture is affected by high heels. Flugel writes, "High heels make a great difference in the whole position of the body when standing. They render impossible the protruding abdomen. . . . By the upright carriage that they necessitate, they tend to give a corresponding prominence to the bosom." The high heel also causes a saucy backward thrust of the buttocks. Heavy legs are made to appear slimmer, and thin legs are given a curvier shape.

Millions of Chinese men, remember, believed that the willowy walk of women with bound feet resulted in an upward blood flow that produced more voluptuous feelings in the woman's genital organs and buttocks. But even today, many men in Europe and America believe that high heels, which alter and sensualize a woman's gait, also "raise the sexual temperature" of a woman's genital area, and thus increase her sexuality. This, of course, has never been proven or tested. But the thought of it alone in the minds of these men achieves the same erotic effect as though it was an actual fact.

Everyone knows that high heels can cause a sensuous transformation in a woman's gait. Witness Marilyn Monroe's famous rear-view wiggle which never would have been possible in flat heels. In fact, she was candid enough to pay tribute to them during an interview on the subject of her wanton walk: "I don't know who invented the high heel. But all women owe him a lot. Excuse the pun, but it was the high heel that gave a big lift to my own career."

The association of high heels with sexual awareness and maturity in the female begins very early. Tot-size girls playing the role of adults will don their mothers' high-heeled shoes as the prime symbol of womanhood. The pre-teen girl impatiently yearns for the arrival of that adolescent age when she's eligible to get into "heels." For the very young, the high heel is the launching site of sexual identity.

Psychologist Richard Green, writing in *Psychology Today* on "Children's Quest for Sexual Identity," reports on a study of feminine behavior in small boys. The study involved fifty boys, average age seven, with transsexual tendencies and habits. Cross-dressing, as with transvestites, was the most common sign. Says Green, "High-heeled shoes and improvised dresses are the most popular articles of women's clothing with these boys."

He cites a somewhat typical interview with the parents of one such boy, which reveals "the standard behavioral pattern of the feminine boys." Here's an excerpt:

FATHER: "Well, most of it is that he still wears my wife's shoes to go to class."
MOTHER: "None of [our other children] wore high heels, none of them. He's the first one, and it floored me when he did."
DOCTOR (to Father): "Would he ever wear your shoes?"
FATHER: "I don't think he ever wore my shoes."
DOCTOR: "What was the earliest that your son showed any indication of this [transsexual behavior]?"
MOTHER: "When he started with the high heels."

Many such boys grow up to become transvestites or transsexuals (though not necessarily homosexuals). The important thing, however, is that whether the small child is boy or girl, the wearing of high-heeled shoes is one of the prime items of sexual identity.

Men frequently refer to women's low or flat heels as "mannish." The stereotyped character in fiction or the movies of the prissy school teacher or sombre professional woman is usually depicted as wearing low or flat heels and "sensible" shoes. A verse from the *Saturday Evening Post* "Postscripts" of some years ago aptly captures the image:

> The girl with low and
>   sensible heels
> Is likely to pay for her
>   bed and meals.

There's a dramatic difference in the look of a woman when standing or walking in a flat heel and in a high heel. The whole personality and physical impression undergoes a distinct change. A burlesque queen or stripper will discard every article of clothing except her high heels. Those heels make the difference of whether she's simply a naked woman on stage, or a voluptuous and sexy one.

Edward Weeks, distinguished former editor of *The Atlantic Monthly*, expressed his own observation: "Now, the ballet slipper may be the perfect mount for the perfect leg but, brother, what does it do for those that aren't! Women look different when you see them flat-footed. Not till I saw Bostonians in ballet slippers did I realize how many of them were bow-legged. . . . The shoe that men really like has a high, thin heel, a sleek pointed toe; it fits tightly enough to arch the foot."

Weeks' comment strikes at the heart of the truth. It has forever been the male habit when sizing up the physical attributes of a woman for his eye to start at the bottom, with her feet and shoes, and gradually move up the body column. Women have always known this. This is why they have such a loyal affection for high heels—so that the male eye gets off to an encouraging start and has reason to complete the bottom-to-top visual tour with admiration.

THE LURE OF THE LEG

In most civilized societies throughout much of history, women's legs have been covered to their ankles. While men's legs were often exposed almost to hip height, even the slightest peek of a woman's legs was considered scandalous. This concealment served only to arouse the male's erotic imagination and give the female leg a high priority on the list of erogenous attractions.

For centuries, in fact, the word "legs" was considered a vulgar term, and in genteel company "limbs" was used instead. In nineteenth-century

England, the legs of tables, chairs, and pianos were covered with lacy pantaloons as a mark of modesty in the homes of the well-to-do.

In the 1920s, when the female leg finally came out of hiding, the exposure in no way dulled the male's fascination with its allure. Even the mini-skirt and bikini that were to follow a half century later, did nothing to diminish the age-old captivation with the female leg. This simply demonstrates the natural erogenous character of the female leg, covered or uncovered. It also explains why, when a marvelous erotic aid such as the high heel comes along, it's universally embraced by men and women alike for its aphrodisiac powers.

But what features give a woman's leg its shapeliness and sex-appeal? The main focus is on the calf—not only its shapely curves but the mobility of the calf muscles beneath. The rhythmic tensing and untensing of these cords, slimming down to the Achilles tendon just above the heel, can hold a male eye fascinated with its sinuous movements in walking. Our word "muscle" is derived from the Latin *musculus,* meaning "little mouse." That's because a bulging muscle such as in the calf or the biceps of the arm, looks like a tiny mouse running up and down beneath the skin. It's the movement of a shapely calf muscle that infatuates the male eye.

"Million-dollar legs," such as those that won fame for Betty Grable and Marlene Dietrich, are always posed on high heels. It's the pedestal, the high heel, that creates the sensuous illusion. The right legs on the right heels have brought fame and fortune to many women. Even the wrong legs on the right heels take on an added value that would never exist without them. Women long ago discovered that one part of them that doesn't deteriorate with age is legs. So they strive to make the most of this asset with high heels.

HOW IT ALL STARTED

No one is quite sure how or when the high heel got its start, except that its origins are ancient. Despite all the legends, perhaps the most credible story is that the high heel was invented by a pretty girl who was always being kissed on the forehead.

Though the high heel dates back to the pre-Christian era, it was Catherine de Médicis, daughter of an illustrious Florentine family, who really gave the high heel its universal fashion launching in the sixteenth century. When this petite, short-statured young woman went to Paris to marry Henry II, she brought with her several pairs of shoes with high heels, designed by an ingenious Italian artisan, to make her look taller. At the wedding and reception, Catherine's heels were a sensation. She was suddenly the sexiest looking woman at the royal ball. Shoemakers throughout Europe were soon besieged to make similar shoes, and with even higher heels. In fact, high heels became such a status insignia of the aristocracy that for many years commoners weren't allowed to wear them. And from this exclusivity came the expression of being "well-heeled."

But it required skill to walk on these slender stilts. Women practiced for hours in the privacy of their rooms to learn the art. It was common for ladies to remove their high-heeled shoes before going up or down stairs to prevent a fall. A popular couplet of the day went:

> Mount on French heels when you go to a ball—
> 'Tis the fashion to totter and show you can fall.

These heels were so thin and high that women often had to use long walking staffs to keep their balance. Slender and pretty girls were carried up or down steps by chivalrous escorts, while the less fortunate struggled to make it on their own. The same situation prevailed in America when the new heel fashions were imported from Paris. Even in Japan, after World War II, when Western shoe fashions with their high heels were introduced to the Japanese women, classes were held all over the country to teach women how to walk in them.

Casanova, in his memoirs, amusingly described the action of the court ladies when they needed to move quickly in their high heels. He said they lifted their crinolines to their chins, bent their knees and leaped like kangaroos. Fashion historian R. Turner Wilcox reports on sixteenth century Europe: "It was considered an art to walk moving the hips so that the hooped skirt would swing backward and forward. Another part of the gesture consisted of lifting the skirt to display the heeled foot and silk stocking."

Thus the high heel opened still another erotic door for men and women alike. The long skirts could catch easily on the heels. The solution was simple. Lift the skirts to avoid any calamity. This treated the men to great leg shows—and the women delighted in putting on this performance of erotic badgery.

But early in this new adventure, women made other delightful discoveries about the high heel. It pulled in the abdomen, caused more bust thrust, gave a flirtatious sway to the hips and a wanton wiggle to the buttocks. The erotic dynamics of the high heel made such fringe benefits inevitable. Such a heel rests on a tiny, dime-sized base that provides little stability. With each step the foot and ankle must wobble precariously in trying to gain a secure "heel hold" on the ground. This undulation travels up the leg to the hips and buttocks, making each step a kind of quivering stride that is an erotic stimulus to the male eye.

As usual, America was late in keeping pace with European fashion. It wasn't until 1880 that the first American factory to make high heels was established, in Massachusetts. Before that, however, elite American women were ordering sexy "French heel" shoes from Paris. In the 1850s, a well-known New Orleans brothel known as Madam Kathy's was patronized by the local upper-class gentry. One of the new girls, a recent French import, had brought with her several pairs of high-heeled shoes, an innovation at the time. As she pranced scantily clad around the premises in her high heels, her leggy look and mobile torso magnetized the lustful eyes of every waiting customer. An overnight sensation, she quickly became the girl most in demand in the bordello.

Madam Kathy knew a commercial opportunity when she saw one. She placed a standing order with a Parisian shoe artisan for twenty pairs of high-heeled shoes in different sizes and styles to be shipped to her every three months. Now all her girls were wearing them. Her business skyrocketed to new peaks of prosperity. She spasmodically kept a diary. In it was found the following:

"We learned we could double the fees when the girls sashayed around in those high heels. It gave a look of class to the ass. The men went crazy just watching them. They drank more, paid more, stayed longer, came back more often."

The news spread and soon other bordellos, locally and elsewhere, were equipping their girls with high-heeled shoes. The male patrons were now urging their wives to buy high heels, or ordering them themselves from Paris for their wives. The fashion and demand for high-heeled shoes spread so rapidly that that first American high-heel factory was started so that these shoes could be bought in America.

Thus the high heel in America owes its launching and success to the nation's whores of an earlier day. And while the high heel has long since gained respectability, it has lost none of its original appeal for women or stimulation for men.

Meanwhile, in Europe, heels were being subjected to extravagant treatment, covered with bright silks, encrusted with jewels (some were valued up to $100,000 a pair). King Louis XIV, himself a high-heel addict and father of the Louis heel, still popular today, had scenes painted in miniature on his heels by the celebrated Flemish artist, Adam Frans Van der Meulen, and the aristocracy was quick to follow suit.

The high heel was by no means the exclusive possession of women. It was worn also by men, and for the same reason women wore them: sex attraction. Men wore short breeches, the leg covered by ornate and expensive hose. The males, with their narcissistic obsession about their

Shoe designers have always outdone themselves in creating new and bizarre high-heel shapes.

legs, found that the high heel added muscular bulk to the calves, giving their legs a more "masculine" look in the same way as the high heel gives a more "feminine" look to a woman's leg.

All through history men have been wearing some version of high heels. Those worn by young American men in the early 1970s (some of these heels reached three inches or more in height) were no fashion innovation as thought, but merely a return to an age-old cycle. In the early days of the American West, most cowboy boots had heels two or more inches in height (which helped to create the illusion of the "tall Texan"). These were supposed to keep the foot secure in the stirrup. Yet, similarly heeled cowboy boots are sold in many parts of the United States, and even in Europe and Japan—and worn by persons who never in their lives have ridden a horse.

PEDESTALS OF PLEASURE

The original high heel is what we know today as the "platform" shoe—a platformed sole of wood, cork or other materials, one to several inches thick. It dates back more than three thousand years. A pair of 12-inch platform shoes was excavated from a tomb in Thebes, dating back to 1,000 B.C. Aeschylus, father of ancient Greek drama, used these platform shoes, called *korthornos*, for his actors on stage. The more important the actor or actor's role, the higher his platforms. The public soon adopted the style to imitate the same status position.

The Japanese have for centuries worn a wooden platform shoe called the *géta*, a frontless, backless shoe raised several inches from the ground and worn with a mittenlike sock called a *tabi*. In 1926, when Emperor Hirohito was enthroned, his *gétas* were nearly twelve inches in height. Similar styles have been worn in the countries of Southeast Asia.

Platform shoes with heels four to ten inches high frequently reappear in the fashion cycle. Carmen Miranda whipped them back into popularity in the late 1940s. They reappeared in the early 1970s. In 1972, Anania Brothers in New York and Jean Paul Goude in Paris designed and sold women's platform shoes with an eleven-inch sole and fourteen-inch heel, priced at $200 a pair.

Why, with all the safety hazard involved, do men and women continue to wear these perilous platforms? A husband, in a letter to Ann Landers' syndicated column of January 1973, bewailed, "Last night, after dinner, Florence said, 'Sit down. I want to model my new shoes.'

Platform styles of the 1970s are not new. (*Edison Brothers Shoe Stores*) Arab harem ladies have worn them for centuries. These platforms required a delicate walk that increased the exotic lure of the wearer. (*The Bally Shoe Factories, Ltd.*)

In a few minutes she came teetering in on a monstrous pair of stilts and announced, 'the latest thing—four-inch platforms. Sexy, eh?' " And that, simply and eloquently expressed, is why people wear them.

The American Medical Association, the American Podiatry Association, the National Safety Council, and various other authoritative bodies have issued public warnings about the dangers of wearing high platform shoes (as well as high heels). As usual, these well-intentioned spokesmen are out of tune with the realities of female psychology. Just as a courageous soldier is willing to risk his life in war, so a woman is willing to risk hers in the perennial battle for sex attraction, and all the dangers and warnings be damned.

In February 1974, consumer crusader Ralph Nader told the Podiatry Society of New York, "Americans demand fashion and style at the expense of health and safety." He assailed the "fashion tyranny" of stiletto heels and the "ultimate idiocy" of platform shoes. But the well-intentioned Nader, like the doctors, sees only evil in these sensuous stilts. He overlooks a psychosexual reality: these sinful stilts have always given men and women alike more pleasure than pain. And most women prefer to trip to hell in high heels than to walk flat-heeled to heaven.

The platform, forerunner of the modern high heel, reached its peak between the fifteenth and eighteenth centuries. It was a style known as the chopine (in Italy as the *chapiney*). It was a shoe worn on a high pedestal, or a hollowed-out cylinder. The heights averaged six to eighteen inches, though heights up to thirty inches weren't unusual. There were instances where pregnant women fell from them with consequent miscarriages. This happened enough times so that a law was passed in Venice in 1430, banning the wearing of the chopine. But neither the peril nor the law could stop its popularity.

The chopine was the constant butt of jibes. British dramatist Ben Jonson, in one of his plays, spoke of one character as "treading on corked stilts at a prisoner's pace." Shakespeare has Hamlet say, "Your ladyship is nearer to heaven than when I saw you last, by the height of your chopine." A popular jesting comment was that the chopine-wearer was half wood and half woman. Seventeenth-century author Douce, in his *Raymond's Voyage Through Italy*, remarked, "This place [Venice] is much frequented by walking maypoles; I mean the women. They wear their coats half too long for their bodies, being mounted on their *chippeens* (which are as high as a man's leg); they walk between two handmaids, majestically deliberating with every step they take." John Evelyn, an English author and traveler of the same century, wrote, " 'Tis ridiculous to see how ladys crawl in and out of their gondolas by reason of their chopines, and what they appear when taken down from their wooden scaffolds. Of these, I saw thirty together, stalking halfe again as high as the rest of the world."

Nevertheless, the chopine remains alive in various forms even today. The Syrian bride still wears the nuptial, platform-clog *kubbabs*. Japanese courtesans for generations wore fancy clogs six to twelve inches high, as a mark of their profession. Today, in Kyoto's red-light district, either a statue or a living model of Shimabara, The Great Whore, is led through the streets in annual processions. She stands in sandals on twelve-inch-high pedestals, supported on either side by two female apprentices. She moves with small, feminine steps that evoke erotic visions in the minds of male observers lining the streets.

SILLY OR SENSIBLE

High heels have been denounced by doctors for generations. The high heel has been blamed for an alarming array of physical disorders—curvature of the spine, backache, sciatica, a host of abdominal and pelvic conditions, eye strain, headaches, sterility, and even temporary insanity. Some years ago the *Health Shoe Digest* published an article en-

The original platform shoe was the *korthornos* worn in ancient Greek drama. (*From* The Mode in Footwear) The more important the actor or his role, the higher his platform. The Japanese version is the *géta*. When Emperor Hirohito was enthroned in 1926, his *gétas* were nearly twelve inches in height.

The platform reached its peak between the fifteenth and eighteenth centuries, in a style known as the chopine, ranging in height from six to thirty inches. (*From* A History of Shoe Fashions)

titled, "High Heels Cause About All the Evils to Which Woman Is Heir To"—which places the high heel on an even footing with the serpent in Eden. A shoe manufacturer's house organ, *The Miller Defender*, in 1940 stated, "Gynecologists estimate that 60 percent of diseases peculiar to women are due to high heels."

A half century ago, the YMCA and YWCA launched a national poster campaign urging young women to discard their high heels and avoid a long list of bodily ills, along with loose morals. In 1963, Nationalist China's Defense Ministry decreed that all women in the armed forces could no longer wear high heels, on or off duty. Why? Because, read the decree, "good soldiers should have a military stride. Soldiers in high heels appear more suited for love than war."

It's no secret that humans will endure all kinds of discomfort and even pain if there are sexual compensations. The high heel is one good example, and Rudofsky comments on this: "Physical pain is accepted by women if it is a constituent part of pleasure and courtship. The discomfort from wearing any kind of hampering apparel is compensated by the collective admiration of the other sex. Women's birdlike tripping is age-old to her mate. The modern woman will, therefore, furiously defend her high-heeled footwear and her stilted walk because the concept of the foot and walk constitutes—if only felt unconsciously—a focus of sexual attraction."

All of it is summed up nicely in a verse by Jennie Farley, published in *Punch:*

> Italy's shoes are like Italy's gents:
> To foreign ladies they give offense.
> The shoe and the man initially please
> But sinfully soon, they pinch and squeeze.
>
> I hate those heels on the hoof, on the street
> Both make you suffer though each looks sweet.
> I'll not be beguiled, despite their appeals;
> As of today, I'm swearing off heels.
>
> Unless, of course, a Don Juan comes by
> Who likes me with heels impossibly high.
> Then back to stilts, though the shoe abuses,
> Life's short. Love's long—and worth a few bruises.

Not diamonds but high heels have always been a girl's best friend. They've done more for psychosexual uplift than any other article of fashion or clothing ever devised. That's why the high heel has retained its popularity for centuries. It will continue to do so as long as sex attraction holds its high position on human nature's list of priorities.

13

Walking Is a Sex Trap

Man is the only creature in all nature capable of walking upright on two feet with such grace and poise that his manner of walking is a focal point of sex attraction and erotic arousal. This applies especially to the female.

We take our walking for granted, seldom realizing how sex-involved it is. Yet, as we saw in Chapter 6, this distinctive mode of walking gave birth to a new kind of body and body dynamics, plus a host of new sexual and erogenous features, particularly in the female, that are non-existent in other species. Thus, walking not only created those erogenous features in the beginning, but today the walk exploits those assets. In short, walking has developed into a sex trap.

The natural sexuality of the gait applies not only to humans but to many other species as well. During courting or mating periods, many animals and birds strut or walk in a sexually turned-on way more exaggerated than their usual gait. This special gait serves as a sexual signal and contributes to sexual arousal itself. This is seen further in the courting and mating dances, which are simply more elaborate forms of gait and are used for sexual communication and arousal.

Humans are no different. They use their own special gaits and dances for the same sex communication and arousal purposes, whether it be a woman prancing along with her sexy walk, or a young man strutting before the girls, or in the dances common to all fertility rites.

We say today, "You're a man when you're able to stand on your own two feet." We rarely appreciate how absolutely valid this is. Man became true man when he could stand upright on his own two feet. However, even to stand and walk erect wasn't enough. What was vital was a full, fleet and graceful *stride*—a completely new idea in living locomotion. "Walking with a striding gait," declares anatomist John Napier, writing on the evolution of human gait, "is probably the most significant of the many evolved capacities that separates man from the primitive hominids."

Man's unique ability to walk upright may well be the most important phenomenon in the entire span of evolution because of the stupendous changes it brought about in the human species and in the world itself. Says Duke University anthropologist Weston La Barre, "The single most spectacular physical trait of human beings is his bipedality—a fact noticed as early as the ancient Greek philosopher Anaxagoras. The effects of this revolutionary change still echo throughout human anatomy and physiology." Benjamin Franklin, founder of the prestigious American Philosophical Society, suggested that one or several meetings of the Society should be devoted to man's erect posture and gait "because it is one of the true marvels of the human species."

The human stride, along with the erect body posture, established a new kind of body dynamics in nature and made man, but especially woman, genuinely a being of beauty in motion; more marvelous in terms of esthetic and body engineering than even a bird in flight or a gazelle on the run.

This was no quick or small achievement. Scientists tell us that early man was walking on two legs more than three million years ago. But over the past one hundred thousand years there has been a constant process of refinement of this technique to instill the potent erotic qualities it possesses today. Dr. Ernest O. Hooton, the distinguished Harvard anthropologist, once told me during a discussion on human gait and its sexual associations:

"Prehistoric man stalked women as he stalked prey. And he was no less selective in his choices than the modern male. One of the most important things he observed in making his choice before springing from hiding was the gait of the female. Apparently much was indicated about her sexuality, her youthfulness, her fertility capacities, and her physical desirability, by the agility, grace and sensuality of her walk.

It's no different today. The gait of the female is a very important erotic stimulant for the male—and one of the several physical features by which he makes his choice of a mate for marriage or otherwise."

The dynamics of human gait and its consequent sexual esthetics are somewhat awesome to ponder. When standing, a body weighing one hundred and fifty or two hundred pounds is balanced on a base of less than one square foot (an average size dog weighing 80 or 90 percent less occupies more body-base space). In walking or running or dancing, this base is further reduced to half or less because the weight is balanced alternately on only one foot. And even this one foot isn't solidly planted, but may rest on only the heel, ball, or toes, thus reducing the ground-contact area to only a couple of square inches.

So magnificent is the balance structure of the human foot—its bones, muscles, arches and ligaments—that, like the crane, with practice man can stand perfectly erect and balanced on only one leg in a restful stance for hours. This feat is done habitually by the Nilotic Sudanese in Africa.

Further, with four-footed or even other two-footed creatures, the body center of gravity is much closer to the ground. With man, however, this center of gravity, due to his erect posture and height, is much higher above ground, hence is more precariously balanced. It's like the difference in balancing a long pencil and a squat cube.

Surely under these fragile dynamic conditions the body must fall flat on its face. And that's exactly what human gait is, a constant sequence of "fall-safe." Just as we're about to fall forward, the other foot and leg magically implant themselves ahead to prevent the fall. However, with three million years of practice, the muscular arrangement of pulleys and counter-pulleys in the foot and leg have become so expert at this that human gait has evolved into the most graceful, fluid and lithesome form of locomotion in all nature.

But something else has happened. This fragile body balance, along with the smooth rhythm of the strides, has *sensualized* the walk—the *only* sensualized walk in all nature. A whole series of erotic undulations of the body and its erogenous parts are set in motion—limbs, hips, buttocks, bosom, torso. These sinuous, rippling-rolling movements, especially in women, are given further erotic accent by certain types of footwear.

The instinctive sex attraction of the walk is revealed at an early age. By the time a girl has reached the age of puberty, she has begun to make some exciting and delightful discoveries about the way she walks. She finds that *how* she walks has, for some mysterious reason, a curious attraction for the boys. As she moves further into her teens she notes that certain kinds of shoes and heels enhance this attraction even more. By the time she's a mature young lady, experience has taught her that if she exploits certain skills and tactics in her manner of walking, she can magnetize the eye and attention of the male to just about any seductive degree she wishes.

WHAT MAKES A WALK EROTIC?

Why does a man look around and continue observing an attractive woman who has just passed him? He can no longer see her face or front. What continues to fascinate him is the motion of her walk that affects her whole figure, especially if she's wearing high heels. He scans her ankles and legs, the angle of her feet, the rhythmic sway of her hips and buttocks, the lithesome spring of her step, the grace of her carriage, the subtle vibrations of her body in motion. Men have been observing this performance for centuries, and never failing to get an erotic lift from it.

When we speak of a "sexy walk" we refer to women, never to men. "Strutting males are mostly confined to the animal kingdom," says Rudofsky. "The shambling gait of modern man . . . hardly turns a woman's head. But then his walk is not meant to excite her; it is the woman's business to do the prancing. If she is good at it, her gait becomes her main attraction—so much so that it is diagnosed as a measure of sexual allure. A woman's attractiveness is determined less by the degree to which she reveals her body than by the way she walks."

A woman's walk sets in motion many of her erogenous parts, whereas a man has few such parts to activate. Men and women have distinctly different gaits stemming from anatomical differences. The male's pelvis is smaller and narrower, which positions his hips and lower limbs differently. His knees are "looser," he uses more shoulder roll, and he walks with a longer stride because his narrow pelvis permits him to take a more straight-ahead step. Also, due to his external genital organs, he walks with a more open-legged stance.

Because there's so little sensuousness to a man's walk, he tries to gain more sex attraction by emphasizing the "masculinity" of his gait. Many men thus acquire a habit of walking with an exaggerated openleggedness and rolling stride, as if to ensure their own sexual identity. This is typified by the open-legged gait of the cowboy, real or movie version; or the pose of a machismo male in an aggressive, combative mood (James Cagney personified this stance in his tough-guy movie roles). Thus, even in his "sexless" walk the male strives to create a virile-masculine image whose aim is sex attraction.

In Japan, the model of the heterosexual, virile male has long been the samurai, the ancient warrior class which was abandoned generations ago. They walked with two heavy swords hanging from the waistbelt. This forced an exaggerated straddle gait, feet wide apart. Even today, some Japanese men walk in this manner in an effort to convey a strong masculine image. Emperor Hirohito, at ceremonies of state, assumes a modified version of this walk. On one such occasion that was televised, the *New York Times* (December 28, 1968) felt obliged to explain, "His jerky walk is one of style and not of chance or disability."

A woman's gait, on the other hand, when effectively executed, can be an erotic vision. "The goddess is revealed by her walk," said Virgil. A woman's anatomy is ideally structured to create this illusion. The man's rolling motion is in his shoulders, while the woman's is in her hips and buttocks. Because her genitals are internal she walks with a more elegant, close-legged stride. There is a sensuous vibrato to her body parts with each step. Let her walk in high heels and the erotic tempo of these orchestrated movements accelerates.

Anatomist John Napier writes, "The difference in the proportion of the male and female pelvis has the effect of diminishing the range through which the female hip can move forward and backward. Thus for a given length of stride, women are obliged to rotate the pelvis through a greater angle than men do. This secondary sexual characteristic has not lacked exploitation; in our culture, female pelvis rotation has considerable erotogenic significance."

A motionless or standing woman, no matter how attractive, has far less sex appeal than when walking. My friend, the late Dr. R. Plato Schwartz, Professor of Orthopedic Surgery at the University of Rochester Medical School, and one of the world's foremost authorities on human gait, told me:

"Human gait is much more than locomotion. Since perhaps the earliest days of mankind women have used it as an erotic instrument, with great success, in the same way as some forms of dancing have always been used to arouse male sexual response. The eroticism of the gait is most influenced by the way the feet are used, often with the aid of certain kinds of footwear. The foot and shoe—those are the real roots of erotic gait."

SEXY AND DESEXED GAITS

Just as a woman's walk can be sexualized, so also it can be desexed. The position or condition of the feet makes a huge difference in the "sex level" of the walk; that is, whether the walk is sexually turned-on, turned-off, or merely neutral.

For example, a person with seriously weakened arches, no matter at what age, usually walks with a sluggish, labored gait associated with senility or infirmity, hence the walk is sex-negative. A pigeon-toed gait in adults has an awkward, childlike quality that desexualizes the natural grace of gait. An exaggerated toeing-out gait also has a desexualizing effect because it's cosmetically ungainly and the youthful spring of the step is diminished with the foot in this position. Bent knees desex a gait because it makes the graceful stride impossible and resembles the insecure, clompy step of the senile.

A desexed walk occurs when the feet are far apart to widen the base for more security in walking. This is typical of the very aged or infirm; it's common among very stout or overweight persons where the gait is more waddle than walk; it's usually seen with pregnant women about the eighth month. Three of the most telltale signs of advancing years and declining libido in women are: a slowing and loss of springiness of the step; feet wider apart; and more toeing out. If these can be avoided, a woman can cut years from her appearance and reflect a more youthful vitality and active libido.

The real key to a sex-attractive walk is in the position of the feet. The average woman walks with the feet three to five inches apart. More than that *diminishes* the gait's sex-appeal value, and less *increases* its value.

The sexiest walk of all, curiously, is an "unnatural" one. Women have learned to use it as they use. cosmetics—to lend erotic accent to their natural endowments. This unnatural gait is with the feet very close together (less than three inches apart), toes straight ahead or slightly toed out. With each step one foot crosses slightly over the other as though trying to walk a chalk line. This forces a mildly exaggerated semicircular swing of the hips and buttocks. The body, delicately and elegantly balanced, is femininely fluid, its upper half majestically straight, its lower half rhythmically mobile. This walk is learned and practiced by fashion models, show girls, actresses—and by many women who possess and transmit a natural sensuousness, or try to.

Florenz Ziegfeld, whose statuesque show girls glamorized the stages of his lavish musicals of the 1920s, had a format which he often used in selecting these sexy queens. A long white screen was stretched across a darkened stage, except for lighting behind the screen. The girls, scantily clad and in high heels, were told to walk across stage behind the screen. Ziegfeld could thus see only the silhouette of the girl.

He said, "Before I see their faces I want to see how they walk. There's more sex in a walk than in a face or even in a figure. A woman can have the most beautiful face and the most glorious form. But if the walk isn't exactly right, it can spoil the whole damn thing. Any woman who doesn't take advantage of her feminine assets by learning to walk right, loses a lot of her sex attraction."

Psychiatrist Karl Menninger states, "Some women cultivate a gait which emphasizes their femininity." By a simple process of self-training, the sensuous qualities of the female walk can be doubled or tripled in impact. "The female gait can be put on," declares orthopedic surgeon Louis H. Paradies of the University of Texas Southwestern Medical School. "It can be learned without difficulty and easily become a habit."

From the ancient days of Egypt and Persia, very young girls have been taught the "art" of sensuous walking. It has been taught in American finishing schools, though under the more genteel heading of "ladylike" walking. Each era in history brings a different kind of "fashionable" gait. In the 1740s, for example, it was the rigid-erect carriage; in 1800 it was something called the "classic" posture; in the 1860s the popular style was the Greek Bend; in the 1920s it was the Debutante Slouch; in the 1940s, the long-leggy stride. But no matter what the walking style, the motive has never veered from sex attraction.

Another version of the sexy walk—perhaps the most universal of all—is the small, delicate, mincing step. Here again the feet are close together, but the step is very short, like walking tip-toe. This manner of walking has strong psychosexual roots because it's associated with the age-old concept of female bondage, a male chauvinistic idea that prevails as strongly today as in centuries past.

Men have always sought to "confine" their women in one way or another. They wanted their women to feel dependent so that this "helpless" condition could give vent to the male's need to be protective and supportive. The whole romantic concept of chivalry has been built on this. Thus the fragile, mincing step has become a vital part of this image. Over the centuries, and even today, it has spawned many women's clothing and footwear fashions that require the small-step, mincing gait. Men have either forced this fetters-type walk on women, or women have cunningly used it themselves, knowing the sensuous fascination it holds for men.

Havelock Ellis writes that the appeal of fetters is "an almost abstract sexual fascination in the idea of restraint, whether endured, inflicted or merely witnessed or imagined; the feet become the focus of this fascination."

History is rife with such examples. In ancient Palestine young girls were taught to walk with the small, mincing step by attaching light "stepping chains" around their ankles that limited the length of the stride. The slave ankle bracelet worn ornamentally by women today is a carry-over from this. The tight skirt, slit or unslit, has always been an almost universal costume, designed and worn to keep a woman's step short and delicate. Right up to the eighteenth century, bridal ankle chains or cuffs were used at wedding ceremonies, signifying the wife's traditional bondage to her husband.

The kimono has been an essential part of the Japanese woman's costume for many generations. But the kimono isn't as simple as it appears on the surface. Beneath is a complex rigging of cords and undergarments, forcing a restrictive manner of walking—a sort of half-step, toed-in gait (a sign of sexual modesty among Japanese women). With each step, the foot makes a kind of half-circular, scythelike movement.

This walk is so ingrained that it has become second nature to Japanese women. Many use it even when wearing Western clothes. Another version of this is the tight, side-slit dress or skirt worn in various Asian countries. The resulting mincing step is found sensuous by Asian men.

The knobbed, cloglike sandal commonly in use today in Asia is of ancient origin. The Africans adopted it as a wedding shoe. A large, mushroomlike knob rises from the front of the sole and fits between the big and second toe. The knobs are often joined by a short, fine chain that forces a small half-step. The knob was designed originally as a phallic symbol, and is the same today. The snug fit of the phallus between the two toes suggests the obvious. The woman, with her small steps and her attachment to the shoe, indicates her dependency on the phallus. This shoe, when worn by the bride, relates the phallus to promised fertility.

In more modern times, one of the most effective instruments to ensure the small, fetterslike step and the illusion of female bondage is the high heel. In a high heel, a full, natural stride is impossible (this is easily demonstrated by trying to walk on the balls of the feet without shoes). But a paradox occurs. The high heel gives the appearance of a long-leggy look and stride—yet the actual step is small and restrained. This optical illusion adds to the erotic image.

Leathem writes, "A curved leg restricted in movement by a pair of extremely high heels can excite a sadist who takes pleasure in restraining the freedom of movement that most women now cherish." Nevertheless, even today the male "sadists" are a huge breed, and the "masochistic" women who delight in catering to this erotic feeling are also legion.

Such devices as high heels, platforms, pointed toes and tight shoes have helped to serve the purpose of female bondage and all its sexual inferences. The walk, particularly a stylish walk aided by clothes and shoes, plays a singular role in man's love antics and thus in the propagation of the species.

But women have always been more ingenious than men. So they've learned to convert these devices of captive constraint into erotic lures that have, ironically, served to ensnare the men who invented the snares in the first place. Women have built a better trap out of the original trap by the erotic use of their footwear and gait to trip up the men.

VIEW FROM THE REAR

A rhythmic, mobile, female buttocks is a wanton sight that has fascinated man since Adam. And woman, knowing it, has practiced the seductive art of hipswaying since Eve. What draws the wolf whistle of male admiration? Not a face. Not even a figure. It's the wiggle of the walk, the hustle of the bustle.

But what do bouncing buttocks have to do with the sex life of the foot and shoe? Plenty. The foot was responsible for the erect gait, which in turn gave rise to the prominence and erotic character of the buttocks (the human rump is larger and more mobile than that of any other creature, relative to body size). Further, footwear has always had an important influence in accentuating the prominence and erotic movements of the female buttocks. Thus, the foot, shoe and buttocks share an erotic partnership.

The vibrations of a walking woman's buttocks are a silent language flashed to men: Follow me behind. When early women discovered this marvelous optical lure, they lost no time in seeking out devices and methods that would further enhance the visibility of their rear-view assets. Their greatest find was the high-heeled shoe. "The special characteristics of the female hips and buttocks become conspicuous in walking," says Havelock Ellis. "The vibratory movement naturally produced by walking and artificially heightened (such as with high heels) thus becomes a trait of sexual beauty."

Whole books have been written on buttocks fetishism and partialism. Why this bewitched male interest in the female buttocks, especially its mobility in gait? Some authorities think it's because the fleshy, bulbous protuberances of the buttocks closely resemble the breasts, including the cleavage. Says zoologist Desmond Morris (*The Naked Ape*), "The protuberant, hemispherical breasts of the female must surely be copies of the fleshy buttocks."

Another reason cited for universal buttocks partialism in the male is the fact that the buttocks are served by the same nerve system as the genitalia. This often translates into sexual imagery in the male mind. Says Leathem:

"Where the female is concerned, many men think of her buttocks as a surrealist imitation of her vaginal opening—the cleavage is longer and the opening deeper. The fact that the female buttocks . . . also move suggestively as she walks—much as they undulate while she is going through an orgasm—has increased the popularity of female derrières in this contemporary era of voyeuristic fashions."

This fascination is so age-old and universal that it has earned its own intriguing medical term—*callipygia*, meaning lovely buttocks. The word is from the Greek, naturally. But the human species has an in-

satiable desire to improve on nature. So when women ages ago discovered the erotic power of the rolling derrière, they cultivated it as
one of the finer voluptuous arts. So in many parts of the world women
strive to develop not only callipygia but a more advanced condition
known as *steatopygia*—buttocks of very large or exaggerated size.

According to anatomists, buttocks exceeding 4 percent of protrusion in relation to the individual's height, are steatopygous. Nevertheless, this posterior architecture can frequently exceed 10 percent,
especially when cultivated by special exercises.

True or natural steatopygia exists among certain peoples such as
the Bushmen or Hottentots of Africa. Or it may occur with particular
individuals of any race or culture. But among societies where a prominent and mobile buttocks is a prized possession among women and a
voyeuristic treat for the men, the women spend years not only in developing large buttocks, but in training them to oscillate in walking like
a nervous pendulum. In other societies, including our own, women have
utilized the erotic devices of fashion to achieve similar results, such as
bustles, large backside bows, tight skirts and pants, fanny falsies, or
even the use of plastic surgery.

Hottentot women, already steatopygous, further develop their buttocks from childhood, and also by tightly binding their waists to force
an additional protrusion of the hips and buttocks. Darwin reported that
the men of Somali often chose a wife by lining up the eligible women
in a row and selecting the one whose posterior protruded most.

Shapera, in his published study of the African Kgatla people in 1940,
stated that the men prized particularly those women with large gluteal
muscles: "The buttocks, especially, have a powerful erotic appeal, and
evoke many compliments, while much of the love play before coitus
consists of caressing them. Girls with slim backsides are seldom considered attractive; they are disparagingly said to have 'bodies like boys.' "

In many Arab countries today, men admire female steatopygia, a
feature they call *ghung*, in their women. The belly dancers of the Middle East are admired more for the extraordinary vibratory control of
their buttocks than for their belly undulations. The South Sea Papuans
view the large, mobile buttocks of their women with high erotic esteem. At age seven or eight, the Papuan girl is taught the refinements of
vibrato, a subtle exercise. By adolescence she has learned to walk in a
highly provocative way in the presence of men—though she subsides
to a simpler gait when no men are around.

High heels and sexy buttocks share an obvious correlation.

Spanish women have long developed an S-shaped contour of the spine, with a deep curve in the lower portion and a consequent back thrust of the buttocks. This highly admired feature, called *ensellure,* is the result of training and practice. It is further aided by the wearing of the high, curvy "Spanish heel."

The high heel has perhaps been the most effective buttocks-builder and buttocks-mover of all devices known. Women have always been conscious of this. An American, on a recent business trip to Glasgow, entered a restaurant. When the young waitress briskly walked to his table he asked what the day's specialty was.

"Roast and rice, sir," she replied with a heavy Scottish brogue.

"My, you certainly roll your R's," the visitor said.

"I suppose so," she answered, blushing. "But only when I wear my high heels."

A century ago it was taboo to show the contours of the female buttocks, so women devised an illusion—the bustle.

The high heel reshapes the body silhouette. For example, the average angle of the female pelvis, front to rear, is about twenty-five degrees when the woman is standing in stocking feet. When standing on two-inch heels the tilt of the angle increases to forty-five degrees; and on three-inch heels the angle increases to fifty-five degrees, or more than double the natural angle. On these heels not only is there much more posterior thrust, but the mobility of the buttocks is at least twice that when walking barefoot or in flat heels. The body posture takes on the look of a pouter pigeon, with lots of breast and tail balanced precariously on a pair of stilts. Men have never lost their fascination with this look.

Much has been written about the healthful values of walking as a means of exercise, mental relaxation and esthetic enjoyment, which is true.

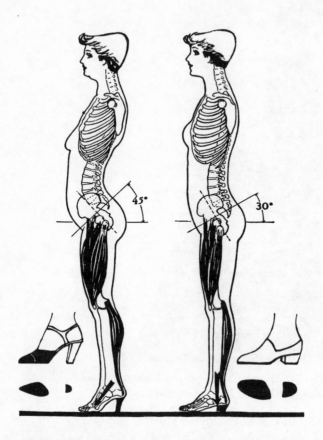

High heels reshape the body silhouette. Note how the higher heel accentuates the calf, buttocks, and lower-back curve.

But we've overlooked the reality that the *chief* tonic value of female gait is as an erotic stimulant. For centuries women have cannily distilled this heady intoxicant, and men have continued to drink with sensuous delight from its cup.

Women seldom walk. They perform. Nothing about this will change as long as men continue to observe this performance as an erotically enthralled audience, which should be to the end of time.

Pedic Sadomasochism

"Man," Darwin said, "admires and often tries to exaggerate whatever nature may have given to him." Man has decorated and adorned his body since prehistoric times. But as succeeding generations became more civilized, they decided that mere cosmetic decoration wasn't enough improvement for sex attraction. So they proceeded to invent ingenious ways of reshaping the body by deliberately deforming and mutilating it, convinced that these anatomical changes add to erotic arousal. And strangely, they actually do.

Every culture and society has practiced the art of body deformation. It's common in civilized as well as primitive societies, and is as prevalent today as in centuries past. Often enduring exquisite agonies, men and women have bent, twisted, compressed, scarred, amputated, fractured, swelled, shrunken, pierced, bruised and otherwise disfigured the natural shape and appearance of their bodies and their parts—all designed to add new sensuous and erotic dimensions to their persons. Karl Menninger calls it "focal suicide" and says it is common to all of us.

In all shoe-wearing societies, no part of the body has been subjected to as much anatomical deformation as the foot.

This is by no means a modern or Western phenomenon due to the wearing of modern shoes. Corns, bunions and other shoe-caused foot ills were as common in ancient Rome, Greece, Egypt, India, Persia, and China. The physician Hippocrates (460–370 B.C.) prescribed for corns and other foot lesions. So did Galen in the second century A.D., whose treatment consisted of Spanish fly combined with arsenic. Pliny the Elder (23–79 A.D.) treated foot ills "galled by shoes" with such concoctions as beef suet mixed with frankincense, or asses' urine mixed with mud.

Critics have always atributed such ills to "abuse" or "neglect" of the foot, with shoes, vanity, and fashion being the chief culprits. But the *real* cause has always been the perverse human desire to reshape the foot to imbue it with new or accentuated sex-appeal features. Shoes have been the chosen instrument to create fresh sensuous illusions by changing the size, shape, and look of the foot. Women especially have always known what they were doing in deforming their feet. Thus, what the doctors and others glibly call foot "ills" or "defects" are, from the woman's standpoint, more realistically regarded as pleasure wounds or sex scars.

No, this doesn't mean that women seek to deliberately deform their

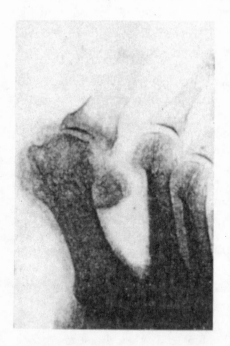 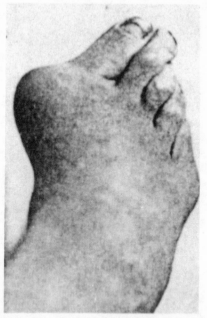

Foot distortion—a price willingly paid for wearing sex-attractive footwear fashions.

feet or acquire foot ills, or that they enjoy foot distress. It means that women subconsciously but voluntarily resign themselves to foot distress and deformity in preference to the alternative of wearing comfortable but desexed or sexless shoes.

Ironically, crippled or deformed feet have long been associated with sensuality. Many observers have related Lord Byron's sensuality to his lameness. The bound feet of Chinese women and its direct link to sexual arousal has already been noted.

"Masochism in women is more a way of life than a neurosis," says British psychiatrist and sexologist Clifford Allen. This may explain in part why women yield more readily to the dictates of fashion and the cycles of new "body forms." But then, compared with men, they have many more erogenous zones to attend to.

"People seem to tolerate rather well any revision of the body if it is done within the framework of social approval," writes Seymour Fisher in *Body Consciousness*. "Various cultures have done such things as cripple the feet of women . . . and these practices have not only been tolerated but eagerly sought after."

The medical term *algolagnia* (from *algos*, pain, and *lagnia*, voluptuousness) was originated by the German psychiatrist Schrenck-Notzing. It is a condition in which physical pain or distress—either experienced or observed in others—evokes a sexual pleasure. Both men and women, but especially women, have endured whatever distresses of body deformation are needed to sexually attract or seduce the opposite sex.

Throughout history we've reshaped heads, ears, lips, noses, eyebrows, necks, breasts, buttocks, legs, arms, waists, penises, skin, hips, ankles—and feet. Especially feet. And always for one reason: to add to sexual magnetism. Every form of body deformation is designed to impart a distinctive look, particularly one having some sensuous or erotic quality. This is why every fashion, whether in a primitive society or in Paris or New York, is called a "look."

All forms of body deformation are fashion, and most forms of fashion are body-deforming either as an illusion or a reality. Art is never a duplication or replica of nature. It's the artist's own interpretation of nature. So he reshapes it to his own vision and imagery. As an art form, fashion does the same with the human form—and shoe fashions with the foot—reshaping the original to a new esthetic version.

This is why men and women throughout history have willingly accepted a kind of "podoalgolagnia," a sadomasochistic experience of foot deformation through foot-constricting shoes to increase sex attraction. This is our own choice. We'll have it no other way because the pleasure is greater than the pain.

THE FOOT GOD NEVER DESIGNED

To assume that the designers, makers, sellers, and fitters of footwear are the sadists behind foot deformation is absurd. These shoemen are dealing with an irresistible force far beyond their control—a mass sadomasochism that demands foot deformation to achieve the desired sex-attraction benefits. If shoes were designed like the natural foot, which they aren't, the public would rebel in protest against the "ugly" shoes fostered on it.

There has always been a supply of "sensible" shoes on the market, and an added supply could be turned on with the ease of a faucet. But because these shoes are regarded as sexless or even antisex, few people buy or wear them. But can't shoes be made fashionable without being footdeforming? Impossible. This would contradict the very principle of fashion, which is to alter body looks, shapes, or sizes to bypass reality.

For example, up until the Civil War there were no lefts and rights in shoes in America. Lefts and rights had appeared from time to time over the past four thousand years, but never gained any popular acceptance. People wanted the symmetrical look of "straight" shoes that could be worn on either foot. After all, all other dual parts of the body —eyes, ears, legs, arms, breasts, buttocks, hands, shoulders, etc.—appear to be symmetrical. Why should the feet be different?

In 1822, a Philadelphia shoe manufacturer introduced lefts and rights but received no public response whatever. They were ridiculed as "crooked shoes." Then, during the Civil War, some military shoes were made for lefts and rights. After the war the ex-soldier tried to buy such shoes for civilian wear. But it took almost another generation before there was sufficient demand to get them into the stores. Thus a sensible and logical idea met resistance for centuries because no one wanted to wear "funny footwear" that contradicted the esthetic principle of body symmetry.

Seymour Fisher makes an interesting and pertinent observation: "The fact that we so carefully assign different clothes to the two sexes reflects our chronic anxiety about matters of sexual identity. . . . It is pertinent to this issue that right-left clothing asymmetries are usually avoided. There are research findings that indicate that the right-left gradients of the body are associated with splits in the sexual identity of the body (for example, 'Am I partially masculine and partially feminine?'). To emphasize differences between right and left may symbolically dramatize the possibility of conflict about the sexual classification of one's body and therefore stir uncomfortable anxiety."

Even today, more than 95 percent of the world's shoes aren't shaped like the natural foot. Many still aren't made for lefts and rights. In the late nineteenth century, when the Japanese army was being modernized, the soldiers were put into Western shoes and boots. None could wear them, and they were permitted to go back to their simple sandals and clogs. The same thing has been happening today among many of the newborn nations of Africa. The feet of these native soldiers are having extreme difficulty getting into "modern" shoes styled on European and American models.

Take, for example, open-toed shoes. The opening for the big and second toes is always in the middle rather than the normal position on the inner side. So the two toes are forced over to the center. Thus the idea of fashion symmetry is maintained.

One foot is always larger than the other (longer and wider). But both shoes of a pair are identical in length and width. Hence one foot is sacrificed for the other. Economically this is necessary, for the only alternative would be expensive custom-made shoes for all. But it's part of the price of wearing shoes, which in turn is part of the price of added sex attraction.

Most shoes don't align with the natural heel-to-toe axis of the foot. On the foot, a straight line starting at the back will go through the exact center of the heel, arch and ball, and come out between the second and third toes. On most shoes, however, this same straight line will divide the shoe into two *unequal* sides. Thus a space conflict is created, with the foot forced to conform to an unnatural distribution of space inside the shoe.

In 1973, one major men's shoe manufacturer advertised in several national magazines: "We Shape Your Shoe the Way God Shaped Your Foot." The picture of the shoe shown was so obviously "off center" regarding this straight-line principle, that God must have winced every time the ad appeared in print.

"Throughout all ages," says clothing historian Robert Riley, "fashionable clothing has been many things, but it has almost never been close to practical. . . . Outside of orthopedic problems, the shoe has never conformed to the 'natural' shape of the foot. It has always been used in the same way as clothing, to create the illusion of the ideal shape. Whether pointed or narrow or round or square, open or closed, high or low, practical considerations of comfort and use run a poor second to the esthetics of the moment."

Among shoe-wearing people all over the world it's almost as impossible to find a straight fourth and fifth toe as it is to find a straight banana. Deformation of the toes—whether as hammertoes, bunions, bent-back toes, curled-under toes, overlapping toes, corns or calluses, ingrown toenails—are the universal insignia or "sex scars" of shoewearing peoples.

Like the Chinese footbinding custom, the modern foot-deforming process starts early. "Never expect the child to complain that the shoe is hurting him, for the crippling process is painless," says Dr. Simon Wikler in his book, *Take Off Your Shoes and Walk*. But again like the Chinese footbinding process, there is no malice intended, only the desired goal of added sex attraction.

The toes of shoe-wearing people have largely been put out of business for podocosmetic reasons. For instance, the toe-grasping ability of the infant, relative to its size, is twenty or more times greater than that of the average shoe-wearing adult. But among *non*-shoe-wearing peoples, this powerful toe-grasping ability actually increases into adulthood. The toes are capable of fanning out like fingers. Among shoewearing adults the immobilized toes are wedged together as though they were a single unit instead of separate digits.

Pointed-toed shoes have for centuries contributed to foot deformation. Says Flugel, "The last form of corporeal decoration is deformation. . . . The prevalent European ideal of a long and slender shoe is one that by no means altogether agrees with the natural form of the foot, and it is also, therefore, responsible for a good deal of actual deformation."

Men and women alike have shown a sadomasochistic affinity for pointed-toed shoes. One reason is that the long, pointed toe has always been a phallic symbol, the *poulaine* style being the ultimate example. But a further podosexual illusion emerges. Combine the long pointed toe with the high thin heel and a sensuous feminine image results—a sleek, slender leg-to-toe look that reaches the male eye with erotic effect.

R. Brody-Johansen, in his book *Body Clothes*, refers to women's shoes in the eighteenth and nineteenth centuries: "The desire for enhanced femininity was demonstrated clearly in women's footwear. No consideration was given for the natural shape of the foot. . . . Self-respecting women always wore boots, but with a high French heel. The effect sought was the grace of the ballet dancer's pointed foot, and the front of the leg and the instep extended in one straight line." The pointed-toed shoes gave the foot the same slenderizing lines women seek for their bodies.

Foot deformation through pointed shoes is hardly a modern development. Egyptian sandals dating back to 1100 B.C. had sharply pointed toes. In every century in almost every shoe-wearing culture for the past three thousand years, pointed-toed shoes have persisted.

Why is the popularity of the pointed toe so universal despite its obvious deforming effects on the foot? It's no mystery. Pointed-toed styles are podophallic, and hence we have a psychosexual attachment to them. And, especially for women, they sexualize a foot. They'll always remain popular because of the human addiction to sadomasochism —"the more it hurts the better I feel"—particularly if the deformation and hurt are compensated by the promise of greater sex attraction.

A psychiatrist recently reported a case of a thirty-year-old woman who used "an unusual approach to masturbation." She purchased shoes that were several sizes too small and narrow for her. These, she said, caused her feet to tingle and burn so intensely "that the burning and tingling sensation goes high up between my legs, then to my vagina. Suddenly I feel so excited I must masturbate."

"But can't you masturbate without wearing those tight shoes?" the psychiatrist asked.

"No, it just isn't the same. What's missing is that hot, tingling sensation. The hurting—that's what gives me the deep feeling of pleasure. After I masturbate, then I can take off my shoes."

This seemingly unusual situation more frequently works in reverse. Not a few men are sexually aroused to erection by observing women walk with obvious distress in tight shoes. One man confessed, "Even when I hear a woman say her tight shoes are killing her—that's enough to bring an instant erection."

Should we bemoan this "sacrifice" of natural foot shape and function to fashion? Not at all. If the wearers receive psychosexual gratifications, then the sacrifice is worth it.

Yet, the foot health alarmists are always with us. An "educational" pamphlet issued in the 1930s by one Milwaukee shoe company, Brouwer's Research Lasts, listed the following ailments throughout the body that had been relieved" by their shoes: insomnia, eye trouble, sciatica, numbness, twisted pelvis, clumsiness, arthritis, muscle spasms, constipation, fainting spells, menstrual pains, aches in the jaw, eczema, vomiting, sunken chest, growing pains, catarrh, nervous indigestion, headaches, pain at the base of the brain, dizziness, among numerous others.

Dr. Dennis White, national director of the Academy of Ambulatory Foot Surgery, recently reported that in a survey of the 1,200 members of the international society, it was found that one of every two women suffers from bunions, hammertoes, ingrown toenails, corns, and similar foot ailments. He declared that these foot ills are frequently the cause of "fatigue, facial wrinkles, and dark bags under the eyes."

Shoe shape and foot shape have always been about as mated as King Kong and Miss America. The objective of the shoe designer has never been to make the shoe look like the foot, but the foot like the shoe. This is the eternal illusion that is the mother of all fashion—to make the individual or his parts appear what he or she isn't, or what he or she wants to look like. Fashion is the universal artisan of masquerade. The public wants it no other way, and it is the business of fashion to serve the public what it wants.

DOES THE SHOE FIT—OR GIVE FITS?

Despite our passion for fashion, Americans have a fixation about shoe fit, as though it were a moral virtue. This mania has made American shoes unique in the world. For example, in almost all other countries, shoes are available in only full sizes (no half sizes), and even these in limited range. And most shoes are available in only one width. Every shoe must be broken in by the foot.

In America, however, shoes come as narrow as AAAAAA and as wide as EEEEEE. And in half sizes of extensive range. The shoes are made in nearly three hundred different size-width combinations, more than all other countries together. In fact, back in 1928 even quarter sizes were introduced, though these had to be abandoned because of high inventory costs.

Shoe sizes came into being about six hundred and fifty years ago when England's King Edward II decreed that three barley corns placed end to end equaled one inch. Thirteen barley corns equaled the length of the longest "normal" foot. Today the same principle of shoe sizes is still in use in America (most other countries use the metric system). A full shoe size equals a third of an inch (one barley corn). Edward, however, did nothing about half sizes or widths. In fact, widths weren't introduced in the United States until 1887.

Despite the foot-deforming nature of footwear fashions, Americans today are the best shoe-fitted people in the world because of the enormous size selection, and also because of the proficiency of most shoe fitters. Yet, paradoxically, *most* shoes don't fit *most* feet for reasons already cited.

Well, if most shoes don't fit, when *does* a shoe fit? Over the years I've asked this question of thousands of shoemen and doctors in the United States and other countries, personally or via surveys. There is no general standard or agreement, and the range of disagreement or variance is enormous.

Ironically, only the wearer can best decide when the shoe fits. Yet the wearer knows no more about "correct fit" than the average shoeman or doctor. The wearer can tell only if the shoe hurts or feels uncomfortable. But even if the shoe feels comfortable, it's no assurance that it fits correctly. A tooth can have a cavity, yet not ache. The feet of most shoe-wearing people have been altered from their natural shape since childhood. So if the shoe feels comfortable, it means only that it accommodates the altered foot. A "comfortable" shoe can be designed for a club foot.

The idea of "perfect" shoe fit is an age-old myth. The paradox is this. The shoe that fits correctly is one that's shaped exactly like the foot. But most people don't want and won't wear such styles. It resolves into a compromise: if the shoe is wearable it's bearable. And what makes it both wearable and bearable is its sex-attractive features. As long as people find more comfort in sex than sex in comfort, fashionable shoes with all their foot-deforming consequences will be chosen overwhelmingly.

15

Cinderella Was a Sexpot

Men sexually appraise women by the size and shape of their erogenous qualities: bosom, buttocks, legs and thighs, waist, mouth, lips, hips— and the foot. The feminine ideal of the small, dainty and curvaceous foot is age-old and almost universal.

This small-foot ideal has psychosexual roots. Some old legends still prevail that the size of the foot is indicative of the size of the vagina. Even today, for example, in rural and semirural Hungary, young and even mature women lie about their foot size as other women lie about their age because of the persistent male custom of judging a woman's genital features by her foot size. And shoes are always purchased two or three sizes smaller than foot size despite the consequences of foot distress and deformation.

However, the centuries-old association of small feet with femininity and even social or aristocratic status has inspired women all over the world to squeeze their feet into too-small shoes. This has also had much influence on the persistent popularity of high heels, pointed toes and other shoe styling features that create the small-foot illusion.

While we are in awe of the "cruel" process of Chinese footbinding, females of many countries have long submitted to comparable forms of deforming footbinding to enhance pedic sex attraction. For example, in seventeenth- and eighteenth-century Europe, girls and women of the higher social castes bound their feet with waxed linen tapes before going to bed at night. During the reign of Louis XIV, ladies of the aristocracy bound their feet at night with long, clipped hair tresses. Right up to the early twentieth century, adult women in America bound their feet with tapes during the waking hours (the tapes were concealed beneath their boots). Sometimes these bound feet were so constrictive that some women fainted in company.

Is it different today among modern, "enlightened" women? Hardly at all. A large share of women (and not a few men) continue to insist on shoe sizes too small—and, ironically, at the same time saying they want the shoe to be comfortable. A long-time cliché among shoemen is that a fortune awaits the man who invents a shoe that's small on the outside and big on the inside. The late shoeman, Harold R. Quimby, put it neatly into verse:

> Oh, why isn't it possible for every grand dame
> To just once in a while take some of the blame
> And acknowledge the truth that it's an impossible feat
> For pint-size shoes to hold quart-size feet.

THE REAL CINDERELLA COMES OUT OF HIDING

The Cinderella fable is the best-known folk tale ever written. Why the universal popularity of this fable? First, the original versions were never intended as a child's tale, but as a romance story for adults—with sexual overtones and undertones. Because the story centered on the theme of the small female foot, every man and woman could relate to it because of the podosexual image involved.

There have been over five hundred versions of the Cinderella fable spread throughout the world, many written long before the Brothers Grimm. There were Cinderella tales in ninth-century China, which may have helped give birth to the footbinding custom a couple of centuries later. Perhaps the oldest version dates back to Egypt in the seventh century B.C. The tale, briefly, goes like this:

A very beautiful girl named Rhodopis was bathing in the Nile. She had been a fellow slave of the famous Aesop. Splashing around, she didn't notice an eagle swoop down and make off with one of her slippers on the bank. The eagle flew for some five hundred miles to the city of Memphis, where it deposited the slipper at the feet of Psamtik I, king of Egypt (663–609 B.C.). The king, certain that this was an omen of great moment, suddenly felt a deep passion about the image of the owner of that small, dainty slipper. Just as Prince Charming did in later versions of the Cinderella tale, Psamtik set out in determined search for the girl. After an exhaustive hunt and trying the slipper on the feet of hundreds of girls, he finally came upon Rhodopis. Of course it was the perfect fit, and she became his queen. To celebrate the nuptials, the Third Pyramid of Gizeh was added to the floor of the desert.

But the best-known version is the one written by the Frenchman, Charles Perrault, in 1697. His original version contained clear erotic inferences. Many of these were lost by faulty translation, and the rest were expurgated—which is how it evolved into a child's fairy tale. In those days, manuscripts were handwritten by authors. In Perrault's original story his phrase for the slipper was *pantoufle en vair* (slipper of fur), but the scribe or translator read it as *pantoufle en verre* (slipper of glass). And so it has remained ever since.

Perrault was fully aware of the age-old eroticism associated with the foot inserted into a fur or fur-trimmed slipper or shoe, and its phallic-yoni symbolism. The "perfect fit" of the slipper indicated the perfect sexual mating, resulting in the ideal marriage. The romantic union of the prince and Cinderella was sexually symbolized by the suggestive union of the virginal phallic foot and the furry yoni shoe.

But the sexual overtones have persisted. The Cinderella fable has served not only to romanticize further the small-foot image, but to dramatize the degree of deformation and mutilation that women will submit to for this pedic ideal of sex attraction. In one of the more popular versions of the Cinderella story, the mother has the elder of Cinderella's two ugly sisters cut off her big toe to fit her foot into the slipper found by the prince, and has the other daughter cut off a slice of her heel to get into the shoe. One such version by Jakob Ludwig Karl Grimm, written in the early nineteenth century, reads as follows:

> "Next morning, the prince went to his father, the king, and said to him: 'No one shall be my wife but she whose foot this golden slipper fits.' Then were the two sisters glad, for they had pretty feet. The eldest went with the shoe into her room and wanted to try it on, and her mother stood by. But she could not get her big toe into it, and the shoe was too small for her. Then her mother gave her a knife and said, 'Cut off the toe. When thou art queen thou will have no more need to go on foot.' The maiden cut the toe off, forcing her foot into the shoe, swallowing the pain, and went out to the king's son. Then he took her on his horse as his bride and rode away with her."

But Grimm's story continues with the discovery of the fraud when the blood showed through her shoe and stocking. The prince returned the girl to her mother, whereupon the mother offers the second daughter after cutting off part of the girl's heel. Again the flow of blood reveals the deception. And here enters Cinderella with the truly small foot that fits the shoe in every detail. In later versions of this Grimm story the portions about the toe and heel mutilations were deleted as being too gory for a child's tale.

But don't be fooled by fairy tales. The truth is that the demure, innocent Cinderella was really a sexpot. What really happened was more likely this. When the prince tried the slipper on Cinderella's foot he exclaimed, "Ah, the perfect fit!"

She replied, "Yes, I know. But do you have it in red, a smaller size, a higher heel, and a pointed toe?"

At heart, Cinderella was no different than most women. If the shoe fits, a woman is sure to find it out of fashion or insist on a smaller size. It's all a paradoxical illusion. A shoe that's too small and tight actually feels better because of the emotional uplift of enhanced sex appeal. It's the pleasure-in-pain principle. Cinderella couldn't have cared less about "the perfect fit." She was more interested in the perfect look.

Time has changed nothing. It isn't uncommon today for women to have their little toe amputated to be able to get the foot into a smaller shoe; or to endure foot deformation and discomfort to squeeze into shoes too small. The sex scars and pleasure wounds found on all parts of women's feet attest to the erotic power of the small-look foot and shoe. It's very common for mothers to bring their little girls into shoe stores and ask anxiously, "Her feet are growing so fast—is she going to have big feet when she grows up?" But, interestingly, they never ask this about the foot size of their boys.

Well, what female foot or shoe size *is small?* Today, in America, it would be about size 5½ or less. Under size 4 is tiny and rare. Prior to the early twentieth century, however, most people in most parts of the world had relatively small feet. For an average American adult male, the average shoe size was 6½ or 7, as compared with 9 or 9½ today. For women it was 4½ or 5, whereas today it's 7½ or 8. It was only in the 1930s that Greta Garbo's "big" size 9 was a constant topic of publicity. Today her foot size wouldn't earn a single line in the press. Elizabeth Taylor and Jackie Onassis both take a 10AAA.

But the glamor queens of decades past really had tiny feet, a feature that was important to their sex-appeal. Shoe size 5B, for example, was worn by the likes of Marlene Dietrich, Joan Crawford, Paulette Goddard, Gina Lollobrigida, the Duchess of Windsor, and Eva Peron. A

4½B was worn by Bette Davis, Jennifer Jones, Carmen Miranda, Agnes DeMille, and Anna May Wong; among the 4B's (the model size) were Jean Harlow, Dolores Del Rio and Ann Todd. Gloria Swanson wore only a 3½B (yet was forever trying to get into a 3B). Mary Pickford wore a legitimate 3B; Mistinguette took a 2½C, and Anita Loos a 2B. Today, these are sizes worn by little girls as young as eight or nine.

However, while the small foot, real or illusory, continues to be the dominant pedic sex symbol, throughout the world there are some people among whom the big foot holds more sex attraction. Just as small feet have had a legendary association with a small or virginlike vagina, large feet, among the believers, have been associated with a large vagina, but in a complimentary sense; that is, voluptuous, carnal, eager.

Shoe sizes got their start in 1324, when England's Edward II decreed that the standard inch equaled three barleycorns laid end to end. Shoemakers found the longest foot of that day measured 39 barleycorns, or 13 inches. This was called size 13, and ever since, shoe sizes have used that grading system, a full size being one-third of an inch. (*Goodyear Tire and Rubber Co.*)

Aigremont comments on the southern Slavs, that "they firmly believe there is a connection between large feet and large, hospitable, female genitals." In some cultures, the large feet of males carry a phallic symbolism, inferring a large penis.

But in America? Yes, the legend of foot size indicating penis size is more common than believed. In the recent movie "Alice Doesn't Live Here Anymore," two women are discussing the real Robert Redford. One character, Bea, says, "I wonder what kind of equipment he has on him?"

"Did you ever see his feet?" asks Alice.

"Feet?"

"I heard one time that's supposed to be an indication."

"Well," says Bea, "I did see a picture once. Wait . . . they're huge!" She spreads her hands apart. "They're like—like *this!*"

The Hangar Club in Camp Springs, Maryland, near Baltimore, features male go-go dancers only. Stripped to bikini or jock strap, their wanton writhings make Elvis Presley's hips arthritic by comparison. Almost all the patrons are women, most of them over 30. Caught in the orgiastic mood of psychedelics, sound and sex, they vie to get to the stage to stuff bills into the jockbands of the dancers.

During the frenetic go-go squirmings a "dancer" will hold up a foot and thrust it sinuously toward the audience, holding his genitals at the same time. Almost everyone gets the message, and a chorus of lecherous "Ahhhs!" rises from the women. The dancer now puts his raised foot in profile and slowly moves the big toe back and forth. Another round of "Ahhhs" and "Ooohs."

One woman turns to her two female friends, both newcomers to the place, and explains, "The size of the foot—it's a sure sign of his jock size. And if he can make that big toe move like that, he can do the same thing with his jock, too."

The male go-go dancers, now rapidly fanning out to other clubs as the new women's lib version of the strip shows that once were exclusive male territory, are increasingly featuring the foot gyrations as part of the act that feeds on the legend that a big foot equates with a big penis, and a large and mobile big toe equates with a large and versatile, mobile member.

The Turks have long viewed large feet of women as a mark of beauty and a desirable asset. In some parts of the world it's believed that the larger the foot the more fertile the woman, and hence the more desirable as a wife and mother. Among the Slavs, their Saint Lucia has always been represented with large feet or shoes. On the evening before the annual Saint's Day, Slavic women will touch the big feet of Lucia. This gesture, they believe, will have any of several effects: enable barren women to have children; make childbearing easier; lead single girls to marriage; or result in a more active and pleasurable sex life in marriage.

In some races or cultures, big feet are simply a natural physical trait. When the Portuguese navigator Magellan first landed on the large island off the southern tip of South America, he and his men were amazed by the large size of the human footprints they saw on the sandy beach. Soon the natives appeared, and their feet confirmed the size of the footprints seen earlier. So Magellan called the island Patagonia, which in his own tongue means "land of the big feet."

Feet are rapidly getting bigger, not only in America but in many parts of the world—simply because people are getting bigger. The average 14-year-old boy today has a foot two sizes larger than his father did at the same age, and three or more sizes larger than his grandfather. The feet of today's girls show corresponding increases in size. The Japanese historically have been a people of small physical stature. But today, due to the introduction of European and American diets over the past couple of decades, an average twelve-year-old boy is 2½ inches taller and 11 pounds heavier than the boy of the same age 15 years ago. And his foot and shoe is almost two sizes larger.

During the Civil War the average soldier was a little under 5 feet 8 inches and weighed 139 pounds. By World War II he stood 5 feet 8½ inches and weighed 155 pounds. In 1975, he averaged 5 feet 9¾ inches and weighed 173 pounds. By 1985, he'll stand 5 feet 10¼ inches tall and weigh 178 pounds. Thus, in less than 125 years he has added two inches in height and nearly forty pounds in weight. His foot has enlarged proportionately—an increase of over two full sizes (nearly an inch) and more than a full width.

But whether the ideal or model foot in any culture is small, medium or large, the human addiction for foot deformation will be no different today or tomorrow than in the long past. The human urge to reshape the foot to the contemporary ideal of sex appeal will never cease as long as the foot itself, especially the female foot, upholds its role as an erotic organ.

TIGHT IS RIGHT

Almost everyone wears tight or snug shoes. What's "tight?" Any shoe that constricts the natural shape and free movement of the foot and toes, and at the same time causes some kind or degree of foot reshaping or deformity. Most shoes, no matter how expensive or carefully fitted, are bought and worn in this "tight" manner. Again, this isn't due to some conspiracy by the designers, makers and sellers of shoes. Most people *want* their shoes to fit this way—and chiefly because of sexual motives, conscious or unconscious.

The wearing of snug or tight shoes has nothing whatever to do with "vanity." Rather, it's linked closely with the touch sense, the sensual tactile pleasure derived from *frottage*, the sensuous rubbing-stroking feeling, which we cited earlier. Gerald and Caroline Greene, in their book, *S-M: The Last Taboo*, write, "The creak of leather, with its inexorable sense of compression of flesh, can produce a delectable *frisson* (a pleasurable sense of sensual excitement) in many."

There is a condition known as "pressure fetishism" wherein the sensation of tight-fitting clothing arouses sexual pleasure. Stekel comments, "The fetish must be something protective, covering or compressive. It is for this reason that shoes are so suitable as (sex) symbols."

However, one doesn't need to be a pressure fetishist to enjoy this. There is a milder form of this—*frottage* or *frisson*—which is found pleasurable by most persons. And, as Stekel pointed out, this is why shoes fulfill this sexual role so well, because most people are pressure-prone in a psychosexual sense, and tight shoes, linked to the erotic foot, ideally satisfy this subconscious want.

There is another motive. The tight fit of the shoe serves as a kind of wrap-around security blanket—a snug, private enclosure that "protects" this erogenous zone, yet at the same time draws attention to it. While the foot is conveying its own sex-appeal messages, it also feels secure within the confines of the tight-fitting shoe.

There's still another sexual undercurrent beneath the wearing of snug-tight shoes. Foot bondage, especially with the use of leather, is the most common of all bondage fetishes. A bondage fetishist, when fettering a woman's ankles or feet with leather straps or cuffs, finds the ultimate sexual pleasure in this sight and act.

But as we saw earlier, foot bondage of women is by no means restricted to fetishists but has been a common practice by "normal" men in many cultures throughout history. It reigned in China with the foot-binding custom, and with European and American women with their linen-wrapped feet. It was seen in the "stepping chains" of the women of ancient Palestine, as well as in other eras, even today.

But today, in our more "civilized" societies, we don't bond or chain feet. We accomplish the same thing with tight shoes. Men continue to satisfy their strange desire to see women foot-fettered, and women continue to wear tight shoes as another erotic lure, and also to satisfy masochistic urges. We're not now speaking of some men and women but most. Add to this the subtle sensation of *frottage* or *frisson* and we find that the *real* motive for the almost universal wearing of tight shoes is esssentially sexual.

The hug-fit shoe, especially when the upper is a light, supple leather or a fabric, adds sensuousness by revealing the contours of the foot and its sinuous movements inside the shoe. R. Turner Wilcox reports that in ancient Rome, "if the shoes covered the toes, the beautiful soft leather was so perfectly fitted that the form of the toes was discernible." Skin-fit shoes were given great impetus in the eleventh and twelfth centuries when buttery-soft, sensuous leathers were developed by the Moors in Spain, where a whole industry rose in Cordova solely to produce these exotic leathers. Then and in later centuries, artisans custom made shoes of these soft leathers where there was a separate slot for each toe, like a glove, to add to the serpentine effect of the toes' movements.

In the seventeenth century, skin-tight boots were popular with men all over Europe. They were fitted so tightly that men often soaked their feet in icy cold water to shrink the feet and legs before putting on their boots. In the nineteenth and twentieth centuries, high laced and buttoned boots of fine kidskin were fitted so tightly so that every contour and movement of ankle and foot was visible. The foot-corseting was so tight that in many cases the ankles and lower legs became atrophied and shrunken to half their normal size. This permanent deformation was considered a podosexual asset because of the trim ankle look that drew male admiration.

Are today's women more "sensible" about tight-fitting boots? Hardly. In 1971, Dr. Paul H. Steel, writing in the *Journal of the American Medical Association*, cited a condition of "boot-leg phlebitis," which was occurring with increasing incidence. The tight fit of the high boots popularly worn by millions of women so compressed blood circulation that blood clots formed in the leg. Doctors warned that thrombophlebitis caused by continued wearing of these leg-tight boots could even prove fatal. But not one woman was known to discard her sexy fashionable boots despite the warnings. Women were ready to die with their boots on.

The sadomasochistic urge to physically deform or distress the self overrides all logic. Men focus on admiration of the shoe, deriving gratification from woman's altered gait and balance. Though our foot-pressing is as old as the Chinese custom, there is no prospect to its end. There is abundant evidence to show that gratifying erotic sensations can be derived from the pressure of tight-fitting apparel.

Throughout history, whenever religious or moral reform forces have strongly imposed their influence, the costumes of men and women alike have become long and loose-fitting to conceal body form. This is seen in the loose, flowing robes of monks, priests, and nuns, or in the straight, somber garments of the Puritans, Shakers, and Amish. By giving the body an uncontoured appearance, this presumably discourages lustful thoughts of the flesh.

It's interesting to note that whenever there is a pronounced decline in the libido, such as with the very old, loose-fitting comfort rather than form-fitting apparel becomes a prime consideration. And so the quip, "You can tell that a woman is getting old when she's more concerned about the fit of her shoes than the fit of her sweater."

Shoes have always been an important part of this syndrome. The same rules of censorship that apply to clothing apply to shoes, which are required to be broad-toed, bluntish, sombre in color, and loose-fitting. In short, sexless. The lower the libido, whether actually as with the elderly, or in profile or appearance as with members of certain religious groups, the looser and more formless the shoes. Tight shoes fall scarcely short of a mortal sin.

In 1970, the deacon of a church in a small English town was relieved of his post for wearing a pair of stylish Winkle Picker shoes, tan in color, tight-fitting, with long pointed toes. Said the pastor, as reported in the British press, "Such shoes have an obscene, lustful look about them. Certainly they are not for the deacon of our church or any church. Who knows what such suggestive fashions could lead to in the minds of our self-respecting parishioners."

When the salesperson in the shoe store says, "It fits like a glove," he means it as a compliment, and the customer accepts it as such. But why should a shoe fit like a glove? Unlike the hand, the foot bears body weight (a cumulative total of nearly one thousand tons a day), and stretches one-half to one inch in length and width with each step. It needs stretch room plus space for toe mobility. Shoes that fit like gloves are faultily fitted—but they look and feel far sexier than shoes that fit like a mitten. And who would ever buy shoes when told that they fit like a mitten?

Women have been tight-corseting their waists for centuries to create the illusion of a curvaceous torso. But the same kind of tight corseting has been going on with the foot, as well. It may be no co-incidence that in the trade the portion of the foot between the ball and instep is known as the "waist" on both the foot and shoe. A laced ox-ford, the saddle portion of a saddle oxford, a wide instep strap—all are designed to pull in the waist and prevent its natural spread.

A sadomasochistic urge is involved in the wearing of tight shoes. The primal need to tactilely feel "things" securely against or around us apparently is not only a psychosexual need but a pleasurable expe-rience. The literature is rich with such examples. For instance, Have-lock Ellis recites the case of a woman who found the idea of fettered feet "erotically arousing." The woman "wore only boots because these seemed to most imprison the foot and ankle. The subject also felt sex-ual stimulation in seeing other persons tightly shod or booted. She re-lated, 'The mere idea of fetters produces the greatest excitement, and the sight of pictures representing such things is a temptation.' "

Ellis cites another case involving a young man who experienced erotic pleasure observing women shod in tight-fitting and obviously uncomfortable shoes or boots. "He was attracted to well-dressed women, especially to those wearing elegant shoes, delighting to imagine them fettered." The man later met one such woman about ten years older than himself, and gradually began taking personal liberties with her. He begged her to permit him to fasten her feet together. "As he did so her shoes slightly touched his sexual organs; this caused erection and ejaculation, accompanied by the most acute sexual pleasure he had ever felt."

The above two cases may seem extreme. Nevertheless, they repre-sent the subconscious feelings of many millions of men and women in a more modified form. In short, men and women alike derive a con-scious or unconscious pleasure from the fettered foot—either experiencing it or observing it. It is one of the important sexual motives for the almost universal wearing of tight shoes.

The world of transvestites is filled with constrictive clothing and footwear that often must feel distressingly binding if the wearer is to derive sexual gratification from it. Psychotherapist Hammond relates the case of a transvestite telling him, ' I bought myself a pair of very elegant women's shoes with French heels, which at first were so tight on me that I limped." Hammond reports the man's story further: "He would wear those shoes publicly while promenading in fine weather and lift up his trousers so the heels would show to better advantage. When the weather was adverse, he would put them on at home once a week and fasten them tightly. This would bring on an erection and sometimes even an ejaculation."

Roubard reports on another transvestite who insisted that his high-heeled shoes be at least two sizes too small. "Nevertheless, with extremely tight and uncomfortable shoes he could walk for miles or dance for hours with the greatest pleasure. It actually appeared as if physical pain was an integral part of his bliss." This, of course, is the algolagnia or pleasure-in-pain principle at work—the sadomasochistic experience in more modified form in the wearing of snug or tight-fitting shoes by most persons.

NOT SO BARBAROUS

So we find that the "barbarous" old custom of Chinese footbinding isn't so alien or strange after all. Europeans and Americans have long been applying their own forms of foot constrictions with deforming results, inspired by the same motive of sex attraction.

One of the first objectives of people of poor or backward nations striving for more advanced status is the wearing of shoes—and, of course, tight-fitting shoes. This is one of the initial signs of progress. These people "progress" with physical agony because of the abrupt change from no shoes to tight-fitting shoes. But they pleasurably endure it. Why? Status is one reason. But equally important is the psychological uplift in knowing that their "modern," fashionable, and tight-fitting shoes enhance their personal sex attractiveness.

Among shoe-wearing people the "pleasure wounds" or "sex scars" of the feet are as prevalent as the common cold. Repeated surveys show that eight out of every ten shoe-wearing adults are foot-defective to some degree. Nearly forty different foot lesions can be traced to the wearing of constrictive footwear—lesions absent among people who don't wear shoes. The medical cost for the treatment of these lesions runs to more than $200 million a year, to say nothing of the additional hundreds of millions for commercial foot aids and special footwear to provide relief.

But again, to lay blame on the footwear industry for these foot deformities is the equivalent of blaming your dinner host for your indigestion from overeating. Yet the overzealous reformists would cure it all by forced decree, as they've attempted to do throughout history. Here, for example, is Ralph Nader, addressing a 1974 convention of podiatrists: "Both [shoe] manufacturers and designers have displayed a callous attitude toward people." He called for "a direct confrontation with the shoe manufacturers and designers" to correct what he termed "ill-fitting and comfortless footwear."

This is abysmal naïveté. It is the nature of the well-intentioned zealot to demand that the world and human nature be reshaped to his design. Nader himself is a habitual eunuch-type shoe wearer. He has been known to wear old army boots when appearing before Congressional hearings, or when attending a posh social event. These simply reflect his ascetic lifestyle. Like most wearers of eunuch-type shoes, he cannot understand the psychosexual motives of fashion nor the sexual inferences of body decoration and reshaping ingrained in humans for thousands of years. His one note of truth occurred when he innocently stated, "Americans demand fashion and styles at the expense of health and safety." This applies to the entire shoe-wearing world.

Our reshaping and shrinking of the foot isn't caused by vanity, ignorance, neglect, stupidity, nor deliberate malice of the designers and makers of shoes. It's caused by the innate eroticism of the foot itself. The shoe, as the foot's covering, has always served like a sorcerer's magic wand in the ceaseless effort to convey erotic pedic illusions.

There is no need to weep for our misshapen feet. In modern civilized societies the foot no longer has need to perform the tasks required of the foot of primitive people. Instead, we now put the foot to decorative use; we cosmeticize and sexualize it. Having relieved the foot from its former hard labor, its purpose now is to look and act sensuous and fulfill its natural erotic role. Its wish is to be pampered like some voluptuous mistress whose chief desire is to please the eye of her lover.

16

The Foot Lovers

There are some men who spend a lifetime in an impassioned love affair with the female foot. Not a mere admiration or infatuation but a full-fledged sexual passion. These are the foot fetishists. Pedic sex arouses them to an emotional heat equal to the highest intensity of sexual intercourse.

Of the approximately fifty different known forms of sexual fetishisms, foot and shoe fetishes are by far the oldest and most prevalent. The more dedicated practitioners probably number in the hundreds of thousands, and those who practice it in milder forms amount to even more. "All men," declares Leathem, "unless they are completely asexual, are fetishists to a certain degree. It's part of the masculine psychosexual makeup."

For the fetishist, the main attraction is to a particular body part, or to an object of wearing apparel, and not primarily to the sexual partner. Flugel describes a fetish as "where the sexual desire chooses as its exclusive and sufficient object some part of the body (e.g., feet) or some article of clothing (e.g., shoes)." Some psychologists regard fetishism as a form of psychic masturbation—which may well open the door for universal membership.

Fetishism is seen as a form of paraphilia—an erotic excursion outside the "normal" center of sexual interests and activities. Says Karl A. Menninger, "In the unconscious, various parts of the body may represent the genitals. This is best seen in fetishism. . . . Such individuals become sexually excited and ultimately gratified by the contemplation and caressing of a foot, a toe, a shoe."

For the foot fetishist, there is an obsessive desire to kiss, lick and fondle the feet and toes of his partner, and to have his penis manipulated by her feet. Like the Chinese lotus foot-lover, the fetishist regards the foot as the most desirable and exciting erogenous zone of the female body. He is a foot-lover in the most complete sense. One foot fetishist perhaps spoke for most of his clan when he told me:

"You can cut off all the women of the world at the ankles. Give me the part from the ankles down and you can have all the rest."

The term "fetish" found its way into the medical and sex literature in 1888, coined by the distinguished French psychologist, Alfred Binet. The word is derived from the Portuguese *fetico,* meaning charmed or obsessive fascination. Binet himself, as well as many prominent psychiatrists and sexologists, believed that *everyone* is to some degree and in some way a fetishist.

Karl Menninger writes, "The unconscious symbolic substitution of one organ for another is by no means limited to fetishists. It is only more obvious to them. But we all do it."

What causes this pedic passion? Why, for so many men, does a woman's foot have such sexual power? Freud, Adler, Jung, Stekel and many others have suggested causes or reasons. Most agree that because the foot itself is an erotic organ, some men are aroused to extremes of sexual stimulation by this organ, and thus move into the special realm of foot fetishism.

But there's an equally important question. Why do so many women, once introduced to the experience, derive such sensual pleasure from a fetishist's or partialist's lovemaking to the foot? It's possible that the "sexual nerves" of the erotic foot remain dormant in many women but are sensually responsive when properly aroused. As one fetishist said:

"Most of the women I've been sexually involved with had never, on our first experience, had a lover bring their feet into the sex act. But once they experience the thrill, especially when it's with a skilled foot-lover, they eagerly look forward to it every time thereafter."

"I'M PARTIAL TO . . ."

Partialism is a form of fetishism, though not quite the same thing. In partialism, the individual is attracted to a particular part of a woman's body—a selective fixation focused on some feature such as the bosom, legs, thighs, hair, buttocks, feet, ankles, toes, neck, hands, arms, even body odors. By contrast, fetishism is partialism carried to extreme, where it becomes a sexual obsession.

Most men are partialists. They have their own personal preferences for women who are tall or short, thin or plump, blonde, redhead or brunette, high- or low-slung buttocks, flat- or full-bosomed, etc. A man will say, "I'm partial to blondes with small feet." Another says, "I like women with large bosoms and small waists." Still another says, "I'm a leg man." Each is a partialist. If the partialism becomes an erotic fixation, they can become fetishists.

The large majority of fetishists are males, and only a small minority females. However, both males and females are partialists—in fact, everyone is—because each individual tends to be attracted by a particular part or parts of another person, or to particular types of persons, in a sexual or psychosexual sense. But whereas there is often only a thin line between partialism and fetishism, it would seem that males and females have the same underlying fetishistic tendencies, except that it is much more frequently materialized in males.

Psychologists and others believe it's almost *necessary* that men be partialists. "Woman as a whole is a desirable object," says clothing historian James Laver, "but man cannot take all of her in at once. He is therefore compelled to concentrate on one particular bit of the female body."

Leathem adds to this: "It is not the beauty queen who has a little of everything, but nothing outstanding, that grips a man's attention. Rather, it is the *specific* part of the female body that becomes a symbol of sexuality to him and thus evolves into a fetish. . . . The woman who possesses each and every item in the size, shape and structure that will greatly appeal to *all* partialists is a very rare woman."

There's nothing abnormal about partialism. It's deeply ingrained in both the male and female makeup. "The field of partialisms is practically inexhaustible," says Stekel. "Everybody has his own sexual predilections and points of preference, the basis of which is part constitutional and part conditional. But the more deeply I delve into my material, the more surprised I am at the inconceivable wealth of 'erogenous' zones which we possess and the number of individual love conditions."

But it's the foot, almost more than any other erogenous zone of the female anatomy, that is the prime target for male partialism. Leathem comments, "A great many psychosexual stimuli reside in any sexual partialism directed at the female feet." Stekel declares, "The most widespread form of partialism is the preference for the feet." Eminent psychologist Dr. Stanley Hall states, "The hand does not possess the mystery which envelops the foot; and hand-fetishism is very much less frequent than foot-fetishism." Krafft-Ebing, who made deep-probing investigations into fetishes, asserts, "One of the most frequent forms of fetishism is that where the female foot or shoe is the fetish, and becomes the exclusive object of feeling and desire."

Foot partialism has age-old roots. It has been related to the ancient earth-contact association of the female foot with fertility and the genital forces of reproduction. There is the persistent phallic symbolism of the foot and big toe, and the phallic-yoni parallel with foot and shoe; and the erotic association of the foot with the sexual dynamics of the female body in gait. There is also the foot's vital role in the development of many of the erogenous zones of the body, along with frontal coitus.

Havelock Ellis comments, "The sexual symbolization of the female foot and its denudation, which we find so characteristic of bygone eras of civilization, and also the fascinating effect which such learning has—these realizations are of importance to us in explaining the many cases of foot fetishism in our times."

The foot fetishist doesn't merely admire or desire to caress the foot of his female partner. He becomes immersed in a passionate love-making with the foot. Whereas the average man seeks "his kind" of woman, the fetishist seeks "his kind" of foot, and the woman herself is usually of secondary importance. He sees the foot as another man sees a woman, with distinct and separate erogenous zones: the size of the foot, the curve of the arch and instep, the toes, the texture of the skin, the contours of the heel, the ankle, the odors, etc. Each is a separate part to caress, bite, lick, kiss and fondle.

He experiences intense sexual excitement and erection from this pedic lovemaking. He achieves ejaculation from it, and from having her foot rub against his body and genitals. He can use this pedic lovemaking as foreplay before coitus, or can exclude coitus and get his sexual satisfaction from his impassioned caressing of the foot. One thing is certain: without the involvement of the foot there can be no coitus, nor even any sexual interest in the woman herself.

PEDIC SEX

Our word "ecstasy" comes from the Greek *existanai*, meaning to drive out of one's senses. This is the intensity of the erotic pitch experienced by the foot fetishist. If this is difficult to comprehend, keep in mind those hundreds of millions of Chinese who were immersed in this kind of ecstasy with the lotus foot for nearly one thousand years.

On occasion a foot fetishist will carry out his own kind of "sexual assault." In October, 1975, the news media across the country ran a UPI story about a man who attacked a thirty-year-old woman in San Antonio, Texas. The police apprehended twenty-four-year-old Faustino Collazo, who had shoved the screaming woman against a car, pulled off her shoes, passionately covered her feet and toes with kisses, and then had run off. This was only one of several such assaults on local women. However, in no instance did he touch the bodies or clothes of these women. Only their feet were the objects of his sexual attentions.

The judge committed the man to psychiatric examination. And one of the arresting police officers later said, "I could've understood if the guy was attempting rape. But just kissing their feet—the guy's gotta be cracked." Thus the irony is that while rape can be regarded as not unusual and perhaps even "normal," its more innocent and harmless form of "pedic rape" is condemned as "abnormal" and dangerous.

Foot fetishism or intense foot partialism is common enough to have earned itself a medical term, *equus eroticus*. The foot fetishist acquires a variety of "sexual positions" with the foot in the same way as other persons acquire skilled techniques or preferred positions of coitus or pre-coital play. Krafft-Ebing speaks of persons of this kind, whom coitus does not satisfy, or who are unable to perform it, find a substitute for it in placing the penis between the feet of women.

Many experienced prostitutes have certain men among their clientele who come to them solely for this "podocoitus." Stekel, who extensively probed the activities of foot fetishists, cites the experience of one foot fetishist, a 26-year-old engineer: "He tries normal intercourse frequently, but despite his utmost efforts has not been able to get an orgasm or ejaculation. Only when the woman touches his phallus with the tip of her foot does he experience complete gratification; it is to this end that he always lays himself in bed with a woman in the opposite position; i. e., with his head toward the foot of the bed."

The foot fetishist often achieves feverish arousal and ejaculation while sucking the big toe of his female partner. Medical observers equate this with fellatio, except that the fetishist does this without any feeling of "homosexual guilt" because the oral action is non-genital. Stekel comments, "His latent desire is to take a sweaty foot or great toe into his mouth . . . from here the path of association leads to the paraphilia of fellatio." As we saw earlier, however, this toe-sucking practice is frequently used by so-called "normal" men and women as one of many variables of sexual foreplay.

Famous trial lawyer Louis Nizer, in his best-selling book, *My Life in Court,* devotes a whole chapter to a divorce trial in which the husband was a foot fetishist—a condition which finally led to divorce initiated by the wife. Minute details of the man's foot fetishism were brought out in the closed-door trial. The sole object of the husband's affection and lovemaking was his wife's feet. The tiniest sign of a callus or speck of soil on her foot would drive him to a frenzy. She couldn't step barefoot on a rug at home. At his demand she had to keep the skin of her feet silky-soft with lotions and creams. In court the man admitted to being "insanely jealous" of his wife's feet—but not necessarily of his wife as a person or woman.

Perhaps the greatest envy of every foot fetishist is the podiatrist who has the privilege of intimately viewing and touching women's feet day in and out. Over the years I've known several foot and shoe fetishists. One, in expressing envy of the podiatrists, told me, "Those foot doctors—what an ecstatic existence! It must be like having a sexual orgy every hour of every working day of your life!"

One foot fetishist I know actually became a successful practicing podiatrist. He of course concealed his fetish behind his professional guise. But he once confessed to me that he had to wear special undershorts—firmly elastic to hold down and conceal his frequent erections, and also moisture-absorbent to protect his trousers from the frequent spontaneous wettings.

I recall visiting him at his office one day. In the crowded reception room, one waiting woman could be overheard telling another, a first-time visitor, "The doctor is marvelous. I've been to other podiatrists, but none has ever been so gentle with my feet. He handles them with such loving care, like a baby."

Some of history's celebrated names were among the foot and shoe fetishists. Charles Baudelaire, the nineteenth-century French Romantic poet, was enamoured with the image and act of kissing women's naked feet. In one of his poems he dwells intensely on the nude foot almost to a degree of open sexual indulgence. Thomas Hardy, the English novelist, showed deep and consistent interest in the feet and shoes of his heroines. Casanova, prominent in the lovers' hall of fame, was no foot fetishist, but very much a foot partialist. He more than once remarked that he always "looked first into a woman's eyes, then at her feet, for beauty rests in both."

The celebrated Persian poet and lover, Hafiz, who lived in the fourteenth century, had an obsession about kissing women's shoes, and about mutual foot-play in bed with his women. But sometimes his lady friends got frustrated when he failed to follow through with coital action. He expresses one such experience:

> From Shiraz I'll flee and I'll dwell in some
>   other city instead.
> She laughed, "Go, Hafiz, thy feet, who is it
>   that holds them," she said.

Ovid, the Roman poet, frequently dwelled on the charms of the feminine foot. Anthropologist Paul Jacoby cites numerous references from Ovid's works bearing on foot eroticism. "In reading him," says Jacoby, "one is inclined to say the psychology of the Romans was closely allied with that of the Chinese."

Among the most famous of the foot and shoe fetishists was Goethe, the poet, dramatist and novelist. While he wasn't one to substitute his fetish for copulation, his foot-shoe fetish was intimately linked to his images and acts of lovemaking. "A pretty foot," he said, "is one of the greatest gifts of nature." At the age of sixty-four he was still engrossed in his fetish. He wrote to Christian Vulpius, a lady friend, "Please send me your last pair of shoes, already worn out in dancing, which you told me about in your letter, as soon as possible, so I can again have something of yours to press against my heart." Goethe had a private collection of women's elegant shoes, and it was unlikely that it was only his heart he pressed them against. In Switzerland's Bally Shoe Museum is a pair of striped, red-and-gold slippers given as a gift to Goethe by another paramour, Marianne von Willemer. She, like other female intimates of his, knew well of his foot and shoe fetish.

D.W. Griffith, the film-making giant of Hollywood's earlier days, had a sensual intoxication about women's feet. He maintained a special collection of shoes owned by some of filmdoms most glamorous women. Salvatore Ferragamo, shoemaker to many of the world's best-known and most beautiful women, relates in his book, *Shoemaker of Dreams*, that Griffith "was fond of pretty feet, and pretty legs and ankles; he suggested that I run a beauty contest for the best feet, legs, and ankles." The competition was run and won by a girl whose name is now forgotten. Second choice was also an unknown, but not for long thereafter. Her name was Joan Crawford.

Author George du Maurier was also among the noted foot fetishists. In his famous nineteenth-century novel, *Trilby*, he repeatedly focuses on the feet of his heroine, an artist's model. Numerous passages contain ardent references to the female foot. Some examples:

> "Her bare white ankles and insteps, and slim, straight rosy heels, clean-cut and smooth as the back of a razor."
>
> Trilby is telling her swain, Little Billee, that she poses for a sculptor "in the altogether." She explains further, "Yes—*l'ensemble*, you know—head, hands and feet, everything—especially feet. That's my foot," she said, kicking off her big slipper and stretching out the limb. "It's the handsomest foot in all Paris." Du Maurier continues, "And in truth they were astonishingly beautiful feet, such as one only sees in pictures and statues—a true inspiration of shape and color, all made up of delicate lengths and subtly modulated curves and noble straightness and happy little dimpled arrangements in innocent pink and white."
>
> Little Billee, himself an artist, is "quite bewildered to find that a real, bare, live human foot could be such a charming object to look at."
>
> Trilby appears before Little Billee in a pair of soft slippers, "originally shapeless, but which her feet, uncompromising and inexorable as boot-trees, had ennobled into everlasting classic shapeliness, and stamped with an unforgettable individuality . . . a fact that Little Billee was not slow to perceive with a curious conscious thrill that was only half esthetic."
>
> Du Maurier comments, "The sudden sight of (the foot), uncovered, comes as a very rare, singularly pleasing surprise to the eye that has learned how to see!"

These descriptions and comments are typical of the foot fetishist. He is pouring out his impassioned feelings about the foot as though it were the beloved woman herself. He is eulogizing it, courting it, urging the reader to see and appreciate the foot not as mere esthetic architecture but as a sexual object—the most sexual part of the whole anatomy.

We'll now see this same approach by another author. While other foot fetishists were more famous, none did more to bring the delights of foot fetishism out into the open than Rétif de la Bretonne, one of the most remarkable literary figures of eighteenth-century France. He was perhaps the first full-fledged foot fetishist to "come out of the closet" and publicly declare and defend his sexual passion for women's feet and shoes. So zealous was he to make converts that foot and shoe fetishism even took his name and was popularly known as Rétifism.

His first literary success, *Le Pied de Fanchette*, or Fanchette's Foot, was inspired by a girl with charming feet. His own enamored zeal about women's feet was deeply interwoven into this novel. At one point he invokes all unattractive females, "Console yourselves, you women worried by your ugliness. There is one way to please, one that will never fail to revive the desire of your husband, to inflame anew the passion of your lover. It is the elegance, the shining cleanliness, of new shoes. The man who is not carved out of dead wood will understand what I mean. . . . Women should only wear clothes that give pleasure and ravish, however uncomfortable they may be. High heels and a high hair style—that is the true charm of a woman."

In his much admired autobiography, *Monsieur Nicolas*, Bretonne gives an explanation of his foot and shoe fetish: "Do physical and psychological factors cause my predilection for beautiful feet? It is so strong that it unfailingly incites my most violent desires and makes me ignore any other ugliness. This desire is very strong in all who are endowed with it. Is it connected with a liking for the buoyancy of a graceful and voluptuous step? The strange attraction which footwear has is, after all, nothing but a reflection of delight in beautiful feet, which make even an animal graceful. In this case, one values the covering almost as highly as the foot itself."

BUT IS IT NORMAL?

Foot partialism, of course, is common among men. But what of its more intense form, foot fetishism? Is it natural and "normal"? Modern investigators, in their extensive interviews with large samples of the population, have found an almost unlimited variety of sexual preferences and practices, including the fetishes. Stekel, certainly in the forefront among the authorities, states, "Normal fetishism aids the man in the conquest of the woman." Note his use of the word "normal" associated with fetishism.

Adler, Sadger, Freud and other eminent psychosexualists also refer to the "normal fetishisms" existing with many persons. Says Leathem, "There existed, for many years, a rather narrow and confining definition of a fetish—'the deriving of sexual arousal from a non-sexual object.' When sex authorities began to point out that all a man sees of a woman, and thus derives eroticism from, are non-sexual, non-genital parts, the attitude toward fetishism was modified somewhat. In actuality, any object, sexual or non-sexual, genital or non-genital, that stimulates erotic activity, both by the view or caressing it, may be said to be functioning as a sexual fetish."

Dr. Lars Ullerstam, in his book, *The Erotic Minorities*, declares, "Fetishism is a comparatively tame expression of sexuality. . . . It provides the individual with a chance to satisfy his sexual urge through looking at or manipulating objects of various kinds."

Thus, instead of the foot partialists or fetishists being regarded as strange or "queer," their special erotic leanings are simply responses to a broader range of sexual stimulants. Alfred Adler contended that "whoever sucked his big toe as a baby will later become a foot fetishist." If Adler is correct, then the world is densely populated with foot fetishists, practicing or potential.

How common is foot fetishism? While there are no statistics, there are the views of qualified observers. Krafft-Ebing declared that foot and shoe fetishists are "a very numerous class." Kinsey finds that these fetishists "are not rare in the population." Havelock Ellis says, "Of all the forms of erotic symbolism, the most frequent is that which idealizes the foot and shoe." Elsewhere he comments, "Eccentric as foot fetishism may appear to us, it is simply the reemergence . . . of a mental and emotional impulse which was probably experienced by our forefathers."

At one time there was a German spa, Wörishhofen, where foot fetishists from all over the country and beyond gathered, much as others might assemble at a nudist colony or health resort. Similar places can be found today in Europe and the United States, though restricted to private membership.

In America today there is a national organization known as the Lotus Love Foot Erotica Club, the membership comprised solely of foot fetishists. Each dues-paying member receives the club emblem, a miniature foot worn on a chain or string around the neck and concealed beneath the shirt. The club, says its literature, "is devoted exclusively to those individuals who enjoy and appreciate the sexually

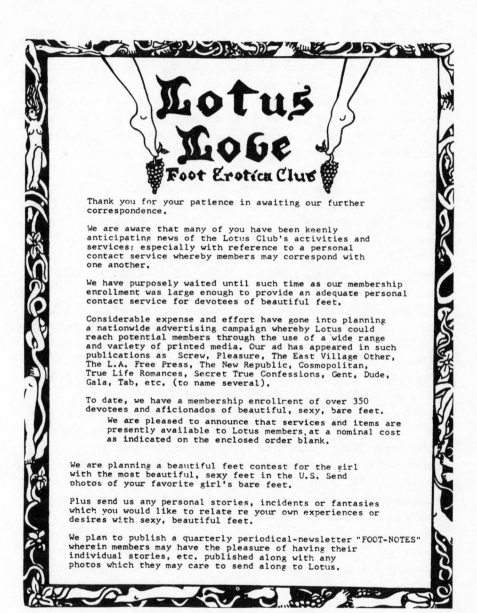

Lotus Love

Foot Erotica Club

Thank you for your patience in awaiting our further correspondence.

We are aware that many of you have been keenly anticipating news of the Lotus Club's activities and services; especially with reference to a personal contact service whereby members may correspond with one another.

We have purposely waited until such time as our membership enrollment was large enough to provide an adequate personal contact service for devotees of beautiful feet.

Considerable expense and effort have gone into planning a nationwide advertising campaign whereby Lotus could reach potential members through the use of a wide range and variety of printed media. Our ad has appeared in such publications as Screw, Pleasure, The East Village Other, The L.A. Free Press, The New Republic, Cosmopolitan, True Life Romances, Secret True Confessions, Gent, Dude, Gala, Tab, etc. (to name several).

To date, we have a membership enrollment of over 350 devotees and aficionados of beautiful, sexy, bare feet.

    We are pleased to announce that services and items are presently available to Lotus members, at a nominal cost as indicated on the enclosed order blank.

We are planning a beautiful feet contest for the girl with the most beautiful, sexy feet in the U.S. Send photos of your favorite girl's bare feet.

Plus send us any personal stories, incidents or fantasies which you would like to relate re your own experiences or desires with sexy, beautiful feet.

We plan to publish a quarterly periodical-newsletter "FOOT-NOTES" wherein members may have the pleasure of having their individual stories, etc. published along with any photos which they may care to send along to Lotus.

A literature sample from the Lotus Love Foot Erotica Club.

stimulating aspect of beautiful feet." The literature further states that "foot lovers tend to be highly sensitive, sensuous, and erotic voluptuaries. They are attuned to bringing themselves and their sexual partners to a keen state of physical and emotional awareness and excitement. A sexual experience that involves oral and genital contact with the feet can result in a most rewarding and delightful orgasm for both partners."

The club provides its members with "a personal introduction service for devotees of beautiful feet." It also provides for exchanges of podoerotic literature and experiences among members; a variety of foot-beautifying or foot-stimulating products and many other items "related to sexy feet." A photo and film exchange or rental service is also available.

In Los Angeles there is a dial-an-obscene-talk phone service (similar ones have started in other cities) called Joy's Jacking-Off Phone Club. Run by "Juicy Joy," whose real name is Dee Boocher, a twenty-seven-year-old, six-foot two-inch tall blonde, the club has hundreds of "clients." They pay a monthly fee of $30, which allows them two fifteen-minute phone calls a week to the club. A crew of three girls, plus Joy, takes the calls.

The unusual twist is that the *girls* initiate and carry through the obscene conversation, fulfilling any sexual fantasy the caller wishes—discussing any form or position of copulation, fellatio or cunnilingus, masturbation, group sex, or lesbian or homo sex—the caller's choice. The callers, presumably, are in a state of constant erection or are masturbating during the everything-goes conversation.

The club has become so popular that a similar service is now provided for fetishists, including foot fetishists, under the supervision of Adrena, the Slave Queen. This specialized service also sells its clients cassette tapes and provides personal letters and fetish-scene photos. For the foot-fetishist caller, the girl on the phone fantasizes about her own beautiful, soft-skin feet—about her own intense sexual arousal and orgasms as her feet are being licked, caressed, toe-sucked, and kissed by the fetishist. These vivid descriptions in passionate voices, intermixed with a steady flow of four-letter words, blow the mind of the foot fetishist listening as he masturbates, his body tremulous and sweating.

A few years ago I attended a private showing of a thirty-minute movie film of a "foot lovers' orgy." The owner of the film was himself a foot fetishist. There were five men and five women in the film—the men, the fetishists, and the women were obviously experienced in such relationships. The feet of the women were genuinely beautiful, clearly the result of meticulous cosmetic care. The men, each with his own partner, caressed, licked, nibbled, and kissed the feet with intense passion. The women played no passive roles, but used their feet to manipulate the penises of the men—and themselves reached high pitches of sexual excitement during these activities. In some instances the men masturbated while caressing the foot, while in other cases there was follow-through to copulation. In one scene the fetishist ejaculated while all five of the girl's toes were in his mouth—and she had a simultaneous orgasm.

Evidence of a fairly large existing population of foot fetishists is further indicated by the magazines and booklets targeted to them. We thus have such foot-shoe fetish magazines as *High Heels*, containing illustrated articles with such typical titles as "Spiked Love," "Boot-Lickin' Good," "Heel-O'-Mania," "Spine-Tingling Spiker," "Kick 'Em While They're Down," "Heel Chicks," "Leather Legs," "Pedestal of Power," "Leather Woman," and "They Suck Shoes, Don't They?" Among other magazine and booklet titles are *Puss 'N' Boots*, *The Fetishists*, and *Fetish Fantasy*, available either by subscription or in adult book stores.

Before World War II, an illustrated British magazine, *London Life*, flourished. It specialized in fetishes, with much space devoted to foot and shoe fetishism. Its popularity inspired an American replica called *Bizarre*, which also enjoyed popular success. In 1972, the publisher of one such magazine told me, "When we started our magazine on sex fetishes, we expected to cover the whole range. But our mail and other feedback quickly told us that the foot and shoe fetishists outnumbered any other fetish group by at least three to one. Today, about 30 percent of our editorial space is directed to foot and shoe fetishists."

After centuries of hiding, the foot fetishists have now begun to come out of the closet. Today, with the greatly liberalized attitudes toward sex, plus the flood tide of sex education literature, they no longer suffer the former guilt complexes that their particular sexual partialism is abnormal or an "aberration." Unconventional, yes. But, as one foot fetishist said to me recently, "What's conventional sex? The Supreme Court would find it as impossible to define as it did pornography."

17

The Shoe Lovers

"Clothes not only serve to arouse sexual interest," says Flugel, "but may themselves symbolize the sexual organs."

That holds precisely true for the shoe fetishist. To him, the shoe equates with the woman and the female genital organs. When he passionately "makes love" to a woman's shoe, in his own mind and feelings he's virtually having sexual intercourse. It arouses an intense erection and finally ejaculation, all accompanied by rapturous sexual images.

But, you say, these are isolated, freakish cases. Not so at all. While there are no reliable statistics, the number of shoe fetishists is estimated to be surprisingly high—likely in the tens of thousands.

For sexual satisfaction, many shoe fetishists need only the shoe of a woman, and not necessarily the woman herself. An example is cited by Krafft-Ebing: "A woman's body and naked or stockinged foot made no impression on him; but the foot, when covered with the shoe, or the shoe alone, induced erection and even ejaculation. Sight alone was sufficient for him in the case of elegant shoes. . . . His sexual desire was powerfully excited by touching, kissing or drawing on such shoes. . . . His nightly dreams were of shoes of beautiful women."

Most shoe fetishists tend to be "bisexual" in their own unique way. They can often be sexually satisfied with lovemaking only to the woman's shoe, without the presence of the woman. Or coitus is enjoyed only when the women's shoes are involved in any of several ways. The eminent Italian physician and anthropologist, Cesare Lombroso, describes a somewhat typical shoe fetishist:

"Nothing in the opposite sex excites his sensual feelings except elegant shoes on the feet of elegant women. The shoes without the wearer is sufficient. It gives him the greatest pleasure to see, touch and kiss them. The feminine foot, when bare or covered with a stocking, has no effect on him. Yet, he is potent; during the sexual act the female must be elegantly dressed and, above all, have on pretty shoes."

The shoe fetishist isn't aroused by just *any* shoe worn by just *any* woman. He's extremely selective. The shoe itself must have elegance, quality, esthetic appeal. And it must belong to, or be imagined as belonging to, a beautiful or elegant woman. After all, to the fetishist the shoe *is* the woman. Further, copulation without involvement of the shoe is unthinkable and usually impossible. Stekel cites a typical case, here letting the fetishist speak for himself:

"Well-shaped women's legs and feet are the objects of my fantasies. I'm not attracted by naked feet, but rather by feet covered with fine shoes carrying half-high or straight heels. . . . In my mind, however, the girl must keep her shoes and stockings on [during intercourse], since this promotes my satisfaction. I then picture myself being embraced with her legs as we press body to body and breast to breast."

The fetishist's skill and techniques in his direct "lovemaking" to the shoe are as expert as a Casanova's sexual sports in bed. He works up to a wanton frenzy of sexual feeling by kissing, licking, biting, sucking, and caressing the shoe or boot. He devotes his attention in turn to each "erogenous" part of the shoe—the heel, toe, arch, sole, straps, lining, ornaments, leather, etc. Each part has its own particular significance for him, symbolizing a different part of the female anatomy. He deeply inhales the odor of her shoe, the equivalent of body odors which to him are sexually intoxicating.

The fetishist takes his "sexual relations" with his favorite shoes very seriously. One fetishist was extremely partial to women's patent leather shoes. He owned many pairs, but one pair in particular was his favorite. One day he noticed a crack in the leather. He confessed his agony: "It was as though I had seen the first wrinkle in the face of a beloved woman. I have not put them on since."

Psychiatrists tell of fetishists who blush when women's shoes or boots are talked about in company. The scientist Mantegazza reported in his *Anthropological Studies* about a fetishist "who considered the exposure of ladies' shoes in store windows as immoral." This, of course, is understandable. To the fetishist, the display of shoes in store windows would be the same as a woman posing naked in the same window.

To avoid ridicule or suspicion, the shoe fetishist keeps his secret passion concealed in the closet. He seeks only those women who will cooperate with his specialized sex indulgence. This sometimes requires that he go to prostitutes, where his identity remains anonymous and he's treated with sympathetic understanding and cooperation. Havelock Ellis writes that "every prostitute of any experience knows men who merely desire to gaze at her shoes, or possibly lick them, and who are quite willing to pay for this privilege." Prostitutes in all countries have special names for this clientele. In America and England, for example, they're known as "bootmen," and in Germany as "Steifelfrier." A national ad for Dingo Boots shows Joe Namath wearing a pair of these boots. The headline reads: "The Bootman. He's no ordinary Joe." The first line of the copy reads: "Boots are his thing." Prostitutes, seeing this ad, must have raised their brows a bit or chuckled. In fact, one of them was overheard to say in a Chicago bar, "Between his pantyhose and his being labeled a bootman, Joe has a lot to explain."

There are even "specialists" among the shoe fetishists. Some prefer shoes, others boots. Some want their shoes with certain materials, such as shiny patent leather or soft kidskin; others lean toward certain styles, colors, or heels. But regardless of the preferences, the shoes must always have beauty and elegance of design. After all, the shoe symbolizes the woman, and hence must be exquisite and also have a voluptuous sensuality to it.

Leathem gives an example of this: "It is amazing the consistency of the male fetishists who admit harboring special feelings for very high boots. Nearly all of them have told of incidents in which they have copulated with a woman while she was wearing her boots, and the resulting pleasure evidently transcended any height of erotic response that they had previously attained. Nearly all of them related the extreme pleasure of lying atop a female, with the penis locked securely into her vagina, and feeling the tough leather boots pressing against thighs, knees, and feet as they went through the traditional coital movements."

Then there are the fetishists who are mad about shoes or slippers that have some kind of furry or softly napped material—suede, velvet, pompons, shearling slippers, shoes or boots with furred collars or cuffs, or expensive shoes with "natural hair" material like unborn calfskin. These trimmings graphically symbolize the pubic area, with the opening of the shoe symbolizing the vaginal entry. In fact, among the initiated, "fetish" is an acronym for Friends and Enthusiasts of Tiny Insignificant Shoes and Hair.

One shoe fetishist told me of a friend of his who delighted in the erotic fantasy that he was living a "polygamous marriage." He owned about ten pairs of luxurious fur-lined or fur-trimmed women's shoes and boots. To him, each pair was one of his "wives," and each had her own name and personality. When it came time for lovemaking, he would select the "wife" that suited his particular mood. And at that moment he always kept the other shoes concealed in the closet.

He said, "How insensitive it would be of me to make love to one while the others watched. Can you imagine the furious jealousy that would stir up?"

Shoe fetishists are found in every segment of the population. There are even homosexual shoe fetishists—males who are sexually aroused by men's rather than women's shoes. Paul Garnier, the French psychoanalyst, cites one such case:

"At twenty-two he felt the first breath of a nebulous desire for passive pederasty and made bashful but fruitful attempts to placate these wishes. He then began to enjoy admiring elegant and handsome young fellows when they happened to be wearing patent leather shoes. He would picture these patent leather shoes to himself when he masturbated at home. . . . He went so far as to insert stereotyped advertisements in the public print which read about as follows: 'I hereby offer my buttocks to handsome men with patent leather shoes.' Even while writing the words 'patent leather shoes' he got an erection."

This man bought patent leather shoes for himself to use in his own private orgies. However, because of his homosexuality, the opening of the shoe symbolized not the female vulva or vagina but the male rectum. Garnier reports the man's own description of how he would stand before the mirror masturbating, with the shoes on a chair or low table in front of him:

"In this position, it is always my purpose to direct the stream of semen that spurts out into the opening of the shoes, and if I succeed in doing this I am seized with a paroxysm of lascivious lust. Another time, I will rub my anus, my legs and my buttocks with a shoe just before ejaculation, meanwhile steadily staring at the reflection from the shiny surface of the other shoe. But I most usually place each shoe on a separate chair near the window, then turn them until they reflect the light the brightest, and then take up a distance which will permit me to squirt into the opening of the shoe. The moment the semen touches the shoe, I feel not only a sensation of fullest gratification, but also one of complete triumph."

The fetishist is as strongly a romanticist about his favorite shoes as is any young man about the girl he's seriously courting. The shoe is a love object as well as a sex object, and he views it with tenderness and adoration. Omar Khayyám, for example, could pay no higher compliment to Heart's Desire when he wrote:

> To kiss, dearest Saki, thy shoes' pretty tips,
> Is better than kissing another girl's lips.

However, it is again Rétif de la Bretonne who used his literary works as a stage for his favorite subject of foot and shoe fetishism to eulogize the shoe as an almost living character. In his popular novel, *Contemporaines*, his hero, Saintepallaire, is a newlywed husband and quite obviously a shoe fetishist. Bretonne writes:

"Nothing more distinguished or precious could be imagined than the shoes of his newlywed wife. Down to the high heels, they were covered with mother-of-pearl and flashing diamonds. They had cost more than ten thousand crowns and were a present from Saintepallaire. In the evening, when the couple were alone in the bridal chamber, the young bridegroom knelt down and, with trembling hands, took the beautiful shoes off her lovely feet. Then he covered them with no less beautiful, though less luxurious, slippers. The other shoes were placed in a small temple of glass with a round support in the middle, resting on Ionic columns, made of crystals and crowned with gilded capitals. There the shoes would be kept as proof and pledge of undying love. Ten years have passed since then, and ten times the shoes have been donned on the wedding anniversary. The erotic passion of the husband has undoubtedly not declined. Perhaps because his cult gives ever-renewed strength to his love. Or perhaps his wife, advised by her admirable mother-in-law, uses means and methods unknown to other women. Or perhaps because men of Saintepallaire's kind are more tender and responsive to the same stimulus repeated over and over again. . . .

"During the first year of their marriage, the shoemaker had to deliver a new pair of shoes every day—colored and embroidered according to Saintepallaire's orders. They were handed over to him. His wife wore them for only one day and locked them away in a pretty wall chest. During the second year, he had only white shoes made. His wife wore in turn all the shoes she had worn only once, as well as a few pairs Saintepallaire had acquired during her maidenhood. This activity kept him continuously concerned with his wife and her charms."

Note how Bretonne is strongly defending his hero's erotic infatuation with shoes. Bretonne is saying in effect, "Just because one is a foot or shoe fetishist doesn't make him any less of a devoted husband, or passionate lover, or less masculine. In fact, these fetishist husbands can be even more tender and attentive than average men." Bretonne's reference to her "admirable mother-in-law" is an obvious effort to entreat women to understand and cater to the desires of their shoe-fetishist husbands and thus sustain the romance of the marriage. But Saintepallaire, a very rich young man, is certainly the envy of every shoe fetishist. Just to think—wedding shoes encrusted with diamonds, and a new pair of shoes every day of the year! This was far more than sheer luxury. To the fetishist it's the equivalent of a perpetual orgy.

Most shoe fetishists have an impassioned affinity for shoes or boots with high heels. The high heel, in fact, is almost essential to his erotic arousal. "When women's fashion decrees high-heeled boots," says Dr. Ullerstam, "many men walk the streets with a perpetual erection." If that applies to ordinary men, it applies tenfold to the shoe fetishists.

Some shoe fetishists have some of their women's shoes custom made —and with heels *eight to ten inches high*. By contrast, an ordinary "spike" heel averages only three to three and one-half inches. These special nine-inch-heel shoes have no platform soles to compensate for the extraordinary height of these heels. To stand or walk even a few steps on such shoes, one must assume the stance of a ballet dancer on tip-toe.

Why such extreme heel heights? First, a nine-inch heel is a greatly magnified version of the penis. But it's the fetishist's own fantasy wish; not any different than the phallic fantasies that ordinary men indulge in about themselves. The only difference is that the fetishist can make his wish a reality on his love object, the shoe, while other men must be satisfied only with the ego dream.

But who can possibly wear nine-inch heels? The fetishist's lady friend or wife—or even himself. He needs only to see these shoes on her feet, even though she may be seated on a chair or reclined on a bed. Or she may even stand and take a few cautious steps on them, holding on to a chair or wall. But whichever way she wears these heels, the fact that these shoes are on her feet is sufficient to send the fetishist into an ecstasy of lust that leads to intense lovemaking of the shoe, the foot, and often even the woman.

PODOEROTIC ART COLLECTORS

Shoe fetishists are avid collectors, and sometimes stealers, of women's shoes. They closely follow the latest footwear fashions. They fill scrapbooks with pictures of beautiful shoes, often with beautiful women wearing them, and frequently write in some tender or lascivious comment beside certain shoes, just as some "normal" men who collect pictures of nude women write in their own graffiti. The scrapbooks become a kind of pornographic collection for the fetishist, although he regards it as an erotic art collection. Each time he opens his scrapbooks, his sexual pulse throbs as he dwells on his favorites, kissing or tenderly touching the pictures.

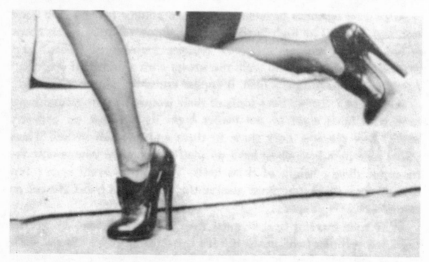

The near-impossible feat: a nine-inch heel. A non-functional shoe custom made for fetishists and worn only in private.

But the fetishist's even greater pleasure is in his collection of real shoes. Stekel remarks that "the fetishist collects his fetishes like a pasha in his harem. There is always a favorite of the moment which receives prime attention." This collection truly becomes a living harem of beauties for him. He doesn't collect just any shoes. His harem must be a cross section of various types of beauties. Whatever his mood, he selects a particular shoe or style to suit it—in the same way an ordinary young man might shift his preference from blonde to brunette to redhead in accordance with his mood.

"His need is usually for possession," writes Dr. John F. Oliver in his book, *Sexual Hygiene and Pathology*. "He is an inexhaustible collector of his kind of fetish; and he may keep books punctiliously about the date and origin of his acquisitions. Periodically, he looks at, fondles, manipulates, smells, or kisses his objects, and this might suffice to gratify him. Some have spontaneous ejaculations during this activity; others use the objects to produce masturbatory orgasm."

We'll call him Fred Blank. That isn't his real name, but he himself is for real. He's one of America's top designers of women's fashion shoes and he's a shoe fetishist. His office and sample room are filled with elegant shoes. Such surroundings are common for shoe designers, so it arouses no suspicions.

But in his home he maintains an extensive collection of some of the most beautiful and expensive shoe fashions in the world, acquired on his frequent "business" trips overseas. He keeps these in a special locked room. He assigns an exotic name to each pair, such as Africia, Dorrine, Bernadette, Ordwina, Bonnilyn, and Abithene.

He calls this special room his "sex quarters." He enters, locks the door, turns on the stereo for soft music, then walks along the rows of shoes, pausing a moment before a pair here and there to speak to them by name with flattering or tender words. Then he selects a pair that suits his mood of the moment, and retreats to his couch to begin his ardent lovemaking to that pair. To him, in this environment, he is constantly surrounded by "beautiful women" in the same way as a Hugh Hefner might feel with his Bunnies in his Chicago passion palace.

Paul Morphy, the celebrated U.S. chess master, died in his bath surrounded by women's shoes. His secret was out. He had long been a closet shoe fetishist and had kept a large collection of fashionable women's shoes.

The fetishist often experiences a lustful satisfaction in stealing shoes for his harem. Even when the fetishist can afford to buy women's shoes, he sometimes prefers to steal them because of the "conquest" feeling, or because they've been worn by a woman he admires. So common is this unique kind of theft that special terms are found in medical literature. "Kleptolagnia" is a theft associated with sexual excitement. This term, created in 1917 by Dr. J.G. Kiernan of Chicago, a pioneer in sex psychology, applies aptly to the fetishist who steals women's shoes. The term "hephephilia" is another specialized aspect of kleptolagnia, and relates to the fetishist who has an uncontrollable urge to steal "his kind" of objects, such as shoes.

"A kleptomaniacal fetishist," says Aigremont, "steals boots, shoes, slippers and socks. With each of these there is a basic erotic representation; that is, that one sticks something into these things, just as one sticks the penis into the vulva. Usually these thieves are rather good people who must steal these things only out of a repressed sex life."

Messalina, the seductive wife of Roman emperor Claudius (10 B.C.– 54 A.D.), liked to play around with men of all ages, depending upon her mood. She was attracted to Lucius, the father of Emperor Vitellius. But in their first clandestine meeting, instead of maneuvering her toward the anticipated horizontal position, Lucius begged of her—as the greatest possible favor—to allow him to pull off her dainty, jeweled sandals. He removed one sandal, passionately kissed it, then suddenly ran out of the house with it. He continued to carry the sandal concealed between his robe and tunic, kissing it in private from time to time with rapturous fervor. He was once caught doing this in public, and suddenly he was "exposed." But none recognized him for the shoe fetishist he was. Instead, his sandal-kissing was misinterpreted as a kind of fawning boot-licking. And so arose the still-popular expression, "He has kissed Messalina's slipper," referring to anyone who flatters and acts servilely to win favor.

Many shoe stores and departments that sell women's shoes are not infrequent victims of men who come in to browse for a pair of shoes "for my wife," but who walk out without making a purchase. Later the store will find a pair or single shoe missing. Store management people, who usually have no knowledge that such a breed as shoe fetishists exists at all, shrug off these thefts as the work of males stealing shoes either out of desperation, or trying to make a favorable mark with a girl friend.

Recently, in Richmond, Virginia, a shoe fetishist was caught after stealing a pair of shoes from an expensive women's shoe store. It was his third theft from this store, and the manager recognized him because on previous visits the man had spent much time browsing and handling the shoes but made no purchase. Each time after the man left a pair was found missing. This time, a salesman was assigned to follow him to his home. Sure enough, a pair of elegant $50 shoes was found missing—and turned up in the man's apartment. The police found a collection of forty pairs of expensive women's shoes there. They asked him:

"Who's the fence?"

"Fence?" he replied indignantly. "You mean that I take these shoes to sell them? That's an insult. Would you 'sell' your wife or girl friend?"

The police couldn't fathom the meaning behind his question. Said one, "What's that got to do with it?"

"Everything. These are my girls—every one of them. They're as dear to me as your wives are to you."

Did the police or store manager realize they were dealing with a shoe fetishist? Not at all. Nor did the judge in court; he assigned the fetishist to a local hospital for psychiatric observation. "Some kind of nut," was the conclusion.

It's not unusual for a shoe fetishist to go beyond merely stealing and to lightly assault and rob a woman of her shoes in a dark street or park. Such robberies are repeatedly reported to the police, who often are as baffled as the victim. No serious injury occurs; no money or jewelry is stolen; there is no attempt at rape or other sexual assault. Simply the shoes are pulled off the feet and the fetishist flees. The fetishist, however, never robs the shoes of just any woman. Very likely he has been watching and admiring a *particular* woman. Unable to gain access to her home to steal shoes from her closet, his only recourse is assault and robbery outside.

The shoe fetishist delights in window-shopping the fashionable women's shoe stores. He thrills at the sight of all these shoes, just as a voyeur might get his thrill peeping through the window of the shower room at a girl's college. He examines the shoes with studied rapture, for he has an expert eye and meticulous taste for shoes. His eye settles on certain favorites which he finds sexually arousing. As he looks and looks, his erection is pulsating, his body sweating in a sexual tremor. As he stands there staring, he'll frequently have an orgasm. He then moves on.

When shoe salesmen from different parts of the country visit New York, they make it a practice to shop the windows of certain shoe stores along Fifth Avenue. A short while ago a visiting shoeman from Toledo, Ohio, was making his window-shopping tour. He was gazing at the elegant shoes in the Andrew Geller window. Standing nearby and looking intently at the shoes was another man, which the Toledo visitor assumed was another shoeman.

Finally the stranger turned to the shoeman and said, "They're all so beautiful it's hard to pick a favorite. Which one would you want to take home with you?"

The shoeman smiled. "I'm not sure. Well, perhaps," he pointed, "that blue pump with the offside red bow on the vamp. She's a real beauty."

The other man's eyes lit up. "She *is* a beauty. You've got real taste." He paused then said, "Look, I've got a closetful of beauties like that at my place. How about it—the two of us and the shoes. We'll have a ball. We'll screw every pair to high heaven."

The shoeman's jaw dropped as he suddenly paled. He turned on his heel and briskly walked away, thinking the stranger was mad—never realizing that he himself had been mistaken for a fellow shoe fetishist who might be interested in a shoe orgy.

But the process works in other ways. I know two shoe fetishists who work regularly as salespeople in fashionable women's shoe stores. One is strictly a shoe fetishist, while the other is both a foot and shoe fetishist. In this occupation they're privileged to handle women's feet and shoes day in and out. For them, it's a never-ending thrill. Both are excellent salesmen and have developed a loyal clientele. This is understandable. The shoe fetishist has an exquisite feeling for fashion. Because he loves both his work and his product, he provides a superb, personalized, and *caring* service for his customer.

We have no idea how many shoe fetishists work "undercover" as salespeople in women's shoe stores or departments. Usually store management is blissfully ignorant that shoe fetishists even exist at all. But it makes no difference. The stores should be grateful if, unknowingly, they have shoe fetishists in their employ, for they're definitely above average in their skills and dedication for this work.

18

Tread on Me

The smallest foot sometimes has a man under it. For the henpecked husband this is merely a figure of speech. For the foot or shoe fetishist it's an erotic reality.

For many fetishists, their most wanton pleasure is to be tread upon, even stomped, by a woman in bare feet or shod in elegant shoes or boots with high heels. This experience, as the fetishist lies supine on the floor, leads him to sexual frenzy. This masochistic urge is not related to the usual flagellation and its sexual satisfactions. Its pleasure-pain syndrome stands as something unique by itself because two vital elements are required: the erotic foot and the sexual shoe.

Says Leathem, "There are in attendance elements of sadomasochism whenever the feet, especially those of the female, are introduced into sexual play. The age-old masochistic sexual fantasy in which a woman literally walks upon a man carries with it very definite overtones of female dominance and masochistic submission."

Many people commonly use the expression, "She walks all over him," referring, of course, to a submissive man or husband and a domineering woman or wife. But both the concept and the expression have definite sexual roots associated with foot and shoe fetishism. In fact, not a few psychiatrists believe that *any* male, single or married, who carries this trait of subservience or obeisance to extreme, also has fetishistic tendencies and strong sexual desires to be tread upon by women. It's no coincidence that we refer to such persons as "bootlicking" men. They may number in the hundreds of thousands.

Havelock Ellis reports a classic example of this tread-on-me desire. Here the subject is expressing his experience and feelings in his own words:

> "When I encounter a woman who very strongly attracts me, my desire is never that I may have a sexual connection with her in the ordinary sense, but that I may lie down on the floor on my back and be trampled upon by her. She must be richly dressed—preferably in an evening gown, and wearing dainty high-heeled slippers, either quite open as to show the curve of the instep, or with only one strap across. The skirts should be sufficiently raised to afford me the pleasure of seeing her foot and a liberal amount of her ankle, but in no case above the knee, or the effect is greatly reduced. Sexually, no other part of her has any serious attraction for me except the leg, from the knee downward, and the foot, and these must be exquisitely clothed. . . . Few women have a leg or foot sufficiently beautiful to my mind to excite any serious or compelling desire, but when this is so, I am willing to spend any time or trouble to get her to tread on me and am anxious to be trampled upon with the greatest severity.
>
> "The treading should be inflicted for a few minutes all over the chest, abdomen and groin, and lastly on the penis, which is, of course, lying along the belly in a violent state of erection, and consequently too hard for the treading to damage it. I also enjoy being nearly strangled by the woman's foot. . . . I must have lain beneath the feet of quite a hundred women, many of them of good social position, who would never dream of permitting any ordinary sexual intercourse, but who have been so interested by the idea as to do it [the treading] for me, many of them over and over again."

This same man tells of one woman, typical of many of the others, who derived deep pleasure from this experience. "She confessed that she loved to see and feel them [her slippers] sink into my body as she trod upon me, and enjoyed the crunch of the muscles under her heel as she moved about. After some minutes of this, I always guided her slipper onto my penis, and she would tread carefully, but with her whole weight, and watch me with flashing eyes, flushed cheeks, and quivering lips as she felt the throb and swelling of my penis under her foot as emission took place. I have not the slightest doubt that orgasm took place simultaneously with her."

This is a fairly classic example of the fetishist's tread-on-me feelings and experience. But note some important features. He doesn't seek this experience with just any woman, but only with those who meet his meticulous standards: the right feet, the right shoes, elegant dress, even a sense of modesty (skirts raised no higher than the knee).

Also significant is the fact these men must feel submissively inferior to their women—socially, educationally or intellectually, in wealth, or simply as domineering personalities. Under these conditions the man is eager to assume some slavish status—and derive great sexual satisfaction from a physical demonstration of it, such as the treading desire. Many non-fetishist men who find themselves in the impassioned throes of love with such women, exclaim, "I will be your slave for life!" never realizing how close they are to the brink of fetishistic urge.

We can understand the fetishist's sadomasochistic pleasure in this treading experience. But what of the sexual arousal of these "normal" women during the process? As in our foregoing case history, many of the women might have resisted or refused a coital relationship, but were eager to participate in the treading activity "over and over again." Sheer sadistic pleasure alone could not be the motive. Or could it? Do women experience sexual pleasure or orgasm in the thought of physically "punishing" a man such as in the act of treading on his sensitive genitals? But if she knows this is pleasing rather than punishing him, how then is her own sexual pleasure experienced? It is a curious paradox.

Bitches in Boots is a quarterly publication by Eros Publishing Company, dedicated to masochistic males who obtain their sex kicks from being stomped or tread upon by accommodating or sadistic females in high-heeled boots. The magazine, whose profuse illustrations are totally uninhibited, contains articles under such titles as "To Stomp a Dude," "The Heels of Dominance," "Heeled & Lusty," "Bitch in Charge," and "Pain Is Her Pleasure." An editorial in its Summer 1975 issue states:

> Historians may well view the current Feminist Movement as one of the most significant movements of all time. . . . *Bitches in Boots* illustrates the most direct and overt aspect of the "female backlash." Here we observe women acting out their wildest fantasies as they unload centuries of hostility upon the male animal who has so flagrantly oppressed them. At the same time we see males ridding themselves of intense guilt, writhing in anguish under the female's lash and boot as they enact their therapeutic, masochistic fantasies.

Almost every experienced prostitute has clients who pay her to tread over their naked bodies, with or without shoes. Some sex "torture houses" even specialize in such a clientele. Dr. Albert Moll, the noted investigator of sexual behavior, tells of one large and powerful man who made a specialty of visiting brothels and fine restaurants "solely to excite himself with the sight of elegant boots [low shoes were less

THE HEELS OF

There is a surprising degree of ignorance on the subject of high heels, and their function. Over the past few years, women have gradually become accustomed to stomping around in low-heeled, ugly shoes provided for them by the dictators of fashion, whose principal motives have certainly been to amuse themselves at the expense of women, rather than to enhance the beauty of women's legs and feet. The clogs and the "Minnie Mouse flats" are a couple of examples of how extremely ugly shoes can be.

One may speculate how these monstrosities came into being. It takes only a moment's thought to realize that most of the designers of women's clothes and shoes are fags, and that they probably spend much of their professional life in the hilarious task of developing new ways of mocking the beauty of women, to reduce their competitiveness in the eyes of men.

Whatever the motives, the result has been that a whole generation of young women have never worn high heels, and understand nothing of the subject. Another great group of women who, five or ten years ago, were accustomed to wearing beautiful shoes with high and slender heels, have apparently accepted the inevitable and become accustomed to the monstrosities that crowd the shoe stores.

Perhaps you will react with surprise to this emotional tirade against present fashions in shoes. If so, it is possible that you, too, do not understand the true significance and nature of high heels and their effect on both women and their men.

If this is the case, I suggest a simple experiment would be appropriate. This will require only two items, a naked woman and a pair of high heels. The women should be beautiful, and the heels at least four inches in height. Begin simply by having the woman stand six or seven feet from you, with her back turned. Study the form and shape of the buttocks, particularly the undercurves of the buttocks. Also study very carefully the shape of the thigh muscles, the backs of the knees, the calves, and the ankle. No matter how elegant and beautiful the woman may be, there is a certain solidity and heaviness to the look of her legs when her feet are flat on the floor.

Now, simply have her move up onto her toes. You will notice an immediate change, a very drastic improvement. First, the form of the ankle alters and

DOMINANCE

The lead page of a story in *Bitches in Boots*, a fetishist magazine. (*From* Bitches in Boots)

attractive to him] . . . The thought to have himself trod upon by ladies in their own boots, or to kiss their boots, gives him the most intense sensual delight. Before shoe stores he will stand and stand, merely to look at the boots."

This individual confessed to Dr. Moll, "It is my greatest delight to be naked on the floor and have myself trod upon by girls wearing elegant boots." Moll himself continues: "Simply a shoe, worn by no one, excites him when he sees it, but not nearly as intensely as when it is worn by a woman. New shoes that have not been worn excite him much less than those that have been used; but they must be free from wear and look as new as possible. Shoes of this kind excite him most. When ladies' shoes are not on the feet, he creates a lady for them in fancy; he presses the boots to his lips and on his penis. He would 'die with delight' if a proud, respectable lady were to tread upon him with her shoes."

One obvious wonder is that the fetishist, submitting to this treading on his body, groin and penis, doesn't experience pain or injury. But the sexual ecstasy erases all thought of injury or sense of pain. It's little different than the Hindu fakir who spends a lifetime on a bed of nails, experiencing a mystical ecstasy without pain or injury. Or, as cited earlier, there is the pleasure-in-pain condition of algolagnia. When the mind and emotions are immersed in pleasure, no room is left for pain.

Medical investigators have sought to "explain" the tread-on-me desire of the fetishist. Havelock Ellis expresses a view: "The focus of beauty in a desirable woman is transferred and concentrated in the region below the knee; in that sense we have foot fetishism. Not only has the foot become the symbol of the vulva, but the trampling has become the symbol of coitus; intercourse takes place symbolically *per pedum*. It is the result of this symbolization of the foot and the trampling that all acts of treading take on a new and symbolical sexual charm."

THE WOMEN SHOE FETISHISTS

Are there women shoe fetishists? Yes, though nowhere near as many as among males. Countless women commonly exclaim, "I just love shoes!" They mean it not merely as a figure of speech, but often bordering on the erotic. After all, the shoe *is* the sexual covering for an erotic organ. It *is* worn primarily for sexual attraction. It *does* have sexualizing effects on the body, such as high heels lending erotic qualities to the gait. It *does* convey sexual symbolism, such as the phallicism of the high heel and pointed toe, and the symbolic yoni character of the shoe's opening. The shoe, therefore, is no "innocent" item in the wardrobes of women.

Shoe industry studies reveal that many women own twenty-five, fifty, seventy-five or more pairs of shoes, and are constantly replenishing these wardrobes. Marlene Dietrich has had a ceaseless fascination with shoes, owning more than one hundred pairs at a time. Ballerina Alicia Markova traveled with two large trunksful of shoes. When Gloria Swanson once complained to an airline about the limit of sixty-six pounds of luggage for transatlantic passengers, she pleaded, "Hell, I carry sixty-six pounds of shoes alone."

Film actress Joan Fontaine owned about three hundred pairs of shoes, and Joan Crawford about the same number. Claretta Petacci, Mussolini's mistress, was constantly buying new shoes despite the two hundred pairs in her closets. Greta Garbo used to think nothing of buying fifty or seventy-five pairs on one shopping trip. Ava Gardner once placed an order for one thousand pairs of shoes—three hundred pairs for herself and seven hundred for her friends. Empress Josephine, wife of Napoleon, maintained a collection of over five hundred pairs, some of which were so fragile they could be worn only while she was seated. Maria Antoinette had so many hundreds of pairs that an indexed book was needed to keep track of the styles and colors.

TV personality Cher owns more than three hundred pairs, almost all of them sexy styles. Singer Diana Ross buys a minimum of $4,000 worth of shoes a year because, as she says, "I've got beautiful legs and I want to show them off with beautiful shoes." Mrs. Walter Annenberg, wife of the publishing tycoon and former U.S. Ambassador to England, has a wardrobe of seven hundred pairs of shoes.

Such a list could continue indefinitely. Hundreds of thousands of women, famous and obscure, rich and not rich, have an obsession about shoes. Significantly, we rarely hear of such a large legion of women having a similar obsession or collection of hats, gloves, hose, coats, handbags, or lingerie. Why this fascination with shoes? No, it doesn't indicate a fetish. But neither is it remote from it. The foot and shoe are among the very few erotic parts that can be exposed. So women "love" shoes because they are free to exploit this sexual symbolism to the fullest without censure.

But what of the *real* female shoe fetishists—those for whom shoes fill the same role of sexual gratification and erotic arousal as for the male fetishist? Psychotherapist R.W. Shufeldt, writing on the subject of female sexual frigidity, tells of an unmarried woman who had "a

Actress Jayne Mansfield, in the 1960s, with some of her two hundred pairs of shoes.

certain uncontrollable fascination for shoes. She delights in her new shoes, and changes her shoes all day long at regular intervals of three hours each. She keeps this row of shoes out in plain sight in her apartment." This obsession was found to be the main cause of her frigidity. She had simply substituted the shoes and their erotic symbolism for an active interest in men.

Stekel reports an instance concerning the daughter of a military officer who developed a sexual fixation about riding boots. She expressed her conviction that "a man shod in boots and sitting atop a horse is the only man." She rejected a variety of young suitors and finally, despite her family's objections, married an ugly old army officer because he always wore high, immaculately polished riding boots.

The marriage failed, says Stekel, because she was frigid. She advised a girl friend not to marry "because naked feet are so ugly. A man with his feet naked is a gruesome sight. 'I shudder,' she declared, 'even at the thought of the great toe' [manifestly a phallic symbol in her mind]. . . . She herself preferred to wear high boots because of the virile and erect appearance it gave her, and also because of the *pleasant sensation of being tightly laced in*."

This woman was an unusual kind of shoe fetishist, though she shared certain things in common with other women. Her admiration of riding boots and a man on a horse as "the only man" was simply an image of strong masculinity and her need for a dominant male. Many women share this feeling. Her "pleasant sensation" from tight boots or shoes again is shared by many women. However, the sight of a man's naked foot and big toe, strong in phallic symbolism, posed a sexual threat to her. In her mind, this was resolved by covering those feet with boots, and doing the same with her own feet. Her boot fetishism served as an iron curtain against the invasion of sex in her life.

I recall another woman, unmarried and about age forty, who maintained a large collection of fashionable men's shoes. I became acquainted with her through correspondence when I served as editor of a footwear magazine that reported on footwear fashion trends. In the beginning she wrote, innocently enough, asking my views on certain men's styles. I presumed the questions were to help her husband select current fashions. But subsequent letters revealed that she had no husband, that she "so loved the men's styles" and was buying such shoes in her own size, mostly via mail order.

Once she confessed that "while I love the look and feel of men's shoes on my feet, all the rest of my clothes are quite feminine." The pace of confession quickened, revealing that she sometimes "spent hours fondling the shoes—and sometimes holding them 'intimately close' to me. I guess it's because I just have 'a thing' about men's shoes." The correspondence ended abruptly when she asked me to send her a pair of my own shoes "because I feel we've become such good friends." She was, of course, a shoe fetishist and was having her "affairs" with men's shoes instead of men.

Shoe fetishism, as we've seen, can take various forms—by heterosexual men or women, homosexuals, expressed by a tread-on-me urge, or other versions. Shoe fetishism in its more extreme forms may be considered a sexual aberration, but in its milder forms it is much more common than realized.

"Such cases of desire for ladies' shoes, without cause, motive, and without demonstrable origin," says Krafft-Ebing, "are innumerable." According to the psychiatrists, many men unknowingly have latent homosexual tendencies. The same may be said of shoe fetishism. Essentially, the difference is that the shoe fetishist thinks sex is better with the woman's shoes on.

19

The Next of Skin

Of all the materials, natural or man-made, that we use for our footwear and clothing, leather is the sexiest and most exotic. That's because leather itself is skin—genuinely the skin you love to touch—and so possesses all the natural tactile qualities associated with sensuousness.

To think of leather is automatically to think of footwear. Leather and shoes are sexual cousins. About 70 percent of all leather goes into footwear, and another 20 percent into articles of clothing. Historically, there has always been a leather-body kinship. Leather is our next of skin.

This intimate kinship with leather dates back to the beginning of mankind. It was natural and inevitable that if man was going to clothe his foot and body, his prime choice would be a second layer of skin. In fact, it was so natural a choice that the Lord Himself initiated it. As told in Genesis: "Unto Adam and also to his wife did the Lord God make coats of skin and clothed them." Thus did God become the first tanner, the first tailor, and the first stylist. He placed the Official Seal on leather, that forever after it would serve as man's "second skin."

This natural affinity and sensory sympatico for leather has been with us ever since, as contemporary as it is prehistoric. The late anthropologist L.S.B. Leakey unearthed fossil bones dating back 600,000 years, some of which had been fashioned by prehistoric men into crude tools, including a "lissor," which is used for softening, smoothing and polishing animal skins. Bone needles used for sewing leather have been found, dating back 25,000 years. Neanderthal man used knives and sharp stones for the defleshing of hides and skins, which when dried were used for clothing. Stone Age wall drawings in Spain and southern France show persons clothed in tanned animal skins.

Leather is not only the world's oldest craft, but also the mother of fashion. Perhaps the earliest known form of clothing was the poncho, designed simply by cutting a hole in the center of a large piece of leather so that the skin draped softly over the shoulders and clung close to the body. This simple poncho was the original parent of most of the basic clothing fashions to follow: the tunic, robe, dress, skirt, coat, shirt, vest, sweater, and jacket. The moccasin, whose origin is also prehistoric, had the same primitive beginnings—a piece of crudely tanned leather wrapped around the foot and held on by rawhide strips.

The first loincloths, later to evolve into the apron and all lengths of pants, were leather. So were the early stockings, caps, turbans, hats, and other head coverings. Even into the nineteenth century, corsets and girdles were made of leather. The bra, invented by a Chinese concubine in the eighth century, was for centuries made of leather.

The idea of leather as man's second skin is dramatized again by an ancient legend of how shoes came into being. In olden days a king was walking barefoot in his garden and ran a thorn into his foot. Angered, he summoned his chief minister and ordered him to cover the whole earth with leather so that he would never again injure his foot. The minister, appalled by the enormity of the project, was suddenly sparked by an ingenious idea. "Your Majesty," he said, "why not cover your feet with leather instead? Would this not be the same as though the whole world were carpeted with leather?" And so the shoe is said to be born.

THE EROTICISM OF LEATHER

Leather, the traditional bedfellow of footwear, has an inherent erotic quality in its touch, its smell, and its esthetics. After all, it shares these same qualities with human skin, which in turn plays a very direct role in sex attraction and sensuous response. Leather and human skin consist of an identical arrangement of layers, identical cellular and protein and fiber structure, the same porous and glandular makeup. Our own epidermal covering and the leather shoes and clothing we wear are skin brothers.

On a recent television program, psychologist Joyce Brothers described leather clothing as "sensuous, sexy and luxurious." Motivationalist Dr. Ernest Dichter, after an extensive study of people's response to leather, and particularly leather footwear, stated that "men like the smell of leather because it has a masculine smell," and women "like the feel of leather because its softness imparts a feminine quality." Leather, he declared in a broader sense, has "a universal sensuous appeal which is characterized by no other material."

Now, combine these natural qualities—the eroticism of the foot, the sexuality of the shoe, and the sensuousness of leather. We can begin to appreciate the podosexual forces that mount to pedic sexual power. Let's take a closer look at the unusual qualities which make shoe leather a further contributing article to podosexuality.

Just like human skin, leather has fat wrinkles, veins, pores and sweat glands, and it gradually puckers with age; also, it responds beautifully to cosmetic treatment. Just like human skin, leather instantly molds to every movement of the body or body part with a constant hugging effect; it expands and contracts with temperature or humidity changes. It even "breathes" via thousands of pores per square inch to help maintain normal body or foot temperature.

Tanners, leather buyers, and shoemen feel a sensuous kinship with leather. While leather's esthetics are important, the real appraisal is by touch. A leather man will often close his eyes when examining leather so that full concentration can be given to his tactile sense. As his hands and fingertips fondle the leather, there's an almost erotic response visible on his countenance. He may as well be exploring the body of a voluptuous woman in the dark.

Leather men even have a special language to express some of the subtle qualities of the leather—terms such as mellow, hungry, open, full, lifty, buttery, boney, firm, round, silky, and supple. They are like old pashas bidding for girls in a slave mart; the younger and more exotic the subject, the more eager the bidding. This is why calfskin costs more than cowhide; kidskin more than goatskin; lambskin more than sheepskin; colt more than horsehide. The younger the animal, the finer and more supple the skin. Hence the more virginal and desirable, which raises the price, all no different than in the flesh pens of the ancient bazaars.

Leather men try to convey some of this deep-felt sensuousness into the brand names of their products—registered names such as Bareskin,

Anilust, Naked Truth, Playnap, Nude, Caress, Love Leather, Lambskin Chemise, Feel Leather, Barehide, Cuddle, Angelskin, Godiva, Ooze, and Nudy.

Shoes are made from many different kinds of leather, each with its own distinctive qualities. Each type of leather transmits a particular sensuous quality of its own. By using certain kinds of leathers, the "sexual temperature" of a shoe or style can be turned several degrees up or down because some leathers are naturally sexier in touch and look than others.

Men and women respond differently to leathers. Women lean more toward more exotic leathers like calfskin, kidskin, lizard, patent, suede, and ostrich—leathers that cling close and stimulate a skin-touch awareness (men's sensuous shoe styles use similar leathers). Or they'll favor fluffy shearling slippers, or shoes and boots with fur trimmings which reflect femininity and which, subconsciously, symbolize a vulva-phallus relationship when the foot is enclosed in them. (Interestingly, men never wear this fur-trimmed, female-symbol footwear.)

Snakeskin has long been one of the most exotic of leathers used in women's shoes. While some women are repulsed by snakeskin, far more are magnetically drawn to it. In either case, there is a very definite phallic and psychosexual link with snakeskin and a strong erotic connection with snakeskin shoes, because of the age-old phallicism associated with the snake itself. Again, interestingly, men almost never wear snakeskin shoes. The phallic symbolism of the snake appears to be exclusively female territory.

Salvatore Ferragamo tells of making a pair of "serpent shoes" for Esther Ralston, one of the early Hollywood queens. These were black and gold with a spike heel. "To the vamp of each shoe I glued the head of a snake, and their sleek, flexible bodies with golden scales painted as lifelike as I could make them, writhed halfway up her beautiful legs. They cost her $150." Here was Cleopatra reincarnated, with artificial snakes substituted for real ones, but no change whatever in their direct phallic or sexual inferences.

Men, too, have their own sexual leanings in the leathers they choose for their shoes. These are usually heavier and firmer to convey a masculine of macho feeling. So they select leathers like cordovan, kipskin (heavier than calfskin), steerhide, buckskin, brushed leather (a coarser nap than suede), and waxy leather. These are incorporated into sturdy-look shoes such as rugged boots or wing-tipped brogues with solid soles, extended heels, notched welting around the sole edge, and heavy stitching. Even today, many men resist the softer, lighter, and more exotic leathers—but only in America.

In the 1960s, patent leather gained enormous popularity in shoes, boots, and clothing, and was hailed by fashion as the "wet look." But according to some psychologists, underlying the popularity of this look was probably a psychosexual motive and subconscious association called "undinism." This term, originated by Havelock Ellis, applies to any condition or image of wetness that arouses sexual excitement. Those who respond to this are known as "hydrophiliacs" or wetness-lovers. The wet look was regarded everywhere as a contemporary sexy look. Hence a large share of the population may have been sub-consciously caught in a wave of undinism. This happens in other psychosexual cycles such as periods of popularity for such leathers as snakeskin, napped leathers, soft-buttery leathers, or waxy leathers.

Next to touch, odor is the sense most erotically aroused by leather. Ellis made a special inquiry into this phenomenon. "There is no doubt," he says, "that the smell of leather has a curiously stimulating sexual in-fluence on many men and women. It is an odor which seems to occupy an internal place with the natural body odors and the artificial per-fumes for which it serves as a basis; possibly it is to this fact that its occasional sexual influence is owing, for there is a tendency for sexual allurement to attach to odors which are not the specific personal body odors, yet which are related to them."

Ellis gives an example of this: *"Peau d'espagne* is of all perfumes that which most nearly approaches the odor of a woman's skin; it also suggests the odor of leather in a more subtle way. They are related." On the market today are any number of fragrances with a dominant leather odor, and sold under a variety of "leather" names.

Aigremont, however, is much more direct regarding the leather-body association: "The intensive smell of leather is akin to the smell of the cunis, especially when intermixed with foot odors." This association of leather and genital odors has been corroborated by other investi-gators, such as Hagen, Pyle, and Gould. Ellis states, "The secret of its [leather's] influence may thus be not altogether obscure; in the fact that leather is animal skin, and it may stir the olfactory sensibilities which had been ancestrally affected by the stimulus of the skin odor, lies the probable foundation of the mystery."

Thus, as stated earlier, the natural eroticism of the foot and shoe is further accented by the natural erotic properties of leather. Combine the three erotic forces—foot, shoe, and leather—and we have a further insight into the influence of podosexuality in our lives.

LUST FOR LEATHER

Just as there are shoe fetishists, so there are leather fetishists. The leather fetishist weaves a sexual imagery around things of leather, usually leather shoes and boots. But many of the sadomasochistic fetishisms are closely related to leather. For example, the bondage fetishist almost always uses leather cuffs, straps, and body harness. The flagellation fetishist requires whips with leather thongs. For them, leather is vital to sexual satisfaction.

The celebrated Monique von Cleef operated her world-famous "House of Torture" in her luxurious sixteen-room home in Newark, New Jersey. She specialized in many sadomaochistic services for fetishistic males with a sexual affinity for leather. She and her girls (whom

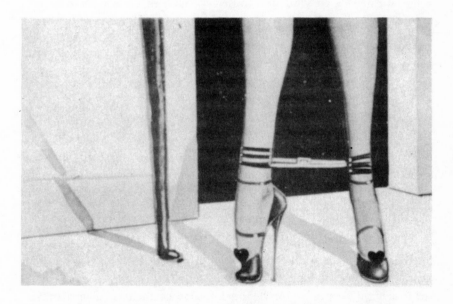

Female helplessness arouses many men. One extreme example—ankle bondage—goes back at least four thousand years. (*From* Bondage Enthusiasts Bound in Leather Magazine)

she called "leather social workers") always wore knee-high or hip-high leather boots, as well as other sensual leather clothing. When the police raided her establishment in December 1965, her clientele card files revealed a list of 15,000 patrons, an indication of the popularity of this sexual sport.

Leather fetishists aren't a tiny, isolated minority. But here again we're dealing with degrees of erotic response to leather. *Most* people feel at least some emotional response to the touch and odor of leather. The fetishist, of course, carries this reaction to extremes.

For example, there are men (and some women) who frequent leathercraft shops just to smell the pervading scent of leather, and to touch and fondle the leather articles. Sometimes they'll buy a whole skin to take home and add to their collection. By rubbing the leather against their body or genitals, and also deeply inhaling its smell, or licking and kissing the surface, the fetishist achieves instant erection, often followed by ejaculation.

Among the dozens of male-audience "sexist" magazines on the newsstands today, many carry ads appealing to leather fetishists, as well as to "normal" men who are aroused by women dressed in leather. A typical example is an ad by Unique Imports, of California, showing a photo of a sexy leather-clad girl, including knee-high leather boots. The headline reads: "You'll Love Her in Leather!" The copy follows: "Help her to turn you on! Strictly for the sensuous! All custom made. Plus a selection of bizarre turn-ons."

In recent years there has been a tremendous increase in sales of leather garments, now running well over $150 million a year. It's apparent that more and more Americans are now discovering what has been a reality since earliest civilization—that leather not only has a sensuous effect against the skin or body, and that its odor is a subtle aphrodisiac for many, but that the leather-clad person often arouses an erotic response in persons of the opposite sex.

I know of one leather fetishist who works as a salesman for a leading tanner. He follows this occupation, of course, so that he can have daily contact with leather, though neither his employer nor his customers know of his fetish. He's an excellent sales performer and is held in high esteem by his customers. One of them, a shoe manufacturer, once told me, "Now *there's* a leather salesman. He's not like so many of the others. He doesn't just show me samples. He practically makes that leather come alive the way he enthuses about it, strokes it.

You can tell that he cares—that he not only knows his product but loves his work." Little did the manufacturer realize, of course, how true his words were.

Many leather fetishists have an expert knowledge of leather that would be envied by even a tanner. One leather fetishist was sexually aroused by women's leather boots. One evening he took a woman out to dinner, which was followed by a few drinks. They ended up in his apartment. She was obviously ready and willing to be bedded. After a few minutes of petting on a divan, he fell to her feet and started kissing and caressing her boots, which was normal sexual foreplay for him. Suddenly he paled, drew back, his erection abruptly disappearing.

She looked at his face, which was now twisted almost into a snarl. "What's the matter?" she asked.

"You've cheated me!" he snapped. "You're a goddam phony."

"I—I'm what? Phony? About what?"

"Your boots. They're artificial leather. I need *real* leather. Sex—that's real leather, not this artificial stuff."

Women can also be leather fetishists. Stekel recounts such a case. "She becomes sexually excited only when the man in question wears shoes made of Russian leather. The very odor of such leather alone excites her to the pitch of orgasm. . . . She possesses quite a collection of leather pieces which she cuts out of boots and shoes."

Sexologist Magnus Hirshfield reports on a woman who "once showed me a small piece of shoe leather which she carried under her dress on a string hung close to her bosom. Using the strongest superlatives, she described to me the significance of this leather's odor for her sexual life." Ellis adds to this: "The odor of new shoes—that is, the odor of the leather—is sometimes desired as an adjuvant to coitus. It is in the experience of prostitutes that such a device is not infrequent."

Since early man, the human species has shown a natural affinity for leather and articles of leather. It is a subconscious sensuous affinity. The age-old kinship in this skin-against-skin feeling and odor for many persons borders on the erotic, and for many others, such as the fetishists, evokes a much more intense sexual response.

There need be no mystery to this. Because leather is essentially skin, we instinctively relate to its odor. And touch, the most sexual of all the senses, is inseparably linked to skin. This may well explain why leather and leather footwear is the skin almost everyone loves to touch.

20

Podocosmetics

The prime purpose of all cosmetics is to enhance personal sex attraction. The foot has always played a prominent role in this body-decorative art. We can call this podocosmetics—the art and practice of accentuating the foot's naturally erotic or appealing qualities.

In 1975, podocosmetics lured an estimated one-half billion dollars in consumer spending. The Dr. Scholl organization alone accounted for about $185 million in sales, much of it in podocosmetic products. Scores of other companies add to the total. A good share of the treatments rendered by podiatrists, valued at nearly $200 million annually, is essentially podocosmetic. There are also the pedicure treatments given in beauty salons, plus millions of additional dollars spent for pedic ornamental items such as decals, paints, jewelry, and tattooing. And none of this includes a penny of the $11 billion spent on footwear, at least two-thirds of which is for "fashion" that is essentially podocosmetic in purpose.

Podocosmetics is as ancient as it is contemporary. In early Egypt it was the custom in more affluent homes to bathe the feet daily in perfumed waters—and also before lovers got into bed, since foot-kissing was part of sexual foreplay. Cleopatra and Queen Hatshepsut, among many others, had slaves massage their feet with scented oils and dry them with peacock feathers since it wasn't uncommon for the feet to be kissed with the same gallant gesture as a modern Continental kisses the hand of a woman.

The exotic women of Turkish and Arabian harems painted their toenails with henna. Sometimes the nails of each toe had a different letter or symbol painted on it, so that the toes together spelled out some sensually suggestive meaning that might entice the sultan or pasha.

But the same exotic podocosmetic atmosphere can be found today. In New York, for example, one is received as a "guest" in Revlon's plush Pompeian Palace, a rococo salon where ladies recline on luxurious chaise longues in a Doric colonnade. For about $15 they dabble their toes in tepid, scented waters, later followed by a pampering indulgence in the hands of a podocosmetologist.

Available today in many stores are foot and toenail decals sold under such names as Deco-Nails, Finger Art and Toe Art Too, Skin Sees, Nailers, and Skin Scenes. Bonwit Teller advertises "Fleurs de Feet," a combination of sixteen different flower decals to apply on the instep and other parts of the foot. Clairol's toenail polish ads proclaim that "Now You Can Be a Blonde Right Down to Your Toes."

A short time ago the Chemway Corporation introduced a new product called "Pretty Feet," which promised to remove blemishes and soften and beautify the skin of the feet. A full-page ad in the *New York Times Magazine* offered a sample bottle for 25 cents. The ad was headlined, "Why Aren't Your Feet as Sexy as the Rest of You?" The ad drew an almost unprecedented response of 50,000 replies—certainly an indication that legions of women are eager to bring their feet out of hiding and let them fulfill their natural sexual role.

Former King Victor Emmanuel II of Italy gave a new romantic mystique to the toenail. He'd let the nail of his big toe grow for a full year. On the first of each January he had it snipped off. He then sent it to the royal jeweler, where it was polished, framed in gold, set in diamonds and placed in an exquisite velvet-lined box. It was then gallantly presented to his favorite mistress of the moment. These royal "memen-toes" were much scarcer than his mistresses, and hence were highly prized. It was Countess Mirafieri, his favorite over several years, who acquired the largest collection. She eventually married the king, which put the final nail into his quaint diversion.

Skin tattooing has its origins lost in antiquity, although it has been used in most societies. Today, in America, increasing numbers of women are being tattooed on toes, insteps, and other parts of the foot. One aspiring young actress had the back of her heels tattooed with the words, "Follow me."

Why aren't your feet as sexy as the rest of you?

A silly question.
    You have a legitimate reason for not having sexy feet. You ignore them. And you have company. Millions of women ignore their feet.
    Women who spend hours making a wisp of hair casually fall out of place won't spend two minutes on their feet. Why?
    Simply because up until now, all a woman could do about unattractive feet was stare at them... hide them... forget them.
    Things have changed, thank goodness. Now there's a product named, appropriately enough, Pretty Feet.
    Pretty Feet is a pleasant roll-off lotion. Pour a little on your fingers every day of the week and rub it into your feet. Then see the rough, dead skin roll right off.
    Soon you'll have beautiful feet that can wear open sandals... lovely feet that won't hide in the sand at the beach... smooth feet that won't run stockings.
    If you're genuinely interested in making your feet as sexy as the rest of your body we'll be happy to start you off with a free sample bottle of Pretty Feet.
    Just write to Pretty Feet, Dept. T5, Chemway Corp., Fairfield Road, Wayne, New Jersey.

We invented it because too many attractive women have unattractive feet.

This clever ad for a cosmetic foot lotion evoked enormous audience response, suggesting that legions of women are eager to bring
their feet out of hiding. (*Pretty Feet Co.*)

It's not uncommon for the wife or girl friend of the foot fetishist to have some love symbol tattooed onto her feet. The big toes of one foot fetishist's wife are tattooed as an almost perfect replica of a penis. The fetishist uses these for simulated acts of fellatio. He says, "The beautiful part is that they're always in a state of erection." This, however, doesn't deny the wife the coitus which always follows the husband's sexual foreplay with her feet.

In central Sumatra, some natives still practice the custom of elaborately tattooing their feet with colorful or erotic decorative effects. In the 1960s in England, a popular fad among teen-agers was to have the initials of their current "steady" tattooed on the sole of the foot—a custom dating back more than two thousand years when adult men and women had the initials of the beloved carved into the sole of their sandals so that "a trail of devotion" was left behind with every step.

THE FRAGRANT FOOT

Americans, unlike most other people of the world, have a mania about foot odors, goaded by the barrage of advertising designed to implant a self-conscious odor awareness. In 1975, sales of foot deodorants amounted to $70 million. In 1974, Gillette alone spent $700,000 in advertising Foot Guard, a foot deodorant. The makers of another foot deodorant, Desenex, spent $3 million. Morton-Norwich Products, makers of NP-27, expended over $700,000 in advertising. Mennen spent several hundreds of thousands of dollars in advertising its Quinsana foot anti-perspirant.

There may well be an unexpected sexual reason behind this self-consciousness about foot odors. Says Aigremont, "The smell of the feet, which reminds one of the odor of the genitals, is a sexual association that has implications worthy of further investigation."

It's perhaps no coincidence that the feet and genital area, along with the armpits, perspire more than any other parts of the body. A pair of feet contains some 120,000 sweat glands which give off a half pint of foot moisture a day. Thus the *natural* odors of the foot (as distinguished from shoe odors) can be as much a sexual stimulant as odors from any other erogenous parts of the body. As is well known, body odors are vital to the sexual attraction, courting, and mating behavior in virtually all terrestrial species, especially humans.

In 1975 Dr. Benjamin Brody, a New York psychoanalyst and clinical professor at Adelphi University, read a paper titled "The Sexual Meaning of the Armpits," at the New York Center for Psychoanalytic Training. He declared that biochemical and psychoanalytical researchers have proved that the odor of the armpits plays a part in sexual attraction. He said that the preoccupation of Americans with deodorizing the armpits and other body parts is a form of sexual coverup. The same psychosexual process may apply in the attempted coverup of *normal* (not shoe-induced) foot perspiration. If the foot is by nature phallic and erotic, then to conceal its natural odors suggests a subconscious sexual camouflage.

An Austrian psychiatrist several years ago reported a case of a man who was aroused to sexual pitch by rubbing the perspiration from the feet of his lady friends onto his penis. He'd vigorously massage their feet until a sweat was worked up on the skin, then would apply the moisture to his penis. The psychiatrist at first thought this was an isolated case, but on further probing found that several colleagues had similar cases. He said: "In each of these instances the 'explanation' of the men was almost the same. They said that the women's foot perspiration had a strong 'sexual odor' which they found highly stimulating, and that the perspiration itself felt like the vaginal fluids against the penis."

Among non-shoe-wearing people there is rarely found any excessive foot perspiration (hyperidrosis) or excessive foot sweating accompanied by offensive odors (bromidrosis). This has been confirmed in thousands of foot examinations among natives in Africa by Morton, in China and India by Shulman, and in other parts of the world by other investigators.

Only people who wear shoes speak of foot odors as being "offensive." A foot tightly encased in a shoe for some sixteen hours a day creates a bacterial reaction of the perspiration with the materials and chemicals in the shoe, resulting in shoe odors. Also, foot perspiration has less chance of normal evaporation.

Leather, for example, is almost wholly protein. The inside climate of a shoe is warm, humid, moist, and dark—the ideal culture for the millions of bacteria that feast on the protein. The gradual decomposition of the leather fibers from this bacterial action, plus the reaction of the shoe chemicals, dyes, and adhesives, develop shoe odors that are mistakenly called foot odors.

Then why do we scent the foot? For the same reason that we add fragrance to any other part of the body, particularly its erogenous parts—to supplement the body's natural forces of sex attraction. Nacht tells us that "the daughters of Zion were excoriated for placing perfume in their shoes and by its fragrance exciting and confusing men as they passed." In Lydia (600 B.C.), a thriving trade was done in dainty, aromatic footwear for women. Sappho, a poetess of the time, encased her feet in "broidered shoes fragrantly scented." The Babylonians perfumed their shoes with a special fragrance that became so popular that the scented footwear from this region was admired and known in other countries as "Babylonian shoes."

In seventeenth-century Europe, many shoes and boots had little sewn-in pockets to carry a sachet of perfume that gave the foot and shoe a permanent fragrance. Many women today place similar sachets in shoes before they store them in closets. A Parisian manufacturer in the 1960s did a thriving business with a line of women's exotic bedroom slippers with perfumed soles "to provide the proper romantic mood for the boudoir."

THE ORNAMENTED FOOT

"Among the most primitive races," says Flugel, "there exist unclothed but not undecorated people." This certainly applies to the foot. Almost nowhere in the world is the foot permanently or continuously left "unclothed." If it's naked, it's frequently decorated to cover its nudity or to erotically exploit it. If it's dressed, as with a shoe, then the shoe is made ornamental for sex attraction.

The undressed or undecorated foot has always been associated with a deprived or impoverished condition. Plutarch wrote that "bare feet are the sign of the slave's degraded state." Rudofsky states, "The intuitive esteem which the antique world held for the foot, gave room to the Talmudic tradition with its emphasis on adequate foot coverings. Only people of the lowest social order—slaves, prisoners, penitents— went unshod. For they were looked upon as not in God's graces."

But the shoeless or unclothed foot is much more than a social stigma. It has strong sexual inferences. Among many people, the unshod condition equates with a kind of emasculation or castration. Plato, Aristotle, and other noble minds of their day believed that going barefooted diminished the libido—that the wearing of shoes or sandals added to one's sexual powers. In recent years some governments, such as that of Mexico, have subsidized the cost of shoes for millions of school children. The motive is more than economic. As one fervent Mexican legislator declared, "Naked feet disgrace a civilized people. It is a condition which denies us our manhood and dignity."

There is an innate psychosexual urge or need to decorate the foot. Among non-shoe-wearing peoples this is done with such ornamental

The psychosexual urge to decorate the foot is inborn. The platform, high heel, surface decoration, open toe and heel—and feathery anklet—of this shoe are all frankly sexual in nature. (*Edison Brothers Shoe Stores*)

effects as feathers, tattoos, painting, rings on the toes, anklets of strung colored shells or beads, and cicatrization.

Among shoe-wearing peoples it's done with footwear—not merely the shoe alone, but the further accent of *ornamented* shoes. Today in America an estimated $10 million a year is spent just on shoe ornaments —buckles, bows, buttons, beads, bells, bangles, tassels, sequins, and rhinestones. They have but one purpose: to lend more seductive appeal to the shoe and foot.

The Eskimo isn't satisfied merely to have warm, protective boots. He must decorate them with bright beads or colorful lacings. He even has special "courtship" and "marriage" boots designated by special types of erotic decorations. The American Indian ornamented his moccasins with intricate decorative effects. For fertility or courtship rite dances, tribal natives of Africa or South America paint sexual symbols on the instep, often with a clear phallic message.

The women and girls of ancient Palestine wore tiny bells and clinking trinkets around their feet and toes (one of the few exposed parts of their anatomy). The prophet Isaiah rebuked these deliberate seductions: "Walking and mincing they go, and making a tinkling with their feet." The Greek historian Herodotus reported that the contemporary women bound their feet and ankles with strips of colored leather, each strip or color denoting a lover or love affair.

Historically, many people who could afford it, as well as many who couldn't, have often spared no expense for shoe ornamentation. The Roman Hadrian wore shoes and sandals with soles of solid gold. Emperor Heliogabalus' footwear was encrusted with valuable gems, and he seldom wore the same pair twice. Nero's sandals were trimmed with solid silver, and those of his wife Poppaea with solid gold. Such ostentatious displays became so common in Greece and Rome that Plato issued a public plea for all to return to unadorned sandals. But it was to no avail. A century later the Attic orator and state treasurer, Lycurgus, repeated the same appeal, and was also ignored.

Two thousand years later, the aristocracy and royalty were still at it. King Richard wore shoes with jeweled buckles valued at $2,000 a pair. Louis XVI made him look like a penny-pincher with his own gem-studded shoes that cost $20,000 a pair. But such luxury wasn't reserved solely for royalty. In the eighteenth century, England's Honorable John Spencer, at his marriage, wore shoes that sparkled with jewels and cost more than $100,000 a pair. In early America, the use of expensive jeweled buckles on elegant shoes inspired the oft-quoted verse of the day:

A pair of smart pumps made up of grained leather,
So thin he can't venture to tread on a feather;
His buckles like diamonds must glitter and shine—
Should they cost fifty pounds, that would not be too fine.

When Thomas Jefferson decided to protest the increasing ostentation of shoe buckles, he switched to the "new" fashion of shoes with laces. The upper classes were shocked and his outspoken critics charged him with "obnoxious informality" and the "shameful adoption of effeminate French notions."

The craze for luxuriously adorned shoes for sex-appeal purposes never loses momentum. Salvatore Ferragamo relates that one of his customers, the Maharani of Cooch Behar, was so taken by a particular style of shoe he had designed for her in the 1920s, that she not only ordered one hundred pairs in different colors and materials, but sent him a bag of genuine pearls and another bag of small diamonds to ornament the shoes.

But were these pedic luxuries only in the old days? Hardly. In 1973, the Tony Lama Company, a major cowboy boot manufacturer of El Paso, Texas, produced a special pair of cowboy boots priced at $10,000 for a wealthy customer. The boots were covered with one hundred and ten diamonds, eighty rubies, four star sapphires, and the leather trimmed with gold leaf finish.

In Europe today, it isn't uncommon for leading shoe artisans and designers in the fashion centers to produce a pair of shoes priced at $1,000 or $1,500 a pair for special customers. The shoes themselves might be worth $100 at most. But the special jeweled ornamentation accounts for the difference. In 1975, three wives among a group of Arabian oil sheiks on a visit to Paris made a total purchase of two hundred and fifty pairs of custom-designed shoes. The price totaled over $20,000. But over half the shoes were ordered with special gem encrustings. Total price: over $100,000. Lobb, the exclusive English bootmaker of London and Paris, sells his fine men's shoes and boots for from $500 to $1,500 a pair, and even the shoe trees are priced at $250 a pair.

In the sixteenth century, the lavish "shoe rose" fashion swept through Europe, and later to America. This started as a modest decoration on the front of the shoe. It had originated three thousand years earlier as a pompon that served as a genital symbol to ornament the tip of the turned-up toe, itself a phallic symbol. In Europe, the shoe roses grew in size and ornateness. Many fanned out five or six inches or more in diameter, some of them lavishly embroidered and jeweled. An aver-

A $10,000-pair of boots. (*Tony Lama Boots, El Paso, Texas*)

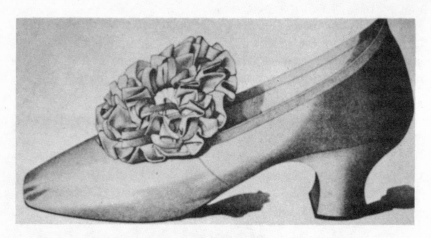

The shoe rose, which in the sixteenth century reached diameters of six inches, was (and is) a female genital symbol.

age man could pay a week's wages for a very modest pair. A wealthy man could spend the equal of a year's income for an average working family for his own luxurious pair. England's King James I at first scoffed at the shoe rose fashion, declaring that he didn't intend to become "an effeminate ruffle-footed dove." But before the end of his reign, his own shoe roses were among the largest and most ornate of all. Today, shoe roses are still part of the picturesque costume of the Beefeaters of London and the Guard Extraordinary, which originated during the reign of Edward VI.

When the aristocratic gentry of early America adopted the silk roses that adorned the fashionable shoes of Europe, some of the working class began to wear similar shoes. In 1639, the Massachusetts General Court issued a public proclamation denouncing those members of "the common classes" who tried to rise above their designated social position. The Massachusetts Colonial Legislature in 1651 proclaimed its "utter detestation" that men of low income, occupation and education "should take on the badge of gentlemen by wearinge . . . boots with roses affixed."

Many of the shoe ornaments that adorn shoes today are carry-overs of the frank genital symbols that have been used to decorate footwear for centuries. For example, large dual buttons or knobs often represented testicles; or a large, semirigid, flapping tassel sometimes represented a penis. The fur trimming around the shoe's collar openly suggested pubic hair for the yoni-symbol shoe. Such ornamental items, common today, have always contributed to a kind of sexual shoe-speak.

Let's cite one other example, the tongue of the shoe. We assume this to be a simple cushioning or buffer device for the instep against the lacings of an oxford; also, one of its early uses was as a "mudguard" to protect the hose against splashings. But long before either the oxford or hose appeared, the tongue of the shoe was serving romantic or prurient uses. More than two thousand years ago, and in subsequent centuries, many shoes had heart-shaped tongues, sometimes with romantic messages inscribed on them (the high-rise, heart-shaped tongue can be seen on some shoes even today).

High-rise tongues on shoes of the past and present. Even today, shoe tongues are sometimes twisted and rolled to simulate the phallus. A modest version of this is seen in the sandal from India. (*The Bally Shoe Factories, Ltd.*)

But creative men and women put their erotic imaginations to work. Shoes were worn with the high-rise tongue fashioned into more obvious phallic shapes. It was narrowed, rolled, twisted, rounded, thickened, lengthened and stiffened so that it resembled a variety of creative versions of an erect phallus. It was a modified adaptation of the earlier *poulaine*—but with the phallic action on the instep instead of on the toe of the shoe.

One Italian shoe manufacturer has a small, private collection of erotic footwear, some historic, some contemporary. One shoe, a relic of the court of France's Louis XV, is called "The Self-Sufficient Sexual Shoe." It's a woman's shoe with a thick collar of fluffy fur that almost covers the shoe's opening. A high-rise tongue shaped like a phallus curves back so that its tip is buried in the fur-covered opening.

To view foot and shoe ornamentation simply as a natural appendage of "fashion" is to be naïve about the erotic realities historically associated with the foot and shoe. Podocosmetics is much more than merely decorative pedic art. Podocosmetics is sexually motivated because its prime purpose is sex attraction.

Fashion designer Kenneth Jay Lane recently stated, "As feet get more prominent, women will pamper their legs and spend more money on their feet than on their hair. And the day will come when elegantes will invite pedicurists, not hairdressers, to their snobbiest dinner parties."

Centuries ago, that was the actual case in Europe. The creative shoe artisans were held in high social esteem. It may well happen again as the art of podocosmetics is rediscovered and appreciated for its exotic potential.

21

Censored!

Censored! For centuries that label has been stamped on both the naked and shod foot. Often the exposure of the foot and the shoes has been denounced as lewd and obscene, supposedly inciting lustful thoughts and lascivious actions. From this have emerged decrees, laws and bans charging the foot and shoe with seduction, pimping and procuring.

We've already seen how the foot, for reasons of "modesty," has been covered by shapeless shoes to conceal its contours, or covered to conceal its nakedness. We've seen how certain types of footwear—the *poulaine*, duckbill, and chopine—have been censured by kings, popes, and press. Is it different today? Not at all. We continue to see the wearing of high heels, platforms, or sexy shoes criticized by certain moralist groups. And millions of women still have psychosexual blocks about exposing their naked feet in public or to the eyes of males.

Such attitudes and acts have a long history. A decree of the British Parliament in the fifteenth century read: "Any woman who, through the use of . . . high-heeled shoes or other devices, leads a subject of Her Majesty into marriage, shall be punished with the penalties of witchery." A century later the law was still in effect, but had now crossed the Atlantic. In 1770, while New Jersey was still a British colony, the law was directed to all women, "whether virgins, maids, or widows, who shall after this Act impose upon, seduce or betray into matrimony any of His Majesty's male subjects by virtue of . . . high-heeled shoes, shall incur the penalty of the law now enforced against witchcraft, and the marriage shall be null and void."

In 1640, several Massachusetts citizens were arrested and fined for violating the sumptuary laws and the wearing of "excess in bootes, ribands, gold and silver laces." In 1720, the women of Pennsylvania were warned not to wear "shoes of light colours bound with different colours, and heels white and red, with white bands, and fine-coloured clogs."

The temptations of the devil himself were seen lurking behind the exposure of sexy shoes. In 1709, the Censor of Britain issued an order against stores selling "indecently styled footwear." He selected one leading London shop on which to spew his wrath for violation of the standards of modesty. The public announcement read:

"The Censor has observed that there are fine wrought ladies' shoes and slippers put out to view at a great shoemaker's shop toward the St. James end of Pall-Mall, which create irregular thoughts and desires in the youth of this realm; the said shopkeeper is required to take in these eyesores, or show cause the next day in court-day why he continues to expose the same; and he is required to be prepared particularly to answer to the slippers with green lace and blue heels." Even *The Tatler,* an influential London newspaper of the time, published a sermonish editorial warning parents to keep their young away from "the perils of exposing their view to the immoral temptations" of the shoes shown in these windows.

You can reach far back into history and extract countless examples of this persistent censure of footwear because of moral and sexual inferences related to the foot and shoe. In the seventh century B.C., the Greek philosopher Zaleucus prepared a detailed code of proper dress. He decreed that ornate or revealing sandals that "lured the eyes of men" were to be worn only by courtesans. But the women ignored his rulings, confirming the age-old reality that the lures of women are more powerful than the codes of men.

A seductive shoe imported from Sicyon in Greece by the Romans was called the *sicyonia.* It was made from soft, light-colored leather, an over-the-ankle sandal with intricate cross-strappings and many apertures, a distinctly sexy and daring style of the day. Cicero, among other notables of the day, denounced it as "flagrantly indecent."

Dfor, in his *Historie de la Prostitution,* tells of the sexual attitudes regarding the foot and shoe in ancient Rome: "Matrons having appropriated the use of the shoe (*soccus*), prostitutes were not allowed to wear it, and were obliged to always have their feet exposed in sandals or slippers (*crepida* or *solea*), which were fastened over the instep with gilt bands. . . . Nudity of the foot in a woman was a sign of prostitution, and their brilliant whiteness acted afar as a pimp to attract looks and desires."

But certainly all that censorship of footwear is ancient history and has no application to modern times. Not so at all. Not a thing has changed. Social and moral censure of footwear is found everywhere in contemporary society. We still have sex-based mores about our footwear fashions.

Many women deliberately avoid wearing "sexy" shoe styles or shoes with bright colors, for fear of being taken for women of "questionable character." In the early 1970s, many mature men criticized the wearing of high-heeled, platform shoes by young men as "obscene and effeminate." Many American men look askance at the sensuous, Continental shoe styles worn by other men, and label them "faggy." There are still many women who self-impose censorship and will wear only "sensible" heels, not for more comfort, but because they feel the sexier high heels may give men "a wrong impression."

One old Boston Brahmin club which only recently opened its doors to women (but only on certain days), has a dress code which includes the rule that "no lady patron may be seeen on the premises in heels higher than two inches." Vassar College, in the 1960s, imposed a regulation that no girl should be seen barefoot on campus or in the classroom because "the traditional rules against indecent exposure must be upheld." Today, at the Frick Art Reference Library in New York City, according to the rules set by its wealthy founder and director, Helen C. Frick, no woman can enter the library wearing high or spike heels.

Mothers even today continue to resist the wearing of high heels by early-teen daughters because of the "dangerous" sexual implications. As one mother bluntly told a shoe store manager, "The moment a very young girl starts prancing in high heels, it's the same as telling the boys she's ready for it."

Written and unwritten dress codes are common in the business world and reflect their own kind of censorship. The personnel manager of one large insurance company that hires hundreds of women each year states privately, "One of the first things I look at is their shoes. If the shoes are what I regard as 'sexy,' the applicant has little chance, no matter what her clerical skills. I've learned that girls who wear sexy shoes tend to disrupt the attention of other personnel, especially the men."

A few years ago in St. Louis, a woman took her employer to court for firing her for wearing bright-red shoes and high heels each day at work. She won her case. Her employer had argued before the judge that "we have to worry about what our customers will think. And you know, as a man, what you think when you see a woman wearing shoes like that."

In the 1930s, an annual convention of the Daughters of the American Revolution issued a dress code applying to members attending its conventions. Included in the code was a ruling against the wearing of "bright-colored shoes, high heels, open toes, or any other suggestive features of footwear."

In 1959, the minister of a large congregation in Akron, Ohio, told his parishioners in a Sunday sermon, "Women who walk in high heels are walking hand-in-hand with Satan. By the wicked movements of their bodies they are a temptation to the eyes of men. We shall have no such carnal visions aroused among the parishioners of this church."

THE TABOO OF THE NAKED FOOT

Why should exposure of the naked foot be regarded by many as "indecent?" Why do millions of women today still feel an embarrassing sense of immodesty when their feet are uncovered before the eyes of others, especially men? This can be traced to the persistent intuition and tradition of the foot's inherent phallicism and eroticism.

The association of the naked foot with sexual modesty is confirmed by many investigators. Aigremont, for example, states, "The foot has played a legendary role in the fertility of women; the foot has a sexual, indeed an erotic, charm inherent in its nature. . . . From the foot there is a localized modesty or 'shame' that is, for many persons, equivalent to modesty about exposure of the genitals." Havelock Ellis adds to this: "The female foot is covered with the same conscious modesty as European and American women cover their breasts."

During the Renaissance, the baring of the bosom to publicly display "upper beauty" was commonplace among upper-class European women. They had their portraits painted with exposed busts; or entertained company at home, visited friends, or danced in the ballroom with bare or nearly-bare bosoms proudly exposed. Some women had their dresses made with apertures through which the nipples protruded. Yet, their dresses were floor-length because it was "indecent" to show the foot, ankle, or leg.

Recently, in a California court, several strippers were charged with staging a nude show. They pleaded innocent on the grounds that a woman isn't naked if she still has her shoes on. The judge concurred, and in dismissing the case stated, "Stark nudity for public display is obscene. But when shoes are worn, the body can be said to be costumed and the display of the body becomes a performing art."

In September 1974, Wendy Blodgett, a shapely twenty-one-year-old from Burlington, Vermont, held a press conference in the Belasco Room of Sardi's restaurant in New York. It was attended by about thirty reporters and photographers. Wendy, completely naked except for her high platform shoes, introduced herself as "Ms. All-Bare America 1974," and proceeded to make a plea for "accepting our bodies without fear." When one reporter asked how she could claim the "all-bare" title with her shoes on, she replied, "It only goes to prove that modesty and nudity can work hand-in-hand."

A recent full-page advertisement in the *New York Times* by Bonwit Teller is headlined, "Are You Shy about Baring Your Feet?" The copy then proceeds to show how the feet can be made more attractive so there's less shyness about them. But this is naïve. The self-consciousness women feel about their exposed feet isn't because of crooked toes, corns, or other blemishes. The real cause is much more deep-rooted—the instinctual feeling about the foot's erotic character and the sense of nudity when the foot is bared to male view.

Podiatrists frequently have women patients who undergo an agonizing emotional experience when they must show their feet to the doctor. Not only must they expose the foot, but they know it will be *handled* by a man. For many women, this viewing and handling of the foot equates with the most personal intimacy. One podiatrist told me of a woman patient who, during the middle of the foot treatment, suddenly burst into tears. He quickly looked up, thinking he had hurt her with the firm foot manipulation he was applying. "I'm sorry," he apologized, "I didn't mean to hurt—"

"Oh, no," she sobbed. "you didn't hurt me. It's just that I feel—I mean, with my feet naked in front of you—I feel naked all over. And so ashamed!"

Unusual? Not at all. Some women will go only to a woman podiatrist. Other women with distressing foot ills will try every kind of self-treatment at home to avoid going to the doctor and exposing their feet. There are some women who have a corn on the toe, but will expose only the toe portion to the doctor. They cover the rest of the foot with a towel, or with a stocking whose toe part has been cut away especially for this visit. (You'll recall that Dr. Matignon described the same "foot modesty" among his lotus-foot Chinese patients.)

Female foot modesty is commonly seen in shoe stores, even though the foot is covered by a stocking. When shoe stores first became part of the commercial scene (America's first shoe store was opened in 1794, in Weymouth, Massachusetts, though such stores didn't become commonplace until almost a century later), most women wouldn't go into these stores to be fitted. This would mean that the salesman would catch a glimpse of their ankle and actually touch their feet with his hands. So they measured their feet with a piece of string and sent a male relative to buy the shoes. A Philadelphia shoe merchant in 1809 advertised in the local newspaper that "elegant ladies" would be offered "special sittings in a private apartment" in the rear of the store. Moreover, they would be measured and fitted "by one of your own sex."

In the 1960s, Mrs. Ellen Robbins, who at age seventy-four retired after working forty-seven years for the Marott Shoe Store in Broad Ripple, Indiana, vividly remembered selling high button shoes to women in the early part of this century. In her recollections, published in a story in the Indianapolis *Star*, she said, "We couldn't even raise the skirt above the ankles, and if a salesman slipped and touched the woman's ankle, it was considered scandalous."

Footwear and clothing have always played a coy game of sexual hide-and-seek: the more you hide, the more the opposite sex is inspired to seek. In Anatole France's *Penguin Island*, a female bird, by accident, ties a bit of stray cloth around her middle. Every male bird on the island chases her to find out what she's hiding.

The concealing and decorating of the foot reflect conflicting purposes of modesty and sex attraction. This applies to most erogenous parts of the body. The women of the harems were usually selected for their voluptuous qualities. But they were required to conceal their feet. So they sat cross-legged, their feet hidden under their legs or thighs, a custom still common in many parts of the world. Even in America women will assume this informal position with one or both feet. This could well stem from an "instinctual" reaction to the ancient taboo of exposure of women's feet.

In ancient Rome, women were taught to walk with slow, deliberate steps so as not to "agitate the movements" of the foot and immodestly draw male attention to it. In the past cultures of Egypt, Turkey, Czechoslovakia, China, and other countries, women went to bed with special "sleeping slippers" that were dainty, ornamented, and scented. The removal of these slippers in bed had, for the husband or lover, the same sexual invitation as the removal of a nightgown. The wife of Alexander the Great reportedly seduced Aristotle "by the temptatious sight and movement of her bare feet" by her bedside.

The sexual implications of exposure of the female foot existed strongly in old Judaic law. Anthropologist Paul Jacoby writes, "To uncover the feet of a person of the opposite sex is a sexual act, and thus becomes the symbol of sexual possession, so that the stocking or footgear becomes the emblem of marriage, or later the ring. (This was practiced by the ancient Jews, Ruth, 3:4 and 4:7, 8). Nacht also refers to the ancient Jews: "The Rabbis went even further in considering as a transgression the baring of certain parts of the body. Attention was therefore paid to the footgear of women." A husband could punish his wife by forbidding her to wear shoes for a given period. This virtually imprisoned her because it would be indecent of her to expose her naked feet in public.

According to Freud and also Jung, to dream of having one's shoes forcefully removed by another person symbolizes castration. For women this could suggest the loss of sexual or fertility powers; for men, the loss of potency or emasculation. The important thing is that forced exposure of the foot is associated with some form of sexual loss.

As we saw earlier, it was a rare privilege for the Chinese husband to view the bare leg or lotus foot of even his own wife. It was even considered in bad taste for a Chinese male to offer a woman the leg of a chicken—though he could offer her the breast. The goddess Kwan-Yon was worshipped as the divine harlot, and the many paintings and sculptures of her highlighted her erotic features and postures—but none showed more than the bare tip of her lotus foot. In Japan, up until recent years, men and women bathed nude together in community baths or pools. But when the first Jesuit missionaries came and showed pictures of the Virgin Mary, the Japanese were shocked to see her feet exposed.

The Christian church long bore enormous influence on dress codes. The clergy seemed to give inordinate attention to the foot and shoe. St. Jerome, one of Christianity's early leaders, solemnly counseled women to wear shoes that would cover the whole foot and thus "subdue the carnal inclinations lurking in men's eyes." In the third century, St. Clement of Alexandria commanded women not to bare their toes in public, condemning "the mischievous device of sandals that evokes temptations." The Puritans of America also forbade the wearing of sandals by women for the same reason.

The Hutterite religious sect, founded in Moravia in 1533, still exists today in North America, its believers living in communal-type groups. It has rigid codes of dress. A woman can paint her toenails, but only if they're covered with shoes and stockings. For the painted toenails to be visible would be sinful. In short, keep your sins covered.

But the Christian church also had problems of "modesty and morality within the confines of its own house. Between the eighth and eleventh centuries, many nuns were as lavishly shod as any fashionable lady of the times. A girl or woman of means who entered the convent brought all her finery with her, including her stylish footwear. Whereas her long dresses covered her body, the revealed foot and shoe became a focal point of attraction, especially for the priests and monks. In fact, the clergy itself was putting on its own podosexual performance, with the monks and priests wearing ornately decorated sandals and shoes and leg garters. The Council of Nicaea in 787 A.D. issued a formal complaint about the exotic footwear worn as "sensual lures" by clergy and nuns alike.

The church codes required that clothing and footwear be designed so as not to show the contours of the body parts—codes which prevail even today. Even the wearing of left and right shoes was prohibited because they revealed the shape of the foot. Right into the twentieth century, the Shakers of America were prohibited from wearing lefts and rights for the same reason.

"The idea of the impurity of the feet," says Rudofsky, "is as old as the shame for the body. . . . The shoe's purpose is hiding. The Christian idea of the shoe was to achieve near-oblivion for the foot.

Every respect for anatomical reality was abandoned, and the shoe was built on the most rigid principle of symmetry."

Have we changed in this "modern" day? Hardly at all. We still insist on the idea of symmetry in our footwear. But we use this to reach the opposite extreme—for sex attraction rather than sex concealment. The one thing that never changes is the self-awareness about the innate erotic character of the foot and its covering, the shoe.

CENSORED ART

The arts have long been the subject of pedic censorship. Right into the early twentieth century, both in England and America, stage actresses couldn't perform in shoeless though stockinged feet, much less in bare feet, no matter what the requirements of the role. An English actress in 1910 was reported in a London newspaper review to have performed on stage without shoes. She brought libel action, charging as "a calumny the statement in the press that she appears on the stage barefoot." She won substantial damages against such a serious charge.

In nineteenth-century Europe, the same prohibition prevailed among female dancers and actresses. One dancer was brought to court in Paris for performing in bare feet. The charges read that "the sight of light blue veins against the white skin was a deliberate act of indecent sexual attraction." Isadora Duncan shocked audiences during World War I with her barefoot dancing on stage. This nevertheless inspired Fokine to have his Russian ballet dancers in Paris abandon their corsets and to perform some of their repertoire in bare feet—a scandalous gesture.

Among the ancient Romans, Greeks, Etruscans, and later the Germans, the feet of the statues of their virgin goddesses were covered "to protect their chastity," even though the bodies often were stark naked. It was common for nineteenth-century painters to "paint out" the feet, and photographers focused their cameras only from the ankle up, or cropped out the feet of the Victorian women, making it appear as though they were practicing the art of levitation.

But it has been Spain, perhaps more than any other Western nation, that has retained its tradition of the foot as the focus of feminine modesty and sexual censorship. This has been evident for a long time in Spanish art. During the Inquisition period in seventeenth-century Spain, artists who dared expose the feet of their Madonnas in paintings and sculptures did so on threat of excommunication. Murillo was severely reprimanded by the Inquisition for painting the Virgin Mary with toes exposed—though no criticism was made of the exposure of one of her breasts.

Pacheco, the art master and father-in-law of Velasquez, wrote in 1649, "What more foreign from the respect we owe to the purity of Our Lady the Virgin than to paint her sitting down with one of her knees placed over the other, and often with her sacred feet uncovered and naked. Let thanks be given to the Holy Inquisition which commands that this liberty be corrected!" It was Pacheco's official duty in Seville to see that these commands were obeyed, with threat of severe punishment to transgressors. At this time in the court of Philip IV, the full-length portraits of any of the women of the court never showed the feet, as the works of Velasquez and others demonstrate.

In Spain, the privilege of viewing a woman's foot was referred to as "the ultimate favor"—the equivalent of bedding her. For a woman to remove her shoes and expose her feet to the privileged man was a more explicit invitation than the bluntest words.

A recent discovery in art history deals with the great Spanish painter Goya, and one of his renowned paintings of the Duchess of Alba. The painting shows her pointing with the toe of her foot to Goya's name written in the sand beneath her toe. Goya was obviously forced by the censor to paint over the area beneath her feet because of the intimacy suggested. When the painting was recently reexamined, careful scraping revealed the area that had been painted over. Such association of a woman's foot and a man's name carried sexual inferences, and hence was taboo.

In some of the Spanish paintings, such as those reproduced in Polss' *Das Weib,* the women are virtually nude, yet wear shoes and stockings. Max Dessoir, a pioneer in sex psychology at the turn of the last century, tells of the many Spanish pornographic pictures in which naked women are shown in various poses of sexual activity—yet always with their shoes on. The extreme modesty associated with the female foot in Spanish art imposed its influence in other countries. For example, Van Dyke's paintings of English women never showed the feet.

During the reign of Philip II in seventeenth-century Spain, when his bold queen suggested that a decree be issued to allow the wide, long and heavy skirts to be raised a couple of inches to avoid picking up all the dust and soil from the ground, there was a vehement mass protest from the men. Many vowed they would rather see their wives and daughters dead than to have them expose their feet to the sight of other men. The skirts continued to drag the ground. Only married women were permitted to wear high heels which allowed the slightest peek of the shoe when the skirts flared out a bit during a breeze or when dancing. Even the carriages of the day had special doors with a collapsible mechanism in the floor that could be lowered to hide the feet of a disembarking lady.

Martin Hume tells us that when extreme unction was about to be administered to Queen Isabella, "she exhibited a curious instance of her modesty by refusing to allow her foot to be uncovered to receive the sacred oil, which was then applied to her silken stocking that covered the limb, instead of the flesh."

On one ceremonial occasion, the Queen of Spain fell from her horse. She was dragged along the ground by the frightened animal as her foot remained trapped in the stirrup. The scene was viewed with horror by the many troops and dignitaries present. Yet, no one could rush to the aid of the Queen, for it would mean touching her foot, the ultimate blasphemy. Finally, one young officer, losing self-control at the sight, leaped to the Queen's aid, stopping the horse and removing her twisted foot from the stirrup. What was his reward? He was exiled to a lonely monastery to do long penance and await a royal pardon.

How could this fastidious sense of foot modesty be carried to such extreme? Enrique Casas Gaspar, writing on the origin of modesty in *El Origen del Pudor*, claims that the covering up of the foot was woman's invention, because man did not share her prudery. Yet it has been man who has been chiefly responsible for upholding the perennial taboos associated with female foot exposure.

Foot censorship remains a persistent force in our lives today. While we all come into the world naked, we insist on leaving it shod—either wearing our own shoes or special "burial shoes" provided by the undertaker. To be buried unshod is the same as being buried unclothed.

In the "liberated" 1920s and beyond, when short skirts revealed the leg and lower thigh and swim suits were form-fitting and body-exposing, the beaches saw most women wearing "bathing shoes"—lightweight, rubber foot coverings. These weren't worn for protection but were "modesty shoes" (men and children didn't wear them). They are still sold and worn in the 1970s.

Thus, regardless of all the trends in "body emancipation" and the relaxation of sexual attitudes, the foot remains a stubborn hold-out. Millions of people, women especially, retain a self-consciousness about foot exposure, and society itself continues to impose its censorship, whether by official decree or social attitudes, about foot exposure and certain fashions of footwear.

It is perhaps no coincidence that even in nudist camps, the ultimate in free expression of body exposure, shoes or other foot coverings are still worn. It almost makes us believe that something was left out in the story of Genesis—that with the fig leaf certainly there must have been a pair of shoes, especially on Eve's feet.

The Talking Foot

In one of Shakespeare's plays a character says, "Nay, her foot speaks." Those words are valid. The foot is one of the most sensuously expressive and "talkative" parts of the body. It has a language all its own. Podolinguistics is my own name for this language.

Your foot is constantly "speaking" to your body, your brain, your emotions. In turn, it is constantly being spoken to by these same sources. It's a two-way communication. Through its postures and movements the foot communicates moods and attitudes. It is an ever-present guest and participant in your sexual, emotional, and psychosexual stirrings. Your foot's movements and "feelings" reveal much about your innermost secrets of personality.

The foot responds to situations, people, and emotions similar to the way countenance does. The difference is that you can see a countenance, while many of the expressions of the foot are concealed within the housing of the shoe. We often say that the hands "speak the mind" in their gestures. The television or movie camera focuses on the hands of a nervous witness to dramatize what the person is thinking or feeling. But what are the *feet* doing at the same time? They too are just as clearly "speaking the mind" via both visible and invisible movements: curling the toes; the pressing of the foot hard against the floor; the rhythmic rotation of the ankle; foot-tapping; a back-and-forth swinging of the foot; the various positions of the feet; the tensing of foot muscles; the increased temperature and perspiration of the foot.

The foot is pouring out a whole stream-of-consciousness communication, a parade of inner messages.

When our moods or feelings are sensuous, podolinguistics actively transmits them. Fashion designer Kenneth Jay Lane catches the rich flavor of podolinguistics: "If only I could get women to practice sensuous gestures with their feet: how to cross the leg at the ankle; how to sit at an angle so that the foot is in sharp focus. Few people realize there's a great language to feet. It's less explored than 'body language' but terribly powerful."

Noted psychotherapists such as Wilhelm Reich and Alexander Lowen have done some pioneer probing into the communicative links between the foot, the body, and the mind. They believe these ties have primal origins. For example, the foot represents a child's relationship to its mother—such as the small child who runs after its mother for protection, who steps cautiously in anticipation of rejection, who in rebellion digs in his heels, who tiptoes to avoid criticism or punishment, or who stomps his feet in a tantrum. Even in childhood the foot is speaking what's on its mind.

Oscar Ichazo, noted psychologist and mystic, and head of the famed Arica Institute, states that "the idea of the body having a mind and psychological functions of its own is both ancient [Zen] and new. . . . It is a mistake to consider thought the result of one specialized organ, the brain. Each thought is as much a product of the eye or foot as of the brain-computer."

The brain-foot link is again seen in an ancient Zen technique whereby pain is demolished by concentrating on the pain in its location. The process is illustrated by Peter Mezan, a writer, reporting on an experience while preparing an article on the noted psychiatrist, R.D. Laing. One night he was in a deep meditation circle with a group at Laing's home. Later he wrote:

"There is a terrifically painful corn that simply will not let me past, it is making such a racket. For the next ten minutes or so I give myself over to that corn, all the attention I can muster. . . . At first, the harder I concentrate, the more intense the pain seems to become, until I am virtually alone and excruciated by it; then, after a while, it ceases to be painful exactly, and then suddenly, it seems, it ceases altogether.

Gait also plays a role in podolinguistics. There is a "personality" to each person's walk, and no two are exactly alike. In the Middle

Ages, specially endowed wise men or shamans were believed to be able to detect witches by the tempo of their footsteps. We ourselves commonly say, "I can tell it's him by the sound of his footsteps." Or, sometimes we're caught by surprise and we say, "Oh, I thought it was So-and-So coming. Your footsteps sound like hers." It's well known that the blind can almost unfailingly recognize persons by subtle differences in footsteps. Thus there is a gait-speak just as there is a foot-speak.

Palmistry has millions of believers to match perhaps the same number of skeptics. Whatever the validity of palmistry, the art has been practiced for several thousands of years. But there is also "podistry," the art of reading a person's character or personality traits by the lines and marks on the foot, or the shape of the foot itself. This may well be as old as palmistry itself, and has been practiced in China, Asia, the West Indies, and elsewhere. The skin and tissue patterns of the foot aren't essentially different from those of the hand.

One such podistry practitioner, Elizabeth Martineau Dawson, a Haitian-born psychic, appeared on the Johnny Carson "Tonight Show" on May 10, 1973. She had been practicing this art, which she calls "podologia," since she was a small girl, having learned it from other native practitioners. Whatever podistry's merits, it is nevertheless another form of podolinguistics. It has its own symbolism which, like all forms of symbolism, comprises a genuine language for the initiated and believers.

HOW THE FOOT SPEAKS

One of the most common and tragic mistakes is to view the foot with the cold objectivity of the doctor or shoeman. They see an anatomical mechanism in need of repair, or something to be dressed like a lifeless mannequin. What is lost to sight is the foot's age-old mystique, its exotic and erotic nature, its sensitive communicative powers, its expressive personality. But these "secrets" have long been known to painters, sculptors, poets, choreographers, mimes and mystics. Among them was the late Salvatore Ferragamo, who in truth was more artist than artisan shoemaker. He approached the feet of his clients, many of them famous personages, as though each pair had its own voice and personal identity.

"I love feet," he declared. "They talk to me. As I take them into my hands I feel their strength and vitality. . . . What do I mean when I say feet talk to me? Just that. They communicate the character of the person. Let a nervous woman place her foot, perfectly relaxed, into my hand, and I know at once that she is of a nervous nature because a current, powerful as a small electric shock, passes through her feet into my palm. I feel the reaction as clearly as I feel the sun when it is warm and the wind when it is cold. The degree of nervousness I can tell you by the degree of shock. When there is no shock, I can tell at once that she is without temper, without nerves. I do not mean that she is without sensitivity, but that she is not a tense or high-strung person."

Another form of podolinguistics is dancing. In all forms of creative dancing, the foot directs and communicates the movements of the body and reflects esthetic and emotional feelings. The body language of the dance has its own vocal chords in the foot. No posture or maneuver of the body is possible without first a corresponding posture or maneuver of the feet. The feet are the rhythm section for the orchestral movements and harmony of the body. Soft-shoe or tap dancing is an example of the rhythmic foot-speak clearly understood by all. Even foot-tapping to rhythmic music is instinctual foot-speak. Thus the foot speaks, or listens and then speaks.

Miriam Winslow, nationally prominent in free-form dancing several decades past, said, "I let all my feelings flow like a torrent into my feet, and suddenly my feet respond. No, it's not just a mental command from the brain. It's a command of feelings that instantly is felt in the feet. The feet move under *emotional* impulse, as though they possess a heart of their own."

Like all magnificent dancers, all the great mimes and pantomimists have a high-level foot sensitivity or pedic vibratory powers. These are the pivot of the silent body language that is the core of the mime's art. The postures and movements of their feet are not only highly articulate communicators in their own right, but are of enormous influence in the esthetic or sensuous language of the whole body.

What does the foot speak about? What do its postures and movements tell us about ourselves and others? Most of us intuitively use a kind of "foot reading." We speak of someone "nervously" tapping his foot; shifting his feet; rocking back and forth on his heels; kicking up his heels; dragging his feet; fidgeting with his feet or toes; digging in his heels; or treading softly; etc.

Each movement transmits a particular image of the person's feelings, attitudes, or personality. Thus, unconsciously, we're using podolinguistics. There are dozens of different foot postures or movements that people habitually assume when seated or standing—habits that are revealing insights into the person. If one learns by practice to interpret these stances and foot movements, it can be almost as revealing as a polygraph test.

For example there are such common foot postures or movements as feet always held close together when seated; leaning on their outer edges; spread wide apart; foot and toes pressing hard into the floor; feet crossed; ankle rotating; foot-tapping at a particular pace; one foot entwined behind the other leg; rhythmically rocking on one's heels; or the direction in which the toes are pointed. And so on *ad infinitum.*

Each foot position or movement is subconsciously sending a clear message in response to a group, another person, or a situation. Whereas words can be devious or evasive, podolinguistics is not.

And it is *especially* valid in sexual encounter situations, in revealing psychosexual attitudes or the person's psychosexual make-up. It's commonly known, for example, that books of etiquette discuss and show the "right" and "wrong" ways for women to position their feet and legs when seated. In short, there are "lady-like" and "unlady-like" foot positions which can convey suggestive sexual impressions to the opposite sex.

A few years ago, a young American businessman and his attractive wife visited Bangkok. One evening they were entertained at dinner by their business hosts at the hotel. Later, they all sat around in the hotel suite talking. The young wife gradually felt more and more uncomfortable because of the stares and ogling of some of the other men. On the following day, while her husband was out on business, one of the men called her at the hotel to make a date. She was shocked and incensed. What she hadn't realized was that the evening before she had sat with her feet wide apart—which in that country is interpreted by most men as a clear sexual invitation.

PODOPSYCHOSOMATICS

Podopsychosomatics is a mouthful of a word. But it nibbles down to digestible size. It's an extension of psychosomatics, and means simply that the foot plays an important role in many of our physical, emotional, psychological, and psychosexual activities and attitudes.

Elmer Green of the Menninger Institute has postulated his much-quoted "psychophysiological principle" as follows: "Every change in the physiological state is accompanied by an appropriate change in the mental-emotional state, consciously or unconsciously . . . and conversely, every change in the mental-emotional state, consciously or unconsciously, is accompanied by an appropriate change in the physiological state."

A pertinent example of this principle might be firewalking. The ability to walk on hot coals without experiencing pain or sensation has been practiced for centuries in many parts of the world, and is extensively practiced even today. It is found among Hindus and Buddhists in Japan, India, Ceylon, Malaysia, Fiji, China, Algeria, and elsewhere. Each year on May 21, several towns in eastern Greece have religious dances and firewalking ceremonies on hot coals, approved by the Greek Orthodox Church.

How is it that hundreds of thousands of participants, including frail old women and small children, are able to walk barefoot a distance of twenty feet or more on burning coals that have been heated for hours to a temperature of 1,800 degrees F.? Some do it several times. Some, learning the process, do it for the first time. And in all instances not so much as a tiny blister on the soles to show for it. And no sensation of pain or distress.

Is it mind over matter? Precisely. The firewalker needs only to concentrate on some religious symbol and chant a religious formula or mantra while walking on the burning coals. If there is proper and sufficient concentration, there is no sensation of pain.

We can understand how intense concentration can nullify pain. But how do we explain the complete absence of blisters or skin burns on the foot? The numerous medical investigators who have observed this phenomenon admit that it is "beyond physiological explanation."

Whatever the mysteries behind it, it does provide another graphic example of the brain-foot relationship.

Anatomically, no two parts of the body are farther apart than the foot and the brain. Psychosomatically, however, the foot and brain share a close association. Emotional and mental states, as well as states of sexual and psychosexual arousal, create reflex actions in the foot. This can also work in reverse.

Everyone belongs to a "foot-type" classification, much as everyone fits into a body-type category. Many years ago I had the opportunity for close-hand observation of body typing processing of students at

Boston University. This was part of extensive research conducted by Dr. William Sheldon, one of the pioneers of modern psychosomatics, who first defined the physique types of ectomorph, mesomorph, and endomorph. The physique of every individual is a combination of these three types, but usually inclined toward or dominated by one of them. Also, each body type corresponds to a personality type. Thus, behavioral and personality patterns can be "read" from body types.

Foot types are identical with body types. The ectomorph—lean and agile, with long, slender bones and muscles, has structural foot traits to match. The mesomorph, big-boned, heavy-muscled, stocky, hairy, with thick-textured skin, has feet with identical characteristics. The endomorph, fat or stout, small-boned and small-muscled, with thin-textured skin, has corresponding feet.

So the sequence is inevitable: psychological makeup usually corresponds to body makeup, and foot types correspond to body types. Thus, if there is a close body-mind association, then there is also a close *foot*-body-mind association. And if a body-psychosexual relationship exists, then a podopsychosexual relationship also exists.

The American Academy of Psychosomatic Podiatry estimates that 20 percent of all foot problems are psychosomatic in origin, and another 30 percent are due to conversion hysteria, a Freudian term referring to emotional or neurotic conditions which cause parts of the body to become permanently tensed or "tied up in knots." For example, some persons walk with their feet and toes doubled up like a fist inside their shoes.

A typical case of the foot's link with emotional or neurotic conditions is reported in *The Journal of the American Podiatry Association:* "During locomotion he claws at the inside of his shoes, causing excess perspiration from an increase in muscle metabolism, and produces undue pressure which may lead to a number of complaints. When he sits down his feet are doubled beneath the chair with the heads of the metatarsals [balls of the feet] forced against the floor with such vigor that symptoms of bursitis and periostitis may develop even after a short period of time. Sleep does not necessarily permit the muscles to relax. Those who have a psychogenic disturbance will usually sleep with the muscles in unrelenting states of contraction and really are physiologically exhausted when they wake in the mornings."

Psychiatrists and others have shown that in certain cases where sexual fears or inhibitions are intense, the feet will "freeze" so that the person, during an emotional or psychosexual confrontation, is unable to stand or walk. Podiatrist J.D.R. Rice states, "The readiness with which unhappily married women tend to develop fatigue or musculoskeletal pain is well known to all practitioners. . . . For example, a patient who complains of limitations of movement of the foot joints may be saying, 'I am helpless. I cannot walk around to help myself.' "

We translate human behavior or psychological states into body language. In fact, we *speak* in terms of body language. We speak of persons being "spineless" or "gutless"; or of having "nerve," "gall," "guts," or "balls." So also do we use a foot language which conveys clear images. We speak of a person "dragging his feet" or "dragging his heels"; we refer to persons being "foot loose" or "down at the heels." Foot language, like body language, reflects our emotions and moods, states of mind, and behavioral patterns.

The immobilized feet serve as a protective wall for the fearful or inhibited person to hide behind. We commonly refer to these persons as having "cold feet." This frequently occurs in sexual or psychosexual confrontations. Actually, the feet *do* get cold; they *do* feel or become immobilized. And here the mind and emotions fulfill their wishes through the feet.

Psychiatrist M. Straker tells of one woman who walked well enough around the house. Yet, she hadn't left her house in three years because as soon as she attempted it "her feet would not carry her and she was on the verge of collapse." The cause was found to be anxiety hysteria with a marked fear of walking in the street. She had psychosomatically "deadened" her feet the moment she stepped out the door. Straker cites another case—a war veteran who hadn't gotten out of his wheel chair without the aid of crutches. Yet, there was no visible disorder of his feet or lower limbs. Eventually a diagnosis of "hysterical paraplegia" was made, and with psychiatric treatment he was walking again. Until then he had been convinced that his feet were useless and could not carry him. And they would not.

The mind-foot association is involved in sexual activity. Says Kinsey, "Some persons tense so severely during sexual activity that their feet and toes develop cramps as soon as they have experienced orgasm. They rarely recognize such cramps during the sexual activity itself, but upon the sudden release of tensions at orgasm, they may have to rise and shake their legs to rid themselves of the cramps.

"Dramatic instances of the development of such tensions are found in the histories of amputees. . . . Although these persons may have nothing but the remnants of the nerves that would serve the muscles of the lower limbs, they may build up a neuromuscular tension in the non-existent portions of those limbs which are quite like those of persons who have complete limbs. Consequently, the amputee may also have to rise after orgasm and shake the cramps out of his non-existent toes."

This phenomenon isn't as mysterious as it appears. The foot is a vital outpost of the brain. Through its vibratory apparatus it is constantly picking up and sending back to the brain a flow of sensory, bioelectric and electromagnetic information from its sustained ground contacts. Even when the foot and toes aren't there, the brain and central nervous system continue by instinct or habit of established neural paths to communicate impulse signals—much as a rescue ship will continue to send radio signals long after the distressed ship has sunk.

Psychologist Stanley Keleman heads the Center for Energetic Studies. The Center specializes in bioenergetics, which relates body motions to emotional, physical, and psychological forces. He states, "Feet show how a person feels about independence and grounding." This grounding factor bears important influence on psychosexual attitudes.

William C. Shutz has spent more than fifteen years as a professional director and instructor in encounter and sensitivity groups, including Esalen. He, along with other encounter psychologists, has found the foot to be a highly refined sensory organ with an important role in sensitivity training. "The feet are of vital importance psychologically," he says, "because they are the contact with reality, the ground and gravity." He cites a case of this influence in his book, *Here Comes Everybody:*

"I remember a woman whose feet looked as though they had always worn shoes three sizes too small. He toes were jammed up against her foot with the joints high in the air, so that there was relatively little foot surface touching the ground. Her emotional problem was that she didn't feel stable, didn't have 'both feet on the ground,' was 'a pushover,' couldn't 'stand her ground.' Her husband constantly did things to hurt her, but she could not 'take a stand,' or 'stand up to him.' These are all phrases that she used spontaneously when discussing her situation.

"She was undergoing a method of deep massage—or, more accurately, tissue organization—called Rolfing, in which the Rolfer manipulates the body to get it back toward normal position. As he worked on her foot the toes began to slide forward. The whole foot began to come down and distribute the weight of the body more evenly. As the days passed the foot slid down futher and further toward its normal position. The following day she went on a fantasy trip that revolved entirely around her feeling of stability and groundedness. She also confronted her husband from her new-found center of strength. Physically, she reported feeling parts of the bottom of her feet she had never felt before. She spent days barefoot, reveling in the feeling of touching the ground with her whole foot.

"The distorted foot had been felt emotionally as a lack of personal stability. Physical correction of the foot aided the stability problem at the conscious level. . . . The physical change was central to her altered state."

This is certainly no unusual case. What's significant is the direct foot-mind, foot-emotions connection. When the vital sensory ground-

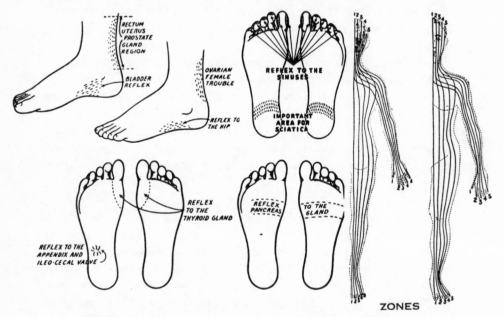

Zone therapy uses the same zone or reflex principles as acupuncture. The entire foot is "charted" with specific pressure points which, contact surface of her soles and toes was diminished, her feelings of security, self-identity, and self-assurance also diminished. Her loss of foot-touch surface had cut off much of those vital electromagnetic and bioelectric currents, with consequent psychological and emotional effects. She had lost some of her sexual identity and sexual response; she felt less a woman, less a person.

Over the past few decades there has been a small, little-known development called "zone therapy," also known as "reflex therapy" and "reflexology." It was introduced in 1913 by Dr. William F. Fitzgerald, who developed its principles after doing medical research in London and Vienna, and later in several U.S. hospitals. His experimental work received little notice or credence in the medical world, and even today its practitioners are regarded as somewhat cultish and hence, suspect.

Zone therapy uses the same zone or reflex principles as acupuncture. However, no needles are used. Manipulation by the hands and fingers is used—with the *foot* as the focal point or source from which the reflexes are "communicated" to any part or organ of the body. The foot is divided into ten longitudinal lines, five on either side of a central axis (the same zoning principle as with acupuncture). These zones

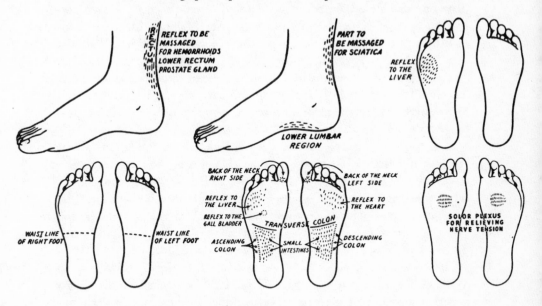

when manipulated, cause a reflex action to the corresponding part of the body above. (*From* Stories the Feet Can Tell)

extend up from the foot and "connect" with specific organs, glands, or areas of the body.

The entire foot is "charted" with specific pressure points which, when manipulated, cause a reflex action to the corresponding part of the body. One practitioner, Mildred Carter, states the basic proposition of zone therapy in her book, *Foot Reflexology:* "One of the most miraculous means given man, and probably one of the least familiar to him, are the electrical reflexes in the bottoms of the feet . . . which correspond to every part of the body."

Are the process and principle of zone therapy mere quackery? Are its practitioners charlatans? Like acupuncture, zone therapy has had a good share of successes, but also its failures as well. This has given rise to the usual proportion of skeptics and critics. But others, probing deeper, are urging further investigation. For example, psychologist Shutz says, "There is a whole method, zone therapy, based primarily on the feet, using different parts of the feet to relate to specific body parts. This is a method worth looking into, a redeveloping, for work on the feet often leads to profound changes [in the body]."

In 1932, an article written by Rex Beach appeared in *Cosmopolitan* magazine and described the equivalent of "miracle cures" being performed by an obscure country physician, Dr. Malhoun Locke, in Williamsburg, a Canadian hamlet near the New York border. Virtually every kind of physical ill, along with emotional and mental disorders and a variety of sexual malfunctions, was being reported as cured or largely alleviated by hundreds of individuals who had received treatment there. Many of these persons had previously undergone prolonged medical treatment elsewhere, to no avail.

Dr. Locke's "magical" treatment consisted of manipulations of the feet, usually lasting less than a minute. He was already treating some two hundred patients a day in what he called his "barnyard clinic," when the article about him appeared in the widely-read magazine. This brought an avalanche of visitors from the United States, Canada, and other countries. For the next ten years he was giving up to 1,200 treatments a day, most of them for ills remote from the foot.

In 1935, accompanied by a young podiatrist friend, I drove up to Williamsburg to see it with my own eyes. The first astounding sight was that long line of patients, never seeming to shorten as it was constantly replenished with newcomers. In summer heat or bitter cold of winter, men and women stood stolidly, sat in wheel chairs, lay on stretchers, or rested on canes and crutches.

The line led to a modest white house with a barn behind it. Locke, in addition to being a physician, operated a prosperous farm. Beside the house was a pasture. This was his barnyard clinic. About thirty persons were seated in a circle, and behind them thirty more in another circle. As soon as those in the inner circle were treated, those in the second circle moved in.

Dr. Locke worked inside the inner circle, continuously moving his small folding chair from person to person. He rarely asked questions, never gave an examination or attempted a diagnosis. Only the shoes were removed from the feet. To each foot he applied less than a minute of manipulation, then moved to the next person. His fee for each treatment was one dollar, though he could have charged much more.

Many doctors came to observe, hoping to detect some unusual technique, or perhaps to expose him as a charlatan. The American Medical Association sent a special team of investigators. They reported that they could find nothing of a "scientific" nature to account for the curative results. But in 1932, the AMA nominated him "miracle man of the year."

One evening, my friend and I, through a coincidence (my friend knew a distant relative of Locke's in the United States), had an opportunity for a twenty-minute talk with him in his kitchen over a bottle of beer. He insisted there was no "magic" to his treatment. He ignored such explanations as "laying on of the hands," "mass hypnosis," or other suggestions of mystical forces at work. Then he said:

"It's been known for centuries that the foot has a definite influence over the body—and also with our brain and emotional processes. Exactly how this mechanism works, I'm not sure. Perhaps it's like a telephone system. The voice is initiated at one end and the message gets through to the other. With the foot and body and brain and feelings, it's the same communication system—except that we really aren't sure what happens between."

The human body is, of course, an interconnected system of parts; each part independent, yet all parts interdependent. The action of one part usually creates a reaction in other parts. All the body parts are an *emotional unit*. When we feel joy or anger it's reflected in the face. When we feel nervous it's reflected in the movements of the hands. When we worry the gastric juices are agitated.

No one part can keep its feelings "secret" from our other parts. The body is like a nation that speaks one common language, but within that language is a variety of "dialects." So we have the "dialects" of hand language, facial language, and foot language—or podolinguistics.

Foot-speak is one of the least known yet one of the most expressive and revealing of all our "inner voices"—not only through the habitual postures and movements of the foot, but in the way we dress the foot with shoes. It is especially expressive in revealing our psychosexual attitudes, along with participating directly in our sexual arousals.

23

Footnotes

Volumes have been written about the human foot in sickness and even some about it in health. But the foot's state of sickness or health reveals no more about its true nature than a physical checkup provides a diagnosis of personality or human nature.

The foot is far more than a marvelous piece of anatomical engineering to fulfill a utilitarian service. It wasn't designed merely to serve us like some domesticated mule to transport us from place to place, or to stolidly carry work loads on its shoulders.

Though the foot has been with us for several millions of years, much about its true nature has yet to be fully discovered or appreciated. Certainly it is one of the more "mystical" members of the human anatomy. It is alive with sensuous and erotic potential. We have only to consider its evolutionary history—the fact that it made the upright posture and striding gait possible; that it gave rise to a host of new erogenous features: legs, thighs, hips, buttocks, frontal abdomen and bosom, gait—all of which, erotogenically, were non-existent before the foot assumed human form. The foot, in short, has played no small role in what we call "human sexuality."

Surely this foot could not itself be expected to remain non-sexual or non-erogenous. Nor has it. We've only to look at its long history of erotic involvement in human behavior and social customs, right to the present day. Thus, just as we are sexual and psychosexual beings, we are equally podosexual beings because of the innate erotic character of the foot.

Much the same can be said of our footwear. Like the foot, we have given the shoe only a superficial view—as a utilitarian covering or as an esthetic decoration. Americans especially have overlooked its deep-rooted and persistent sexual implications. Again, we've only to go back over the historical record to see the shoe's true role as an erotic instrument—a reality as viable today as in centuries past.

This failure to pay homage to the true nature and heritage of the foot and shoe has resulted in many naïve and often ridiculous views about the foot and shoe, such as the popular assumption that we abuse and neglect the foot out of "vanity"; or that fashion imposes a tyrannical dictatorship on our footwear styles, over which we have no control.

To assume that the "logical" thing is always the best or right thing is to show a disregard for the forces of human nature and psycho-sexual realities. It's more logical to wear "sensible" shoes. But human nature and behavior are also governed by deep personal desires and needs that defy or contradict logic. So we wear fashionable shoes that reshape the foot and even cause some discomfort because sex appeal has always been more potent than sense appeal. If in our own minds this makes us look and feel better, then logic and the "sensible" thing must play second fiddle.

If man hadn't invented shoes he would have invented other devices (as done in many shoeless societies) to reshape and ornament his erotic foot. Women acquire and endure more foot problems and foot reshaping than men, by a rate of at least seven to one. To assume that this is because women are more vain than men is absurd. The female foot is endowed with far more erotic power than the male foot. Hence the female foot has naturally been subjected to more cosmeticizing and reshaping to accentuate its sex-attraction qualities.

In contrast, because men have only limited erogenous features, they've had to compensate for these shortcomings by becoming artificial peacocks—a role they've assumed throughout all history except for the change during the past couple of centuries. But even men have been willing to undergo the same process of body and foot reshaping for the same sex-attraction purposes.

Thus the foot, because of its erotic nature, begs to be pampered and tampered with. This truth should rid us of persistent, but futile, complaints such as: Why don't we wear sensible shoes? Why can't they make fashionable shoes that are comfortable? Why do so many people wear those silly styles? Why do women insist on wearing those ridiculous high heels and platform shoes? Why do we stuff our feet into tight or pointed-toed shoes, or shoes too small? Why do we neglect or abuse our feet? Why do we let vanity rule our feet?

All the "whys" have the same answer: Sex has more power than sense. The reality, as the evidence so overwhelmingly demonstrates, is that the foot is an erotic organ and the shoe is its sexual covering. The influence of this truth is interwoven in human history and human behavior, and will continue so into the infinite future. We can no longer be naïve. "Foot" and "shoe" are new four-letter entries eligible to be included in the dictionary of erotica and the language of sex.

Bibliography

Aigremont, G., *Foot and Shoe Symbolism and Eroticism*. Leipzig: Verlags-Aktien-Gosellscraft, 1909.

The American Family Shoe Wardrobe. New York: National Shoe Institute, 1963.

Anspach, Katherine, *The Why of Fashion*. Ames, Iowa: Iowa State University Press, 1967.

Bombaugh, Charles Carroll, *The Literature of Kissing*. Philadelphia: J.B. Lippincott & Co., 1876.

Brachman, Philip, *Shoe Therapy*. Chicago: Universal Publishing Co., 1951.

Broby-Johansen, R., *Body and Clothes*. New York: Reinhold Book Corporation, 1968.

Caprio, Frank S., *Variations in Sex Behavior*. New York: Citadel Press, 1967.

Carlyle, Thomas, *Sartor Restartus*. New York: E.P. Dutton & Co., Inc., 1967.

Carter, Mildred, *Helping Yourself with Foot Reflexology*. New York: Parker Publishing Co., 1969.

Cohn, Walter E., *Modern Footwear Materials and Processes*. New York: Fairchild Publications, Inc., 1969.

Dichter, Ernest, *Why Men Buy Shoes*. New York: National Shoe Manufacturers Association, 1956.

Dickson, Frank D., *Functional Disorders of the Foot*. Philadelphia: J.B. Lippincott & Co., 1953.

———, *Posture: Its Relation to Health*. Philadelphia: J.B. Lippincott & Co., 1931.

du Maurier, George, *Trilby*. New York: E.P. Dutton & Co., Inc., 1931.

Ellis, Albert, and Abarbanel, Albert, *The Encyclopedia of Sexual Behavior*. Vols. I and II, New York: Hawthorn Books, Inc., 1961.

Ellis, Havelock, *The Psychology of Sex*. Vols. I and II, New York: Random House, 1936.

Ellis, T.S., *The Human Foot: Its Form, Structure, Functions and Clothing*. London: Churchill Co., 1899.

Fast, Julius, *Body Language*. New York: M. Evans & Co., Inc., 1970.

Fellowes, C. H., *The Tattoo Book*. New York: The Pyne Press, 1971.

Ferguson, Marilyn, *The Brain Revolution*. New York: Taplinger Publishing Co., Inc., 1973.

Ferragamo, Salvatore, *Shoemaker of Dreams*. London: George G. Harrup & Co., Ltd., 1957.

Fisher, Seymour, *Body Consciousness*. New York: Prentice-Hall, Inc., 1973.

Flugel, J.C., *The Psychology of Clothes*. London: International Universities Press, 1930.

Foot Dimensions of Soldiers. Fort Knox, Ky.: Armored Medical Research Laboratory, 1946.

Gold, Annalee. *How to Sell Fashion*. New York: Fairchild Publications, Inc., 1968.

Greene, Gerald and Caroline, *S-M: The Last Taboo*. New York: Grove Press, 1973.

Gregory, W.K., "The Upright Posture of Man: A Review of Its Origin and Evolution." Philadelphia: American Philosophical Society, Vol. LXVII, No. 4, 1928.

Hall, J. Sparkes, *The Book of the Feet*. New York: William H. Graham, 1847.

Harris, R.I., and Beath, T., *Canadian Army Foot Survey*. Ottawa: National Research Council of Canada, 1947.

Heard, Gerald, *Narcissus: The Anatomy of Clothes*. New York: E.P. Dutton & Co., Inc., 1924.

Hide & Leather & Shoes Encyclopedia. Chicago: Rumpf Publishing Co., 1941.

Hiss, John Martin, *New Feet for Old*. New York: Doubleday, Doran & Co., 1933.

Hooten, E.A., *Up from the Apes*. New York: The Macmillan Co., 1931.

Horn, Marilyn J., *The Second Skin*. Boston: Houghton Mifflin Co., 1968.

Ingham, Eunice D., *Stories the Feet Can Tell*. Rochester, N.Y.: Arrow Publishing Co., 1941.

Kauth, Benjamin, *Walk and Be Happy*. New York: The John Day Co., 1960.

Keith, Arthur, *Man's Posture*. London: British Medical Journal, March–April, 1923.

Kinsey, Alfred C.; Pomeroy, Wardell B.; Martin, Clyde E.; and Gehard, Paul H., *Sexual Behavior and the Human Female*. Philadelphia: W.B. Saunders Co., 1954.

Krafft-Ebing, Richard, *Psychopathia Sexualis*. New York: G.P. Putnam's Sons, 1965.

Krich, Aron, *The Sexual Revolution*. New York: Dell Publishing Co., 1964.

La Barre, Weston, *The Human Animal*. Chicago: University of Chicago Press, 1954.

Lake, Norman C., *The Foot*. Baltimore: William Wood & Co., 1935.

Langner, Lawrence, *The Importance of Wearing Clothes*. New York: Hastings House, 1959.

Laver, James, *Clothes*. New York: Horizon Press, 1953.

———, *The Concise History of Costume & Fashion*. New York: Horizon Press, 1969.

———, *Modesty in Dress*. Boston: Houghton Mifflin Co., 1969.

Leathem, Harvey T., *What You Always Wanted to Know about Sex Fetishes*. Wilmington, Del.: Eros Publishing Co., 1971.

Leather in Our Lives. New York: Leather Industries of America, 1963.

Levy, Howard S., *Chinese Foot Binding*. New York: Bell Publishing Co., 1972.

Lewin, Philip, *The Foot and Ankle*. Philadelphia: Lea & Febiga, 1947.

Lewinsohn, Richard, *A History of Sexual Customs*. New York: Harper & Co., 1959.

McGuire, William, *The Freud/Jung Letters*. New York: Bollingen/Princeton, 1974.

Malinowski, Bronislaw, *The Sex Life of Savages*. New York: Halcyon House, 1929.

Menninger, Karl A., *The Human Mind*. New York: Alfred A. Knopf, 1961.

———, *Man against Himself*. New York: Harcourt, Brace & Co., 1938.

Montagu, Ashley, *Touch—The Human Significance of Skin*. New York: Columbia University Press, 1971.

Morton, Dudley J., *The Human Foot*. New York: Columbia University Press, 1935.

———, "Human Origin." *American Journal of Physical Anthropology*, Vol. X, No. 2, 1927.

———, "Significant Characteristics of the Neanderthal Foot." *Natural History*, Vol. XXVI, No. 2, 1926.

Morton, Dudley J., and Fuller, Dudley D., *Human Locomotion and Body Form*. Baltimore: The Williams & Wilkins Co., 1952.

Napier, John, "The Antiquity of Human Walking." *Scientific American*, April, 1967.

Nelson, George E., *Your Feet*. Minneapolis: George E. Nelson Publishing Co., 1947.

Picken, Mary Brooks, *Language of Fashion*. New York: Funk & Wagnalls Co., 1939.

Pullman, M.J., *Foot Hygiene and Posture*. Los Angeles: M.J. Pullman Publishing Co., 1933.

Quimby, Harold R., *Pacemakers of Progress*. Chicago: Rumpf Publishing Co., 1946.

———, *Shoeman's Holiday*. Chicago: Rumpf Publishing Co., 1952.

———, *The Story of Style*. New York: National Shoe Manufacturers Association, 1947.

Randall, E.E.; Munro, E.H.; and White, R., *Anthropometry of the Foot*. Fort Knox, Ky.: Army QM R&D Division, 1946.

Romance of Leather and Its Importance to Mankind, New York: Tanners Council of America, 1937.

Roper, Elmo, *A Study of Consumer Attitudes Toward Shoes*. New York: National Shoe Institute, 1965.

Rosencranz, Mary Lou, *Clothing Concepts*. New York: The Macmillan Co., 1972.

Rossi, William A., *Podometrics*. Chicago: Rumpf Publishing Co., 1947.

———, *Your Feet and Their Care*. New York: Emerson Books, Inc., 1955.

Rudofsky, Bernard, *The Unfashionable Human Body*. Garden City, N.Y.: Doubleday & Co., Inc., 1971.

Ryan, Mary Shaw, *Clothing—A Study in Human Behavior*. New York: Holt, Rinehart and Winston, Inc., 1966.

Schuster, Otto F., *Foot Orthopaedics*. New York: The First Institute of Podiatry, 1927.

Schutz, William C., *Here Comes Everybody*. New York: Harper & Row, 1971.

Severn, Bill. *If the Shoe Fits*. New York: David McKay Co., Inc., 1964.

Spink, Walter M., *The Axis of Eros*. New York: Schocken Books, 1973.

Standard Dictionary of Folklore, Mythology and Legend. New York: Funk & Wagnalls Co., 1971.

Steindler, Arthur, *Mechanics of Normal and Pathological Locomotion in Man*. Baltimore: Charles C. Thomas, 1935.

Stekel, Wilhelm, *Sexual Aberrations*. New York: Grove Press, Inc., 1964.

Strauss, Maurice B., *Familiar Medical Quotations*. Boston: Little, Brown & Co., 1968.

Sulser, Wilhelm, *The Bally Exhibition Felsgarten*. Schoenenwerd, Switzerland: Effingerhof Brugg, 1948.

Sussman, Aaron, and Goode, Ruth, *The Magic of Walking*. New York: Simon & Schuster, 1967.

Szasz, Thomas S., *Pain and Pleasure*. New York: Basic Books, 1957.

Talbot, Percy A., *Phallicism*. New York: Barnes & Noble, 1967.

Taylor, John, *It's a Small, Medium and Outsize World*. Cleveland: World Publishing Co., 1966.

Towle, Herbert C., *The Shoe in Romance and History*. Boston: A. Carlisle & Co., 1934.

Turner, E.S., *A History of Courting*. New York: E.P. Dutton & Co., Inc., 1955.

Ullerstam, Lars, *The Erotic Minorities*. New York: Grove Press, Inc., 1966.

von Buddenbrook, Wolfgang, *The Senses*. Ann Arbor, Mich.: University of Michigan Press, 1958.

von Cleef, Monique, *The House of Pain*. New York: Lyle Stuart, Inc., 1974.

Waldeman, Charles, *The Mystery of Sex.* New York: Lyle Stuart, 1960.

Walker, Morton. *Your Guide to Foot Health.* Chicago: Follet Publishing Co., 1964.

Whitman, Sidney. *Fetish Worship in the Fine Arts.* London: Remington & Co., 1885.

Wikler, Simon J., *Take Off Your Shoes and Walk.* New York: Devin-Adair Co., 1961.

Wilcox, R. Turner, *The Mode in Footwear.* New York: Charles Scribner's Sons, 1948.

Wilson, Eunice, *A History of Shoe Fashions.* London: Sir Isaac Putnam and Sons, Ltd., 1969.

Wright, Thomas, *The Romance of the Shoe.* London: C.J. Farncombe & Sons, Ltd., 1922.

Index

Taki, Empress of China, 33–34
tatooing, 213–215
Taylor, Elizabeth, 161
Taylor, John, 72
thighs, evolution of, 56
throatlines, 91
thumb, big toe and, 67
"Tit Mats," 23
toe, big, 4, 31, 153
  as dildo, 39–40
  evolution of, 54
  functions of, 67
  phallic symbolism of, 11, 13, 67, 108,
    163, 202, 215
toe-grasp ability, 49–50, 154
toenails, 213
toes:
  deformation of, 153, 154
  female symbolism in, 13
  in natural state, 66
  in sexual activity, 9, 10, 122
  use of, by armless, 66–67
toe-sucking, 11–12, 27, 40, 67, 176, 215
toe tips, sensory areas of, 20
touch, sense of, 20–21, 22
transsexuals, 123
transvestites, 33, 123, 169

Ullerstam, Lars, 180, 189
undinism, 208
unisex fashions, 97–99
United States:
  men's shoes in, 113, 116–118

negative foot-consciousness in, 5–6
  women's shoes in, 82, 99–100
Unthan, Carl, 67
Urban V, Pope, 106

vagina, shoe size and, 158, 162–163
Van der Meulen, Adam Frans, 128
Van Dyke, Sir Anthony, 234
Veblen, Thorstein, 116
Velásquez, Diego Rodriguez de Silva
  y, 234
Victor Emmanuel II, King of Italy, 213
von Cleef, Monique, 209–210
Vinci, Leonardo da, 65
Virgil, 139

walking, *see* gait
wedding shoes, 15, 142–143
Weeks, Edward, 124
Weidenreich, Franz, 52
White, Dennis, 156
Wikler, Simon, 154
Wilcox, R. Turner, 126, 166
Winslow, Miriam, 240
women's liberation movement, 92

yoni (vulva) symbolism, 13, 15, 16, 17,
  108, 109, 160, 200, 222–223

Zaleucus, 226
Zen, 238
Ziegfeld, Florenz, 141
zone (reflex) therapy, 247–248